Michael Paterson is the author of *A Brief History of the Private Life of Elizabeth II* and *Private Life in Britain's Stately Homes*, also published by Constable & Robinson.

Recent titles in the series

A BRIEF HISTORY OF

THE HOUSE OF WINDSOR

MICHAEL PATERSON

RUNNING PRESS
PHILADELPHIA · LONDON

Constable & Robinson Ltd.
55–56 Russell Square
London WC1B 4HP
www.constablerobinson.com

First published in the UK by Robinson,
an imprint of Constable & Robinson Ltd., 2013

A copy of the British Library Cataloguing in Publication Data
is available from the British Library

UK ISBN: 978-1-78033-803-3 (paperback)
UK ISBN: 978-1-78033-804-0 (ebook)

1 3 5 7 9 10 8 6 4 2

First published in the United States in 2013 by
Running Press Book Publishers,
A Member of the Perseus Books Group

Books published by Running Press are available at special discounts for
bulk purchases in the United States by corporations, institutions, and other
organizations. For more information, please contact the Special Markets
Department at the Perseus Books Group, 2300 Chestnut Street, Suite 200,
Philadelphia, PA 19103, or call (800) 810-4145, ext. 5000, or e-mail
special.markets@perseusbooks.com.

US ISBN: 978-0-7624-4804-3
US Library of Congress Control Number: 2013931823

9 8 7 6 5 4 3 2 1

Digit on the right indicates the number of this printing

Running Press Book Publishers
2300 Chestnut Street
Philadelphia, PA 19103-4371

Visit us on the web!
www.runningpress.com

Typeset by TW Typesetting, Plymouth, Devon

Printed and bound in the UK

This book is dedicated to
PHIL AND ROSEMARY RIPLEY
to convey a lifetime's love and gratitude.

CONTENTS

ACKNOWLEDGEMENTS

I would like to thank several people for their time or trouble or interest with regard to this book. My wife Sarah has, with customary good grace, put up with the disturbance to our lives. Duncan Proudfoot and Becca Allen at Constable & Robinson have both shown a good deal more kindness and patience than I deserved. I have relied on my charming editor, Lynn Curtis, to make sense of the text. Her criticism has been very useful and her chatty emails a pleasure to receive. I would also like to thank two young friends: Yasmin and Adam al-Hassani, whose interest in the royal family spurred my efforts.

ROYAL WEDDING

'The genius of an event like this is its simplicity. It's
simultaneously magnificent and very simple.'

Simon Schama, historian

April 2011

London is about to witness a national celebration that will – it
is taken for granted – also be of interest globally. It will be followed with fascination, in some quarters even with hysteria,
in countries all over the world. The audience will run into
the tens of millions and the television rights will command a
king's ransom.

In the city all is in readiness. The flags and bunting are hung
out, the souvenirs are in the shops, the bands and troops are
rehearsed, the journey to Westminster Abbey has been timed
to the second. The route has been scoured by anti-terrorist
officers and the public chastened by the reminder that such
a high-profile event provides a tempting opportunity for
extremists.

On the day itself the crowds, blessed on this occasion by
unseasonable, summer weather, have slept in the parks and on

kerbsides, or have caught trains at hideous hours of the morning to ensure that they will see something. In a televisual age it goes without saying that the whole event can be more comfortably, and more comprehensively, enjoyed by those who have stayed at home. Such is the magnetic pull of atmosphere, however, that the desire to 'be there' has driven many thousands to the pavements of Westminster and St James's. There they will endure long hours of boredom and discomfort for the sake of the few minutes' excitement they will experience. It is obviously worth it, to judge by their swelling numbers.

The crowds wait, fortified with thermos coffee and by anecdotes swapped about similar events, or about the adventures experienced in getting here from Croydon, Rochdale, Toronto or Auckland. Vendors patrol up and down the crush-barriers with armfuls of little Union Jacks, calling their mantra: 'WAVE yer flag!' Where do these men go between such state occasions? One only sees them here.

Somehow the interminable hours will pass, the anticipation and excitement will increase. Eventually there will be cheering in the distance, swiftly coming closer. The noise will swell into genuine, spontaneous delight and the flags will be waved with impressive vigour. There will be the slow purr of a car engine or the swift clip-clop of carriage horses. Though the principal participants – the bride and groom, the queen and the Duke of Edinburgh – will be immediately obvious, many others will not be recognized until their vehicle has passed. People will ask: 'Who was that? Who did we just see? Was that Beatrice and Eugenie? Which was which?'

In the Abbey itself there are television cameras everywhere. Can it really have been within living memory – the time of the queen's own wedding and then her coronation – that there was reluctance to allow filming of the ceremonies, or even their broadcasting on radio? The arguments that these are either private family occasions or religious services too holy to be treated as public entertainment have been decisively lost. Now it is entirely expected that the viewing public will see the occasion from start to finish. This even includes the empty moments before the service begins, as the congregation arrives. Men dressed in suits or uniforms or tailcoats wander in, sit down, gaze about them. Most are unknown to those watching at home, though a smattering of foreign royals will be recognized by those who read the glossy social magazines. Here is Prince Albert of Monaco, there is Haakon Magnus, Crown Prince of Norway, over there is what's-her-name from somewhere else. The faces are known although the names and even the countries are not. In attendance, too, are the usual celebrities, picked out by the cameras as they sit and fidget. No state occasion seems to be complete without their over-familiar faces appearing somewhere in the background, a blurring of the boundary between ceremonial and entertainment. The royals arrive, the men mostly in uniform. Where does this notion come from that they dress to attend a wedding as if they were going to a war? Nevertheless, the splendour of scarlet and blue and gold adds considerably to the look of the occasion. This is one of those rare moments when it is the costume of the men and not of the women that most impresses.

There are reportedly not so many of the Great and Good – if that term can be applied to official guests – as might be expected. The couple allegedly chose the attendees largely themselves, so protocol has been kept to a minimum. Such was the level of worldwide interest that the public has heard the story of a Mexican woman, apparently obsessed with Britain's royal family, so determined to attend the wedding that she has gone on hunger strike. If her plight fails to move the Palace into issuing her with an invitation, she has let it be known that for her to be given one would go some way to erasing a recent insult to her country that was broadcast on a British television programme. The British Ambassador has presumably been asked to tell her, as gently as possible, that this is not the basis on which wedding guests are chosen. If she got away with it, imagine the scale of self-inflicted harm that might result on future occasions. Populism can only go so far. But it is ironic that those who stand in the very shadow of the Abbey will, unless they are within sight and sound of one of the big screens that relay the service, see far less of what goes on than the woman watching in Mexico.

Why is there such interest in this occasion? Other countries have royal families too, and these are often filled with people who are attractive, charismatic and interesting, yet lack the same widespread appeal. In 2002 the Crown Prince of the Netherlands, Willem Alexander, was married in Amsterdam to a charming and beautiful young Argentinian woman. Interest within the country itself was immense, but scarcely a ripple reached the wider world. Two years later Felipe, son of Spain's King Juan Carlos, married in Madrid. The television audience was huge . . . within the Hispanic world. The occasion made little impact elsewhere. Each groom was heir to a throne, his marriage a matter of national interest. In both cases the brides were middle-class women, sharing with Kate Middleton a comfortable background and an unfamiliarity with court protocol. They represented, in other words, the same fairy tale come true as she did. Yet no one, as far as is known, went on hunger strike in the hope of being invited to these weddings.

The British monarchy sets more store by ceremony than any other monarchy in the world. The United Kingdom is larger than any European country – other than Spain – that is ruled by a royal house. There is therefore an expectation that Prince William's wedding will be bigger, better, more spectacular, than such an occasion would be elsewhere. There is also a feeling that – principally because the BBC has such experience and expertise in relaying state occasions – it guarantees to make good viewing. The British monarchy, like the Spanish, can stir a sense of affinity not only in their home country but wherever in the wider world their language is spoken or their culture has taken root. In the case of Britain this is, of course, greatly helped by the existence of the Commonwealth. For viewers in Australia, New Zealand, Canada and a host of smaller countries, the wedding they are watching is a matter of immediate interest because the queen is their head of state and this couple are their future rulers. Even other lands – principally of course the United States, whose citizens have long since rejected monarchical rule – still enjoy certain aspects of royalty: the televised ceremonial, the sense of continuity, even the occasional juicy scandal.

Naturally there has been general fascination with a photogenic young couple whose relationship has been followed by the media almost since it began. Celebrity magazines have made William and Kate their own, despite the fact that royalty and celebrity should be two entirely different things. It matters, of course, that the two of them appear to be so similar to other young people of their age group. He has managed to seem, despite an upbringing in surroundings that few would find comfortable, a very ordinary young man. Today he is wearing, for the first time in public, the uniform of the Irish Guards (he has just been appointed Colonel), and this is perhaps the most formal he has ever looked. His grandmother's subjects are accustomed to seeing him in more casual attire – the jeans and sweatshirts of his teenage years, the combats of a soldier during his military training, the green jumpsuit of a helicopter pilot while serving in the Royal Air Force. Because these images are familiar to people and represent the stages of life through which they have followed William's progress, they feel they know him well. The bride, naturally the focus of attention today, is also well known. The details of her short life and her family background have already been extensively raked over by the media. Everyone with an interest in these matters knows that her mother was an air stewardess, that her parents run a company that supplies accessories for children's parties, that she was bullied at one of her schools and was captain of the hockey team at another. Even Kate's childhood piano teacher has been interviewed on television to say that, though a pleasant little girl, she was not destined for greatness as a musician.

People of course enjoy the Cinderella aspect of the story – the notion that someone without social prominence or connections could win the heart of a prince on the basis of personal merit. If Kate could do such a thing, so could thousands, millions, of others. It is as if fate has reached into the crowd and plucked out one of them at random. She comes, of course, from a solidly upper-middle-class and public-school background, and has lived in a wealthy community in one of the most snobbish corners of England ('the M4 Corridor'). There is no rags-to-riches element here, though the media has been able to score one or two points by tracing the differences in background between bride and groom. One newspaper published photographs of their respective great-great-grandfathers, taken during the First World War. Hers was a private in the Army, his was Commander-in-Chief. It has also been revealed that she has relations who run a chip shop in Sunderland, an emphatically working-class part of the north east of England, a world away from the green acres of Bucklebury in Wiltshire where she grew up. Though she has never met them, the mere fact that she is linked with Sunderland through her family will enable its inhabitants – and the owners of chip shops everywhere – to feel that they too have a stake in this event.

Her parents have been caught up in this to an extent that they must have been expecting ever since their daughter first brought William home. Their house has been shown on television, their wealth has been speculated about in the press (it is estimated to be costing her father over half a million pounds to finance his daughter's big day), her mother has been criticized for an unfortunate habit of chewing gum during solemn occasions. Her sister will become a celebrity through the events of today, her figure much admired – especially from behind – in her tight bridesmaid's dress. From now on she will appear regularly in gossip columns, though the bride's brother James will, by contrast, be largely ignored both during the service and afterward, despite the fact that he reads a lesson in front of what must be the world's most intimidating audience with complete confidence and absolute perfection.

Once the ceremony is over and the principals have returned to the Palace, the crowd in the Mall is allowed to stream, slowly and under police control, toward the railings. This is the usual climax to any royal event that takes place in London. After an interval, while thousands wait patiently outside, the French windows on to the balcony will be opened by invisible hands and the family will appear, the signal for general uproar. Down on the street itself there is often pushing and jostling. Those who find themselves in the centre of the roadway can see nothing at all because their view is blocked by the great white bulk of the Victoria Memorial. Others are still struggling to get through one of the narrow gaps in the barriers between the pavement and the roadway, and to line up their cameras, when a sudden roar tells them they have already missed the great moment. Nevertheless they will stand there in the crush until the appearance is over and the family retreats inside.

The British monarchy, it is obvious, is popular. Its various celebrations – weddings and jubilees (of which there have been several in recent years) and coronations (the last was in 1953) – are regarded as national events. Though the queen and her husband are spoken of with respect, for the younger generations the public uses first names – Charles, Andrew, William, Harry, Kate – as if they were personal acquaintances. Only the minor members of the family, about whom much less is known, are referred to by their titles – the Duke of Kent, the Duchess of Gloucester, Princess Michael. The immediate family, with its divorces, its outspoken patriarch, its tearaway younger son, is public property. There is a feeling that people know them, and are privy to their secrets. They know about their clothes, their tastes, their sense of humour, their love lives.

Familiarity does not exactly breed contempt, though there is far less respect for them than there was when the present monarch came to the throne. The public likes, and expects, its royal family to be accessible, informal and not aloof, even while demanding that they be dignified. Insofar as this is possible, the family perform the trick of facing both ways at once, of personifying the nation's history and representing it abroad, upholding its ceremonial traditions, while at the same time belonging to the present – wearing the clothes, liking the music, befriending the celebrities, of their generation. Some royals are naturally more serious, some more fun-loving, but because there are now so many of them and they cover such an age span – and because they have between them such a wide variety of interests – they can relate to more or less any sector of society.

A hundred years ago, their predecessors were very different. Then the monarchy was hedged around by rigid protocol, and members of the royal family were not seen in public anything like as much as they are now. Royal weddings were private events held behind the doors of Windsor Castle or the Chapel Royal, though they spawned general enthusiasm and were publicly celebrated. Family members were not seen by the public while informally dressed, though they might be photographed indulging in the leisure pursuits of the comfortably off – golf, shooting, hunting – in the appropriate costume, and a tweed suit would have been the equivalent of being 'dressed down' today. They did not take part in charity events – other than by acting as patrons – and certainly did not help to raise funds. They did not mingle with crowds by undertaking the 'walkabouts' that are now standard practice, and the most that many of their subjects would have seen of them was a distant splash of white dress or scarlet tunic.

They made formal speeches without a trace of levity (King George V warned his sons never to inject humour into their official utterances), and indeed never smiled or laughed in public – a rule to which Queen Victoria had strictly adhered, and which her successors adopted in their turn. They did not tell jokes, and it would have been unthinkable for any of them to give an interview, so that their views on any subject were a matter purely for speculation. Both press and public treated them with what seems today to be exaggerated deference, their male subjects immediately doffing their hats at the appearance of any royal carriage. Their friends were drawn entirely from the aristocracy and the wealthy plutocracy, and no one pretended that they had any understanding of the lives of their more ordinary subjects. They did not go to school, and naturally did not work in any profession. They were deliberately kept apart from everyday life because it was considered important to preserve their mystique. In an age of more rigid class structure it was in any case unheard of for people in their position to court public favour. Members of the aristocracy after all would not have stopped to chat with coal miners or market women, and what was the monarchy if not the apex of the aristocracy? Members of the royal family were, and were expected to be, the remote tip of the social pyramid.

Their business was not to be liked by the rank and file of their subjects – though it was gratifying when this happened, as it did sometimes. Rather it was to enhance the prestige of the nation through their splendour and dignity, to further the country's interests through their relations with their fellow monarchs, to preside over Society (a hugely important function, since they thus set the tone of national life) and to provide a reference point, a nominal leadership, for politics, the Civil Service and the armed forces. Nowhere in their 'job description' were they required to befriend or even to notice the great majority of their people, other than with a distant wave.

In fairness, their isolation was not so complete as might be imagined. They held the patronage of charitable organizations, just as they do today, and made visits to hospitals and orphanages, where they might have brief conversations with inmates who had probably been chosen and groomed in advance (such staged encounters were, and are, standard practice for politicians too). More importantly, the male members of the family served in the forces. The boys were put into the Royal Navy where they might live and work on close terms with men from the lower deck. Nevertheless it was taken for granted that members of the family existed on a different plane and had very little in common with their subjects.

It was apparent, by the beginning of the twentieth century, that a more democratic age was coming. Monarchy had already been cast aside by France not once but twice, and the emerging giant among nations – the United States – was emphatically a republic. The future seemed to lie with big, energetic nations: America, Canada, Australia, South Africa. These were accumulating unheard-of wealth and their frontier nature made them egalitarian to an extent that Europe could never be. If these emerging powers were to dominate the world, monarchies would quickly seem outmoded. The subjects of kings would look enviously at the social freedom enjoyed by the citizens of these new countries, and would become increasingly impatient with their own situation.

At this time there were also a number of murder attempts – many of them successful – against monarchs all over Europe, perpetrated largely by individual fanatics whose only motivation was to kill heads of state. Never before or since have royal families endured such persecution from the bombs and bullets of assassins as they did in the years between 1900 and 1914. The Age of Kings could be coming to an end, and Britain's monarchy might well go down with all the others. That was why Edward VII – who presided over an era of radical upheaval – once introduced a visitor to the Prince of Wales, later George V, with the words: 'This is my son, the last king of England.'

Queen Victoria had identified the family with the morality of the middle class, though in everything else they belonged to the super-nobility. Edward VII, with his extravagance and extensive womanizing, had been a throwback to the more riotous Hanoverians, the sons of George III, and had lived with all the vulgarity of a *nouveau riche* millionaire. His own son was to prove quietly dutiful in a manner that would re-align the institution of the monarchy with safely conservative bourgeois values. Once again its outlook would reflect that of the highly influential and politically important middle class.

Whatever their affiliations with a particular class, one thing the royal family clearly did not have in common with their subjects was much of a sense of 'Britishness'. Their names, their accents, their family customs, were alien, and did not always sit well with British attitudes or expectations. Like most monarchies they were, by force of circumstance, a very cosmopolitan lot. By and large, royals could only marry people from their own social stratum, and suitable candidates could of course only be found in other countries – in courts and palaces equivalent to their own. The result was that although 'imported' members might live most of their lives in England, they remained – subconsciously or deliberately – wedded to other cultures, languages and practices. One example of this was the Duchess of Edinburgh (1853–1920) who was born Grand Duchess Maria Alexandrovna of Russia and married Queen Victoria's second son, Prince Alfred. She never ceased to regard her adopted country with disdain, and continued to order her clothes, her shoes and even her biscuits from St Petersburg. Monarchs spoke German or French to each other – Victoria and Albert had used German as their language while at home – and British royals often spent their summers on the Continent, at health spas or visiting their seemingly endless relations.

The close ties between Britain's monarchy and several of those in modern-day Germany were well known. The most conspicuous of these were with the Royal House of Prussia, a country that had come to dominate its neighbours and whose kings had since 1871 become emperors, or kaisers, of a united German nation. Wilhelm II, who had come to the throne in 1888, was a grandson of Queen Victoria and a cousin of George V. He was a noisy, erratic, opinionated man whose personal behaviour and public statements more than once caused offence in Britain. He was also the head of a state that was actively arming itself, building a huge navy that was intended to rival, perhaps surpass, that of Britain, thus threatening the balance of power and the preservation of peace. His prominent role in European affairs was a source of considerable disquiet. The British public did not like or trust him, yet he was related to their own royal family.

Another cousin, so physically similar to George V that they were even mistaken for each other, was Tsar Nicholas II of Russia (1868–1918). Though personally benign, he was the autocratic ruler of a backward country, and was regarded by many as an oppressive, reactionary despot. It seemed to some that the British monarchy kept highly questionable company. These international hate figures were their friends, intimates, relations. Instead of belonging to the country and its people, the British royal family of the time could be viewed as part of a class of rootless international idlers and troublemakers. Had these monarchs confined themselves merely to dressing up and mounting ceremonial displays, they could safely have been ignored, but in fact they wielded enough power or influence to threaten the political stability of the Western world. When in the summer of 1914 war did indeed break out, dividing the Continent into two armed camps, some of the monarchies were on the same side as Britain (Russia, Romania, Serbia, and later Italy and Greece) while others (Germany, Austria–Hungary, Turkey and then Bulgaria) became her enemies. The British people greeted the war with enthusiasm as a chance to settle the score with a European bully. As stories of German atrocities in Belgium began to spread, and as sons and brothers began to die in the conflict, a state of perpetual fury and indignation replaced the initial euphoria.

It was seen as particularly unfortunate at this time that the British royal family had affiliations with Germany, though over the previous centuries it had never occurred either to them or to their subjects that there was anything negative or shameful about these links. The German states were seen as having much in common with Britain, and were regarded by the often xenophobic British as less foreign than other nations. (This attitude was mutual. When war broke out, the fact that the British were on the other side was viewed by Germans as 'racial treason'.) The links were so close and so obvious that it would be impossible to ignore or to undo them. Since 1714, when the Elector of Hanover had become King George I of Great Britain, the British Court had been dominated by German names and German culture. George I and his son and successor George II had not even troubled to learn their subjects' language.

For members of the British Royal House the choice of marriage partners had been limited. Their brides must of course be Protestant princesses, which meant that they must come from northern Europe, not from the Mediterranean or Austria. There were occasional exceptions: Queen Victoria's eldest son had married a Danish princess, and her second – as we have seen – a Russian grand duchess (Orthodox Russians were generally viewed with as much suspicion as Catholics), but to a large extent young women were recruited from the same tried and tested kingdoms and duchies. Coburg, from which Prince Albert originated, was nicknamed 'the stud-farm of Europe' because its ruling family married into so many dynasties. The range of available girls in the German lands was so wide owing to the fact that the territory contained over three hundred princely states – more than any other part of the Continent, or indeed the world. Germany did not become a united nation until 1871, and even then its ruling families retained their individual titles until the general collapse of the monarchy in 1918. George III had married a German, as had George IV and his brother William IV. Queen Victoria's mother, the Duchess of Kent, was German, and Victoria went on to marry Prince Albert of

Saxe-Coburg-Gotha. The name of her grandson – George V – was a reminder of the Hanoverian connection and of the sheer foreignness of the family.

As the First World War continued the public and the press increasingly looked toward Buckingham Palace and wondered about the real loyalties of those who lived there. Were they as committed as everyone else to a war against their own relatives? How British were they, in hearts and minds? With whom did their sympathies lie – their compatriots or their class?

What was the British monarchy to do in this climate of fearful suspicion and intermittent hostility? How did it change and adapt, to keep its credibility and the loyalty of its subjects – and to ensure its own survival in a world where respect could no longer be taken for granted? How did it turn from the aloof and formal institution that was so much a part of the old European order into the royal family personified today by William and Kate?

The story of this transformation in expectations – both theirs and ours – is a fascinating one. It is filled with colourful characters and exciting events. At the time it begins – the First World War and its aftermath – the institution of monarchy seemed to have no future. Today the British monarchy seems more secure than it was a century ago, and its appeal, judging by international interest in the royal wedding and Queen Elizabeth II's Diamond Jubilee, is truly universal. Its survival, and successful adaptation, is an inspiration to all those who wish the institution well.

How did this successful transformation come about? To a large extent it was a matter of personalities. The twenty-six-year reign of George V represented a clean break in style and tone from the very public excesses of his popular but profligate father, Edward VII. For a long time dismissed as dull by historians, George was in fact a good deal more shrewd – and intelligent – than many give him credit for. He read the mood of the country and set about giving his people a monarchy that suited the time: unspectacular, dutiful and safe. He was aware that respect and goodwill would henceforth have to be earned through hard work, and he ensured that his heirs understood this. His own son, Edward VIII, brought the institution of monarchy to new heights of popularity as Prince of Wales, only to squander this goodwill once he briefly ascended the throne. Edward's brother, George VI, became arguably the best-loved king in British history. His is a story of triumph over personal limitations, but his leadership of the nation during its gravest crisis undermined his health and contributed to his early death. His daughter, inheriting the throne at an age when her contemporaries were busy setting up homes for themselves, has reigned with exemplary devotion ever since.

The crucial year in the process of modernizing the monarchy was 1917, a more important date in British history than most of us realize. Though, quite rightly, the nation was preoccupied at that time with the First World War, it was in this year that a quiet revolution took place. In essence what happened was that the British people told their rulers what sort of monarchy they wished to have, and the royal family – swiftly, willingly and completely – made the necessary changes.

1

THE HOUSE OF WINDSOR, 1917–PRESENT

'The British Empire is very near the limit of its endurance of a kingly caste of Germans. The choice of British royalty between its peoples and its cousins cannot be indefinitely delayed. Were it made now, publicly and boldly, there can be no doubt the decision would mean a renascence of monarchy and a tremendous outbreak of royalist enthusiasm in the empire.'

H. G. Wells, 16 May 1917, *New York Times*

If you travel by rail from Waterloo, you arrive at Windsor and Eton Riverside, one of two stations in this royal town. The immense, battlemented, grey granite ramparts of the Castle loom above you as you come out on to a busy road. Walk along this, in the direction of the High Street, and in less than a minute you will see a monument. It is set back from the roadway in a miniature garden. There are benches, flowers and long wild grasses, and two matching basins in which fountains play. A pair of stone lion's heads, one at either end, spew water into a pool. Perhaps there ought to be a statue here but there is only a plinth, and on it there are the trappings of kingship, carved in stone: a crown, an orb, two sceptres, all displayed on a cushion. It is as if the figure who should be holding these things has vanished on some urgent errand, and if you wait a few minutes he will return and pick them up. On the plinth there is the briefest of inscriptions:

GEORGE V
FIRST SOVEREIGN OF THE HOUSE OF WINDSOR

There is not even a date, though a nearby plaque tells you that the memorial – designed by the great imperial architect Lutyens – was unveiled by the king's successor in 1937. George V, as you may know, reigned during the First World War, and the twenties, and some of the thirties.

The House of Windsor, Britain's royal family, is evidently not very old, as dynasties go. There are millions of people still alive throughout the world who were this man's subjects, who were born during his reign, who might even have caught a glimpse of him. The present queen, now in her eighties, remembers him very well indeed. As a child she often had breakfast with him, or visited in his company the stables where his horses were kept. She and he were great friends. He called her 'Lilibet'. She referred to him as 'Grandpapa England'.

Though the House of Windsor is clearly not ancient, it was the ancestors of George V who built Windsor Castle, and that was almost a thousand years ago. They have lived in it more or less ever since. It is in effect the same family, the same dynasty, that has ruled the country for a millennium, if under different names. The British royal family – and the Crown is the oldest institution in Britain, other than the Christian Church – has 're-branded' itself.

In pictures King George V looks the archetype of a monarch and an Englishman. Yet since his foreign-sounding family name had become a source of embarrassment or even antipathy, he decided – no doubt after consultation with the College of Arms, and whoever else might be interested in these matters – to change it by royal command.

BY THE KING
A PROCLAMATION

Declaring that the Name of Windsor is to be borne by His Royal House and Family and relinquishing the use of all German Titles and Dignities

GEORGE R.I.

WHEREAS WE having taken into consideration the Name and Title of Our Royal House and Family, have determined that henceforth Our House and Family shall be styled and known as the House and Family of Windsor:

AND WHEREAS We have further determined for Ourselves for and on behalf of Our descendants and all other the descendants of Our Grandmother Queen Victoria of blessed and glorious memory to relinquish and discontinue the use of all German Titles and Dignities:

AND WHEREAS We have declared these Our determinations in Our Privy Council:

NOW, THEREFORE, We, out of Our Royal Will and Authority, do hereby declare and announce that from the date of this Our Royal Proclamation Our Royal House and Family shall be styled and known as the House and Family of Windsor, and that all the descendants in the male line of Our said Grandmother Queen Victoria who are subjects of those Realms, other than female descendants who may marry or have married, shall bear the name of Windsor.

And do hereby further declare and announce that We for Ourselves and for and on behalf of Our descendants and all other the descendants of Our said Grandmother Queen Victoria who are subjects of these Realms, relinquish and enjoin the discontinuance of the use of the Degrees, Styles, Dignities, Titles and

Honours of Dukes and Duchesses of Saxony and Princes and Princesses of Saxe-Coburg and Gotha, and all other German Degrees, Styles, Dignities, Titles, Honours and Appellations to Us or to them heretofore belonging or appertaining.

Given at Our Court at Buckingham Palace, this Seventeenth day of July, in the year of our Lord One thousand nine hundred and seventeen, and in the Eighth year of Our Reign.

GOD SAVE THE KING

The spring of 1917 was a dark time for Britain. The war, which was now almost three years old, was going badly. In France and Belgium, the conflict had settled into a static contest in which neither side could defeat the other. The British armies, now no longer made up of regulars but of wartime volunteers whose only asset had been enthusiasm, were being ground down by attrition and decimated by frontal attacks on positions that were grimly defended. The previous summer the biggest of these, along the River Somme, had cost over 20,000 fatalities on the first day alone. The territory gained had ultimately amounted to about six miles. That winter, there had been another costly fight at Passchendaele. Scores of thousands of men were dying for nothing, and no one seemed to know what to do about it.

Elsewhere in the theatre of war, the situation was no better. An attempt by Allied troops to break through the Dardanelles and attack the enemy countries through a side-door had been a costly failure. In the Middle East, Britain had suffered disaster in the siege and fall of Kut. In East Africa the war was unwinnable, and would remain so. Further east the Russian Empire, a staunch ally if an inadequately equipped military power, underwent a revolution in the first months of the year that toppled the tsar. The new government had pledged to keep Russia in the war, but this promise was clearly not popular with a people that had suffered, perhaps, more than any other of the combatants, and the stability and commitment of the country's new rulers could not be guaranteed. If Russia should make peace, or be defeated by Germany, the consequences would be grave if not catastrophic. The Eastern Front would cease to exist, freeing a million men to fight in the West. With so many seasoned troops at the enemy's disposal, the rest of Continental Europe would surely be overrun.

Added to the morale-sapping sense of frustration was the horror of new weaponry. In 1915 the Germans had begun using poison gas. Zeppelin airships had flown over the English coast to bomb centres of population. From the early summer of 1917 there was a new danger – 'Gothas' were long-range German bombers that began mounting daylight raids. Their reign of terror lasted several months. In the course of one attack on London they killed 162 people, including 18 children in a primary school. This was barbarity on a scale never before experienced by the British populace, for whom wars had previously been something that went on in far-distant places.

Equally horrifying was the principle of 'unrestricted submarine warfare'. Germany possessed a fleet of submarines that patrolled the British coast and ranged far into the Atlantic. Their purpose was to starve the country into surrender by preventing food and raw materials from getting through. The Germans were bound by international treaty – as were other countries' navies – to give warning before sinking any merchant vessel and to allow the crew time to abandon ship. Since the surface vessels were routinely armed, the Germans felt that warning them simply invited retaliation and put their own crews at risk. They therefore reserved the right to attack without notice ships that were sailing for British ports, whether these belonged to combatant nations or not. One casualty was the liner RMS *Lusitania*, torpedoed off the Irish coast in May 1915 with the loss of over a thousand passengers. Among the dead were 128 Americans, whose country was neutral. The event caused worldwide outrage (even though later investigation suggested that the ship was illegally carrying huge stocks of ammunition and that the explosion of these, rather than just torpedo damage, was what sank her). It was a propaganda coup for the Allies, doing much to alienate American opinion from Germany, and led to a lull in submarine activity. In February 1917, however, after the policy had been ratified by vote in the German Parliament, unrestricted submarine warfare resumed. The enemy was back scouring the sea-lanes and as dangerous as ever. Only two months later the United States would enter the war.

It is therefore clear that during the spring and summer of that year, several elements – fear and frustration, 'Hun Frightfulness' and British public outrage – built toward a crescendo. Since the beginning of the conflict there had been mass hostility toward symbols of the enemy nations – the sacking of shops and businesses with German names, the banning of performances of Beethoven and Bach, the interning of German citizens, and even the stoning of dachshunds. All of that had long since removed from sight any public reminder of Britain's past teutonic connections – except for one: the royal family.

In this climate of hysteria it was, in a sense, the only target still standing. As soon as the war had begun, the king had returned all enemy uniforms to which he was entitled – he was Colonel-in-Chief of a Prussian regiment – just as the kaiser had handed back his honorary British ones (this swapping of clothes among Europe's monarchs would now cease for good), but a number of buildings still attested to the royal family's origins, such as the Albert Memorial in Kensington Gardens. Prince Albert's coat-of-arms, as well as his wife's, appeared as a motif on the arch spandrels and panels on the roadside of Westminster Bridge, and the crest was the same as that seen on the helmet-plates of some soldiers fighting against the British. In St George's Chapel, Windsor, the home of the Order of the Garter, the personal standards of German members still hung above their stalls. The surname of Britain's ruling family remained as Germanic as ever – a continuing source of discomfort, resentment, anger. Tsar Ferdinand of Bulgaria, ruler of a hostile power – one of the leaders of the enemy camp – even bore the name Saxe-Coburg-Gotha, and Gotha was of course also the name of the aircraft responsible for the recent massacre of civilians.

It got worse. Two of the king's relations were fighting for Germany while holding British titles: the Dukes of Albany and Cumberland. Another, Prince Albert, Duke of Schleswig-Holstein, was commandant of a prisoner-of-war camp that housed captured Britons. An open disrespect for the royal family in Britain was spreading with alarming speed. It was even rumoured that they had been signalling to zeppelins from the roof of Sandringham. The prime minister, and the king himself, received an increasing number of vitriolic letters demanding that something be done to rid the country of these associations. Prime ministerial advice became more pressing: public repudiation of the German connection would not only be timely and welcome, it was now vital.

With King George's decree, the British royal family publicly shed all connections with its German heritage. It did so in the nick of time; waiting even a few months more might have been leaving it too late. A contemporary cartoon in the satirical magazine *Punch*, titled 'A Good Riddance!', showed the king with a broom, sweeping crowns out of the door. Only several years of bitter war could have provoked such an attitude, and the king did not share it. He was yielding to public pressure and prime ministerial advice. It is likely that the decision caused him some private grief, not only because he was abandoning the only family name he had known but also because he saw the gesture as a capitulation to his country's mood of panic. Monarchy takes the long view. One of its most important functions is to represent continuity, to stand above the tides of fashion and the short-term preoccupations of the public, to remain unmoved by the issues of the moment. Another is to symbolize the best of its people's characteristics and aspirations – and certainly not to reflect their hatreds and prejudices. It must have been humiliating to have to yield to pressure from what appeared to be a mob howling for blood. Some supporters of the status quo may have felt that once the war was over the issue would quickly be forgotten, but in this they would have been mistaken. Hostility persisted for years after the Armistice in 1918 and the advent of another war, twenty years after the last, would ensure that anti-German feeling lingered well into the 1960s.

The College of Arms, the ultimate authority on genealogy, was not actually certain that the family was called Saxe-Coburg-Gotha in the first place, so that the change might not even have been necessary. What, in any case, were they to call themselves now? Members had accumulated over centuries a host of other titles – dukedoms, earldoms, lordships – that referred to places in Britain and would therefore sound more appropriate, though these ranks were not exalted enough to be used by a sovereign. One of the first suggestions – The House of Brunswick-Luneberg – was no improvement at all, being if anything even more obviously German. The House of Cerdic was hopelessly unevocative, sounding like the name of some patent medicine. Other dynastic names – Guelph and Wettin – that were equally teutonic had been associated with the family in the past. Both sounded just as alien and, to British ears, frankly silly. A number of further names and associations were dredged up from history, tried on like hats and discarded. Whatever was chosen had to sound unmistakably British and long-established, and to reinforce the sense of seamless national continuity that is one of the major reasons for having a monarchy in the first place. Options considered included Plantagenet, York, Lancaster, Fitzroy. All of these awakened echoes of schoolroom history lessons, of dreary things learned by rote, or of Shakespeare plays. D'Este, another option, was absurdly foreign. It was suggested that 'England' as a surname would suit the purpose, though this would at once have alienated subjects in other parts of the United Kingdom and overseas.

The notion of 'Windsor' as a family name was the inspired proposal of the king's private secretary, Lord Stamfordham. From the moment it was first mooted, it sounded right. It worked on every level and it followed precedent, for to take the name of a castle was established practice in Europe. The Habsburgs, rulers of Austria, had done so. The Oldenburgs had too. The Hohenzollerns, kings of Prussia and German emperors, took their high-sounding family name from their ancestral castle – Burg Hohenzollern – which was not in Prussia but in Swabia (the name literally meant 'high toll', and referred to the levies they imposed on those passing through their lands). Windsor was not only a name already familiar to every citizen of British territories, it also conjured up images of a building that itself symbolized both monarchy and empire. Depicted endlessly on postcards and biscuit tins, the Castle, invariably seen from the water meadows across the Thames from which it rises on its bluff, presented an image of unshakable solidity, majesty and power. The surrounding landscaped parks, crafted over centuries into a royal Arcadia, embellished with houses, cottages, monuments and follies, had loomed large in the life of all British monarchs for a millennium. In the imagination of the public its Round Tower was an instantly recognizable emblem of their sovereigns and their heritage.

The adoption of the new family name was immediately, immensely popular with the public, both in Britain itself and in her overseas territories. It was perceived as representing a massive sea-change in the attitude of the royal family. The monarchy was seen to have redefined its loyalties, and for the first time sided with its people rather than its own class. This decision proved its worth not only in the climate of wartime but in the inter-war period of austerity which followed.

Though their name had been Saxe-Coburg-Gotha, it is important to remember that neither they nor anyone else

had actually *used* it. Royalty did not actually need a surname. Kings, queens and princes signed their first name only;
dukes used only their title ('Gloucester'). With the adoption
of Windsor, the royal family had, for the first time, a surname like other families. It also sounded straightforward and
simple and much like anyone else's – indeed, it is a not especially uncommon name among the British. This added to the
perception that the royal family had joined the ranks of its
people.

The war had changed more than the name of Britain's
ruling family. It had altered the perception of them by society as a whole. Nothing like the experience of 1914–18 had
happened before – a conflict that affected every family and
every individual in the land, in some capacity or other. The
fact that all classes were active participants was a great social
leveller, and the royal family almost at once became less aloof.
There was a vast increase in the amount of charity work to
be done – the war hospitals and comforts funds to be visited
or encouraged – and there was a far greater need for public
appearances. Queen Mary, for instance, extensively visited
the street shrines erected to local people killed overseas or
in air raids. Royalty, both in uniform and out, became much
more conspicuous at a time of heightened patriotism. The
king's visits to the Western Front were well documented.

It was believed that the royals, who for obvious reasons
could not undertake active duty at the Front, were irritated
by this restriction and wished to 'do their bit' like other families. The Prince of Wales did his utmost to be posted to places
of danger, while his brother Bertie actually took part in the
war's most important naval battle. Relatively speaking – but
in a way that had not previously happened – royalty was sharing the day-to-day hardships and anxieties of its subjects.
Members of the royal family were seen to be concerned about
the plight of ordinary citizens, as they had been in peacetime
when some occasional disaster had befallen a community.
Members of the public, in turn, could worry about the safety

of young royals in theatres of conflict just as they would about their own sons.

Once the Armistice had been signed, the former sense of distance between monarchy and public would not return. The age of 'mass media' had by that time begun, with the advent of the cinema and the popular press at the turn of the century. Now there would also be wireless. The magazines and pictorial newspapers enjoying a heyday were always looking for ways to engage public attention, and would focus on the activities of the royal family in a way they had not previously done. The new generation of the family would, in any case, give rise to widespread fascination, either through the sheer charisma of the glamorous young Prince of Wales or the heartwarming domestic contentment of his brother Bertie's family.

The end of the conflict brought an international economic and social climate that was different from anything the king or his ministers had lived through before. With so few monarchies left, and the example of Bolshevik Russia encouraging revolution elsewhere, with a sense of entitlement among those who had fought and with an economic climate that was to prove the worst within living memory, the royal house was sailing through uncharted waters just as much as it had been during the war years. It was necessary to find out what sort of monarchy fitted these times and then swiftly adapt to provide it.

When the war had ended, there was speculation about who the older princes would marry. There would now be no further dynastic alliances – no more brides would be shipped across the North Sea, and no British prince could have courted public hostility by looking in that direction for a wife. (The Prince of Wales, having served in the war, was violently anti-German at that time in any case.) Lloyd George told the king privately that public opinion would no longer accept foreign spouses – a daring concept, since up to that time there had scarcely been any other kind. King George agreed, and he made another announcement, to the Privy Council, in 1917 that was to have enormous, and beneficial, consequences for his family. He stated that in future members of the royal house could wed British citizens. This, more than anything else, was to change the character of the British monarchy and make it into the middle-class-writ-large that it has been ever since.

In the decades that followed, through depression and war, economic boom and bust, industrial unrest, European integration and global terrorism, the House of Windsor has continued seeking to give its subjects the monarchy they want, treading a fine line between ancient and modern, grandeur and thrift, influence and neutrality. There have been mistakes, even disasters, but to an overwhelming extent Britain's royal family has been successful. Its popularity has never been in doubt and, though individual members may lose favour for a time, the institution itself remains remarkably sound.

The marriage of Prince William of Wales and Catherine Middleton in April 2011 appears to have secured the future of the British throne for, at the least, half a century to come. So much about this young man and woman – their casual meeting, their on-again, off-again courtship, the relative ordinariness of their tastes, their friends, and above all their desire to live as unassuming a life as possible – is perfectly in tune with modern attitudes and expectations. They are seen as finding their own way in life, and as having the ability to relate to their future subjects without formality or unease. All evidence suggests that their popularity will continue to grow and that they will be highly successful sovereigns thirty years from now.

In this they are simply the latest in a series of personalities to have benefited the monarchy, for the Windsors have, throughout their short history, been fortunate in those who have led and belonged to it.

There is more to the House of Windsor than its sovereigns; those who have married into it have also made immense contributions to its success. Queen Mary, wife of George V, was a minor princess who became the most regal of queens – but confessed at the end of her life that she would have loved to have had some ordinary experiences. Her daughter-in-law, Elizabeth Bowes-Lyon, was the strong-willed wife of George VI. She put her formidable energies to work in supporting her shy and diffident husband and in preparing her daughter to rule. Her superb ability to relate to people in all circumstances, particularly amid the hardships of war, made the monarchy more accessible and more universally well regarded than it had previously been. It was this Queen Elizabeth who, more than anyone else, created the concept of royalty that is familiar to us today.

Prince Philip, scion of a minor and unstable royal house, was seen as alien and unsuitable when he married the heir to the British throne. Yet he brought to the role of consort enormous energy and intelligence, and – through his interest in technology, sports and conservation – succeeded in making the monarchy more modern and relevant. His outspokenness has entertained – or horrified – his wife's subjects for over sixty years.

Another charismatic young woman, who turned out to share Queen Elizabeth's innate ability with people, married into the family in 1981. Diana Spencer brought to royalty a glamour that was at first very welcome. The tragedy of her subsequent life was to provide the monarchy's greatest challenge since the abdication crisis, yet she created for her sons a legacy of public sympathy and goodwill that bodes well for the future. Kate Middleton, a genuinely ordinary member of the British upper-middle class, has already demonstrated a personal charisma that is winning her more and more admirers and has shown that an ancient institution can still successfully absorb outsiders.

And what of the younger generations of Windsors? The queen's children grew up at a time when royals were having to compete on equal terms with their subjects, in education, in sports, in the armed forces and in employment. Some of these new experiences were decidedly painful, for them and for the country, yet lessons were learned and the adjustment has in general been a happy one. In the space of a single generation of royal youth it has come to seem unremarkable that they attend school (albeit private ones), go on to a provincial university, plan a career, have exposure to – and make friends with – people of all backgrounds. This has been standard practice for decades among other European monarchies, whose children have long been educated locally. The process has surely now gone as far as it can – there must be some distance left between royalty and everyone else, because they must remain an abstract national symbol, and one that reflects the nation's better qualities. This is guaranteed by the homes in which they live, the vehicles in which they travel, the possessions and collections at their family's disposal, the duties they perform and the deference of those who surround them. Informality and ordinariness have probably gone as far as they can go without letting too much 'daylight in on magic' (to quote Walter Bagehot's famous phrase). The result is, perhaps, a royal family that is better adjusted, more comfortable with its people, and more genuinely popular with them, than ever before.

2

GEORGE V, 1910–36

'I am only a very ordinary sort of fellow.'
George V, on the occasion of his Silver Jubilee, 1935

Like his son and namesake after him, George V had never expected to be king. He was a second son, and his elder brother, Prince Albert Victor, was the one who received the training for kingship, at least to a relative degree. The boys were born less than a year and a half apart, Albert Victor (at Queen Victoria's request he was named after both his grandparents, but was known to the family as 'Eddy') in January 1864 and George Frederick Ernest Albert on 3 June 1865. Their father, the Prince of Wales, was not entrusted by the queen with any role in affairs of state and therefore his sons, although they were respectively second and third in line to the throne, did not grow up to be familiar with political or constitutional issues, or with any sense of impending responsibility.

George may have been the second son, but he was far more suited by nature to be king than his brother was. Though somewhat spoiled by his mother, who was devoted to him, he had none of Eddy's languid and unfocused nature. What he did have were good manners and a sense of duty that developed early and became so overriding that it guided his every action for the rest of his life. He was expected to make a career in the Navy – despite the fact that his grandmother thought this an unsound idea – and was ideally suited to the Service. He had a genuine ability in seamanship that would have made him extremely able in command of a vessel. He also excelled in mathematics, a highly important skill in such a technical profession.

At the age of twelve he performed impressively in the entrance exam for midshipmen and then undertook, together with his tutor and brother, a series of three voyages that gave him valuable experience of the Navy, the British Empire and the wider world. By the time he became king he would have travelled more widely than any of his predecessors. While overseas he paid formal calls on rulers and governors, and thus his time in the Navy was in no sense an escape from protocol – or from education, for lessons continued on board.

George probably received a finer education through this process than he could have gained anywhere else. He responded to the sights and sounds and experiences, and to the instruction he received, in exactly the way his elders had hoped he would. Naval discipline had stamped out a previous tendency toward self-indulgence. His inherent abilities as a seaman had been honed by practice to make him a thoroughly professional officer who would have been a credit to any ship and who could, in other circumstances, have enjoyed a successful career. His patriotism, greatly enhanced by his tour of British overseas territories and by the respect with which a grandson of the Queen Empress was received, was to become the hallmark of his character. As his biographer Harold Nicolson was to write: 'Not being an intellectual he was never variable: he remained uniform throughout his life.'

A tutor, John Dalton, had been appointed to teach both the

princes, though he was not to have exclusive charge of them for long. As was normal for young men of their era with exalted future roles, the regime they endured was strict and the curriculum crowded and demanding, including as it did not only 'book learning' but, by way of exercise, military drill. Dalton quickly came to realize that neither of his charges was naturally academic, and Eddy in particular had an attention span of discouraging brevity. While he has been seen by some historians as slow-witted to the point of virtual imbecility, others have suggested that he suffered from mild epilepsy and that his inattention was perhaps characteristic of children born prematurely (he had arrived two months earlier than expected). George was more intelligent, less indolent, more amenable to instruction and to reason, and more aware of the dignity of his position. He was also absolutely devoted to his father, and wanted above all to earn his approval.

Though it has been suggested that their tutor was a dull and conventional man who could have gained more of a response from the boys had he been more flexible, they in fact had a happy childhood that was not spoiled by an excess of discipline or deadening rote learning. Their father believed that the Royal Navy would provide them with the best preparation for life, and it was possible for them to go into the Senior Service at a very young age (Eddy was thirteen and George twelve). Because they worked best whilst together, they stayed together in the Service. Instead of learning about the world through geography lessons in a schoolroom, they would see it for themselves. Rather than receiving their education entirely from tutors in a 'class' that consisted only of themselves, they would have the company of boys their own age, a largely random collection of youngsters with whom they would live on equal terms and whose respect they would have to earn through their ability to carry out the same tasks. It was, for the time, a remarkably democratic upbringing and it gave them common ground with their grandmother's people in a way that very few other experiences could have done.

Their naval careers began at Dartmouth. This training facility – later renamed Britannia Royal Naval College – is today a substantial and imposing collection of buildings over-looking Dartmouth harbour in Devon. At that time it was a fifty-year-old wooden warship – HMS *Britannia*, a veteran of the Crimea – moored in the same harbour, aboard which aspiring officers received instruction. It was as cramped and claustrophobic as being at sea. Dalton joined the ship with his two charges, for he had been appointed chaplain. He would continue to supervise the progress of one or both of them for many years to come.

Following training, the two princes and their tutor trans-ferred to another RN vessel, HMS *Bacchante*, and made three voyages round the world, which took them away for several years (1879–82). They sailed the Mediterranean, vis-iting Greece, Palestine, Egypt and Aden. They also went ashore in South Africa, Ceylon, Singapore, Japan and Aus-tralia, the Falkland Islands, South America and the United States. While in Japan, both of them visited a tattoo parlour and George was, for the rest of his life, to bear on his arm the design of a dragon in red and blue ink. When they returned, their grandmother was horrified to find that neither boy could speak French or German, the latter an outright neces-sity given their overwhelming preponderance of teutonic relations. They studied these languages for a time but in nei-ther case with conspicuous success, despite spending an inter-lude at Heidelberg. Whatever the charms of this town – the 'Oxford of Germany' – George considered it 'beastly dull' in comparison with the places he had seen on his travels, and he hated German, considering it 'a rotten language, which I find very difficult'.

He might have been influenced here by more than mere personal disinclination. Though so many of his relations were German, the relative to whom he was closest – his mother – hated the country. A daughter of the king of Denmark, she would never forgive the Prussians for their war of 1864 against her people. The German states – they were not yet at the time a united nation – had, under Bismarck's leadership, aggressively seized territory from a small and peaceful nation. Princess Alexandra's vehemence can be seen in a statement she wrote after her son had been appointed honorary colonel of a Prussian regiment: 'My Georgie boy has become a real, live, filthy, blue-coated, Pickelhaube German soldier!' (A *pickelhaube* was the brass-and-leather spiked helmet ubiquitous throughout the German armies.) If he had good reason to inherit a dislike of Germany and its language, he had no such excuse for his failure to master French. He managed to communicate in that language, but with the Englishman's perverse pride in speaking it very badly.

George enjoyed his period of naval service immensely. One of those straightforward personalities who recognize at once the path he wishes to follow in life, he took to the sea and the camaraderie of the wardroom with genuine enthusiasm. He had the habit of instant obedience, and would be characterized all his life by an absolute respect for those above him – just as he expected similar reverence from those below. His period of naval service was to last for fourteen years, from 1877 to 1892, when the death of his brother meant that he was called to another type of duty. He was successful in professional exams, gaining qualifications in seamanship, gunnery and torpedoes – achievements that his exalted position alone could not have won for him. The Navy gave him a quarterdeck view of the world that would stay with him for the rest of his life – a bluff, blunt, to-the-point manner that would include fo'c'sle language, paroxysms of anger and loud expressions of impatience with those who failed to match up to his expectations. Deeply conservative by nature and entirely at home in this hierarchical, no-nonsense world, the Navy made him a man of absolutely decided views, which he saw no reason ever to change. Unlike his grandmother, who never travelled outside Europe and who thus never saw the worldwide empire over which she presided, George had first-hand experience of the lives of her overseas subjects. It was ironic that, having spent his early life roaming the world, he would come to hate foreign travel. Once he became king he would make only one significant trip outside his realms – a Mediterranean cruise – and even that was undertaken only on doctor's orders. He did not want to go, and no doubt would have given vent to one of his outbursts when advised to take the trip.

Delighted at being lower in the order of succession than Eddy, George had expected to spend his life as a serving officer. He was given one of the most agreeable postings in the Service – to Malta, where he was under the command of his uncle, the Duke of Edinburgh. (Sixty years later another Duke of Edinburgh would also serve there in the Royal Navy, and his wife would spend a very pleasant interlude on the island before becoming queen.) George was handsome and personable (his only faults, perhaps, his knock knees and the bulging blue eyes he had inherited from his grandmother), and he developed an affection for his uncle's daughter, Marie. She was a spirited girl with both intelligence and a fine sense of humour. They were distant enough relations for a marriage to be possible, but her mother did not want him for a son-in-law. The Duchess of Edinburgh was the only daughter of Tsar Alexander II. Haughty by nature, she had never taken to living in England, and disliked her husband's family. She discouraged the match, and her formidable personality was an obstacle that could not be surmounted. Ironically, in that she considered the British royal family too pro-German, she was to marry Marie to a member of Prussia's ruling house, the Hohenzollerns, which had been invited to occupy the throne of Romania. As queen of that country, Marie would exert influence to ensure that it fought on the Allied side in the Great War. Her children would subsequently marry so extensively into neighbouring royal families that she would earn the sobriquet 'the Mother-in-Law of the Balkans'.

It was during this period that George grew the beard that was to become his trademark (Eddy, though senior in years, was not yet able to manage one), and it was at this time too that he began the stamp collection that was to provide him with stimulus and solace, and which would grow into one of the finest in the world. He also became the first of his family to develop a passion for polo, a game taken up by British officers in India and which had spread throughout the British Empire. Enthusiasm for it was all but compulsory among the officer class, and to play it well was a certain route to popularity.

His brother, who lacked any noticeable passion for anything, had meanwhile moved on to another phase of preparation for his eventual life. He went, still accompanied by John Dalton, to Cambridge to study, though he was to be exempted from having to take any exams. He followed this by going into the Army. Serving in the 10th Hussars, a fashionable cavalry regiment, he settled into a routine of training and garrison duties at Aldershot and Hounslow, though he rebuffed attempts by his fellow officers to 'make a man of the world of him'. A certain innocence was noticeable in his nature. In spite of this, he became mired in scandal when, in 1889, the police raided a homosexual brothel in London's Cleveland Street. He was not among those apprehended, but it was alleged that he had been a visitor. Modern biographers have dismissed this as implausible, but there were persistent rumours at the time. To these have since been added the theory that he was Jack the Ripper, the serial killer whose murder of a number of prostitutes brought a reign of terror to the streets of Whitechapel during the autumn of 1888. Why would he have wanted to do such a thing? Allegedly because he was being blackmailed over involvement in a vice-ring, and sought to silence witnesses. In fact, crimes of this nature must have taken considerable planning. They would have been well beyond Prince Eddy's abilities, even had it not been definitively proved that he was at Balmoral when most of them took place.

Though both his charges might have been a disappointment to Mr Dalton in that neither of them showed intellectual promise, they were good, agreeable young men, dutiful and dignified, whom one observer described as having 'a total absence of haughtiness'.

Eddy began to carry out royal duties. He visited India, and at home opened the Hammersmith suspension bridge. He was created Duke of Clarence and Avondale, and began gradually taking his place as a public figure. While his military career was mere marking of time, he did of course have another significant role to perform. He must marry and continue the succession. He made three attempts to do so. Limited in his choice of spouse to a member of another ruling house, he chose one who was entirely suitable: the curiously named Princess Alix of Hesse and by Rhine. She simply did not like him, however, and refused his offer. She would go on to make a love match with the Russian tsarevich, Nicholas, marrying him in 1894. They would be immensely happy together, though their lives would become increasingly tragic, ending in front of a Bolshevik firing squad in 1918.

Eddy's second attempt at finding a match seemed more promising. His attachment to Princess Hélène of Orléans was a matter of genuine, and mutual, affection. She belonged to the ousted Bourbon family. (There was no reason why a member of a ruling family could not marry someone from a deposed one. It was the blood that counted, not their current status. Queen Victoria, in fact, had something of a weakness for exiled sovereigns, and her country gave sanctuary to several of them.) The Bourbons were former rulers of France, and Princess Hélène was a Roman Catholic. This was a serious obstacle, but both parties attempted to compromise. Eddy offered to renounce his place in the succession. She offered to convert. In the event his family was willing, but hers was not. Her father refused to let the marriage take place, his religious convictions overruling even the prospect of his daughter one day occupying a throne.

In the third instance Eddy was successful. His choice was inspired, for the young woman was eminently suited to be a queen. Victoria Mary, Princess of Teck, was nicknamed 'May' after the month in which she had been born. She was his second cousin once removed and related to the Dukes of Württemberg, an archetypal German dynasty. She had, however, grown up with her mother at the British Court. By the peculiar standards of royalty she was impoverished and obscure, overlooked by members of more illustrious families. Nevertheless she was extremely personable – lively, clever, charming and pretty – and observers could see that she would provide a useful counterweight to the prince's natural inertia. In December 1891 Eddy proposed to her at a house party, to her considerable surprise, and she accepted. Queen Victoria was delighted. Eddy, it seemed, had made a very wise decision.

But his time was running out. Less than two months later, in January 1892, he caught influenza at Sandringham from his sister, Princess Victoria. He rapidly developed pneumonia and within six weeks was dead. It was a tragic loss for the entire royal family. It has been suggested by some writers and conspiracy theorists that Eddy was an imbecile rather than merely slow-witted, and that he was either murdered or his death faked so that he could be removed from the succession to make way for his brother. This is not the way royal families tend to behave, however, or at least not in modern times. His death was witnessed by his parents, his brother, his fiancée and a number of others, so we must assume it really happened; he was known to be suffering from the symptoms of pneumonia. The grief of those he left behind was genuine and lasting – his mother, Queen Alexandra, had his bedroom preserved as he had left it, an echo of Queen Victoria's homage to Albert. George was now the heir. Created Duke of York, he had to quit active service and begin the study of constitutional history that would be important to him in the future.

And he inherited not only his brother's place in the succession but Eddy's betrothed. Princess May was taller than George, by half an inch, but with the piled-up hairstyle of a lady of that era she was to overshadow her husband physically all his life. George and May genuinely liked each other, and a period of mourning for someone whom both of them had loved gave them a significant amount in common. Queen Victoria approved of the princess and felt she would still make a useful consort. Suitable girls of the right background and religious beliefs were not so plentiful that they could be allowed to go to waste. It was with pleasure and approval rather than any sense of impropriety that George's family watched him grow closer to his dead brother's fiancée. Such a match was considered perfectly respectable, and indeed there was a recent precedent. In 1865 the Russian tsarevich, Nicholas, had died. The next-eldest brother had taken his place in the succession and had become Tsar Alexander III in 1881. He had married his dead brother's fiancée, the beautiful Princess Dagmar of Denmark, who was the younger sister of Queen Alexandra. Family affection for a young woman, not to mention dynastic interests, were what mattered most.

It was a year after Eddy's death that George proposed, and the couple were married in the Chapel Royal in the summer of 1893. They remained devoted to each other for the rest of their lives. Their history demonstrates two things. First, that even within royal circles, governed by duty and expectations and with so much arranged by others, there could still be rejected advances and unsuccessful marriage proposals. Secondly, that in such a world there could be genuine romance, mutual passion or close companionship, and lifelong attachment. Though these young people had met within the narrow confines of the Court, their marriage was as successful as that of any couple who had encountered each other by chance and had had no obstacles to contend with. George was, by his own frank admission, inarticulate in expressing tenderness verbally. His letters to his wife, however, give adequate proof of a sensitive and appreciative nature that is surprisingly at odds with the bluff and bad-tempered naval officer that others perceived. This was entirely understandable, however. Among royalty affection was considered to be a private matter, and no hint of it should be displayed in public. That view is still held by many members of the royal family today.

In temperament, George was the opposite of his father, who had in 1901 became King Edward VII. From early manhood Edward was given to keeping raffish company, and indulging freely in games of chance and sexual licentiousness. Respectable people had dreaded the moment he became head of state, though once he was on the throne he managed – without altering his habits in the slightest – to gain a somewhat wider popularity. Though his morals, and mistresses, were to earn him the nickname 'Edward the Caresser', the new century was less censorious than the old, and he fitted surprisingly comfortably into the position of father – or grandfather, for he was almost sixty when he succeeded – of the nation. He clearly enjoyed being king. He had a benevolent charm, and was perceived by his subjects as kindly. His son George, who of course became Prince of Wales, promised however a different and far more widely acceptable style of rule once he succeeded. Both George and May were by nature shy and private. The son had little of the father's outgoing charm. Though George was fond of horses and attended races, he was nothing like as enthusiastic about the Turf as Edward was, and was never linked with the sort of 'fast set' that had surrounded his father. The Yorks in fact derived little pleasure from going out in Society.

They lived a modest country existence on the Sandringham Estate. York Cottage, their home from their marriage until 1926, had been George's dwelling when he was a bachelor, and he seemed happy to remain there as father of a family. The rooms were small and poky, though this endeared the house to him. They reminded him of shipboard cabins, and all his life he was to prefer accommodation of such limited dimensions. The house looked like any large suburban villa, and was remarkable only for its ugliness. A structure of mock-Tudor beams, tacked-on gables and crazy angles, it

displayed the worst excesses of contemporary suburban his-
toricist pastiche (it now houses the Sandringham estate offices). The house was to become increasingly cramped as George
and May added more and more children to their family (there
would be six in total, plus all the servants necessary to look
after them). Despite having the treasures of the Royal Collections to choose from, they had their home furnished from
Maple's store in London's Tottenham Court Road, a place
synonymous with middle-class taste, and hung the walls
with reproductions of pictures from the Royal Academy.
They resembled, in every way, a family of the upper bourgeoisie. While Victoria and Albert had adopted the values of
the middle class, their lifestyle had been that of the senior
aristocracy. George and May not only *thought* like the middle
class, but *lived* like them too.

George was interested in farming the estate and, in an age
that had invented so many new forms of leisure, he excelled
at sports and games. He played golf and tennis well enough,
but his real passions were sailing and shooting. He was both
a fanatical and a highly accurate slaughterer of game birds –
one of the half-dozen best shots in Britain. His record bag
would be achieved in 1913: over a thousand birds in six hours.
He also continued with – surely the most suburban of hob-
bies – his stamp collecting. Harold Nicolson lamented that, as
Duke of York, 'he did nothing at all but kill animals and stick
in stamps'. Perhaps so, but the collection he built, of stamps
from all over the world but specializing, understandably, in
his own various realms, became by far the most complete and
valuable of its kind, and is still kept in its own room at Buckingham Palace. This proved to have been time wisely invested.

As for his wife, she provided him with a settled and tranquil domestic life that was to be the foundation of much
happiness. Like her mother-in-law, Queen Alexandra, she
was quiet, dutiful and supportive. Upright in bearing, she
appeared wonderfully regal – everyone's idea of what a queen
should look like – and when in the course of time she became

one, would set standards of dignity that would influence the family for generations to come. For example, she never, never laughed – at least not in public – because she said it made her look like a horse. She shared to a large extent the unworldliness of royalty, as demonstrated when she visited East End slums and asked the inhabitants: 'Why do you live here?' She was to prove a highly useful confidant and counsellor to George, however, throughout his life. She did not share his rigid conservatism, believing that 'one must move with the times', but she would never have defied her dogmatic husband who was, after all, also her sovereign. One unusual aspect of the Duchess of York was that she smoked (in private), but then so did her mother-in-law, Princess Alexandra. May's parsimonious upbringing, as well as her preference for a modest, unostentatious life, would cause her as queen to do without ladies-in-waiting. Though this was an economy measure as well as a matter of personal preference, it might also have been a gesture of revenge against those aristocratic families that had snubbed or sneered at her during her impoverished upbringing. It was the senior aristocracy whose families traditionally provided the candidates for such posts and she was thus denying them the chance to enjoy the associated prestige. Nevertheless the simple domesticity of the royal couple would win widespread approval, expressed by one peer, Lord Esher, who said: 'We have reverted to the ways of Queen Victoria.' After the extravagances of Edward VII, this was indeed welcome.

One vice that May possessed, however, which was to become more pronounced as she became older, was her insatiable desire to acquire antiques, bibelots, and items of furniture. She bought these – she was a well-established customer of London dealers in such things – but she was also 'given' them. On visits to her friends, or even to strangers, if she took a liking to something she would make it increasingly clear that she wished to have it. If hints were not enough, she might ask outright or use some honeyed phrase such as: 'It's so kind of you to give me this!' Hostesses made a point of hiding their best pieces before she arrived, and some found themselves engaged in unseemly verbal tussles as they tried to save family heirlooms. May's single-minded determination usually won, and she would return to the Palace, in some instances, with her Daimler car filled with treasures. The present queen has, in cases where the original owner of an object can be traced, made a point of having these prizes returned.

Just as George and May defied the stereotype of an arranged marriage by being genuinely in love, they were to do so also by being affectionate parents in an age when the aristocracy was renowned for keeping its children at a distance. The Yorks had, of course, a staff of nurses and governesses to deal with the more mundane chores of looking after their offspring, but both were very fond of them and the duke, in particular, loved to bathe them or sit them on his knee ('I make a very good lap,' he boasted). As his children grew, he took to marching them round the estate for exercise.

Once his father succeeded to the throne, George, now Duke of Cornwall and York and, from November 1901, Prince of Wales, began to train in earnest for the task he might expect to inherit before many more years had passed, for King Edward was over sixty and given to both heavy smoking and overeating. Because Edward had been denied the chance to learn about kingship while his mother was alive, he was intent on leaving his own successor better informed. As soon as he succeeded, he had George's desk placed beside his own at Windsor and the two of them often worked together, examining the contents of dispatch boxes and discussing the procedures for getting through a sovereign's paperwork. As well as administration, George continued to learn more about the public side of royal duty.

He went, on his father's behalf, on a tour of the Empire. His task was to thank the Dominions for their support in the Boer War, and he visited all of them: Australia, New Zealand, South Africa itself, Canada and Newfoundland. He was very good at the protocol and formality that went with his duties. Vintage film of him in Canada, handing out medals to a seemingly endless line of recipients, shows him ramrod-straight throughout. He cut an equally impressive figure when opening the first Australian Parliament. He had mastered the art – essential for members of his family or 'profession' – of standing for long hours without looking either tired or bored. If he did not look bored, however, neither did he look happy. He very rarely smiled in public. 'We sailors never smile when on duty,' he said. (This was an attitude that would also often characterize his granddaughter, Queen Elizabeth II, during official engagements.) George made speeches fluently and well, and he actually sounded English, for he had not inherited his father's Germanic accent. Had he done so, it would no doubt have proved another grave disadvantage once the Great War had broken out.

He made another tour – of India – in 1905–6, gaining personal insight into the British Empire's most important overseas territory. Curiously, one of his most marked impressions was of indignation at the treatment of educated Indians by the British rulers. In this he was both right – the later universal understanding of racism had not of course yet become manifest – and prescient. For some generations the British had been providing education of a high standard to Indians. This meant that many thousands of talented, intelligent and ambitious local men aspired to better themselves and to take a hand in governing their country. There were no avenues to enable them to do so, or to make best use of the training they had received. Within a generation it would be these men who would spearhead the movement for independence from Britain. They had nothing to gain by keeping the connection, and George could see this.

His father sought to ensure that George was gaining equally useful experience for his future role at home. A major reason for Edward's own youthful dissipation had been that he had no constitutional function to fulfil. Pleasure-seeking had therefore become his chief purpose in life. This was a not uncommon experience for those waiting their turn to fill the thrones of Europe. The Italian monarchy, for instance, believed that pertinent knowledge should not be provided until the prince actually succeeded. ('Here in the House of Savoy we rule one at a time!') The result was a dysfunctional dynasty, of which Italians would rid themselves by plebiscite after less than a century of rule.

George's working relationship with his father, who instead of formal training for his role had at least had a lifetime of observing the monarchy at close quarters, gave him considerable wisdom. When Edward died, in May 1910, after more than nine years on the throne, his son would write that: 'I have lost my best friend and the best of fathers. I never had a [cross] word with him in my life. I am heart-broken and overwhelmed with grief but God will help me in my responsibilities and darling May will be my comfort as she has always been. May God give me strength and guidance in the heavy task that has befallen me.' Though these private sentiments were not of course known to his subjects at the time, they demonstrate to posterity that his was a deeply fulfilling marriage.

The era over which Edward VII had presided as king was not one of complacency. In Britain the advance of socialism was obvious in the presence – and increasing numbers – of Labour Members in the House of Commons (the Party had been founded in 1900). The suffragettes, although one can understand their frustration and their cause, left an ugly scar on the Edwardian age through acts of public vandalism. It was a time of militant labour unrest, strike chaos, confrontations with police and with soldiers. Struggling to pay the massive costs involved in the arms race against Germany while simultaneously financing a huge and innovative programme of social reform, the Liberal government imposed punitive taxes on land and income that drove the aristocracy to fury. The 'People's Budget', rejected once by the House of Lords but passed after a general election had returned the Liberals to power, served to emphasize that the era which had begun on 1 January 1901 would be known to history as 'the century of the common man'.

Internationally these were extremely dangerous years for monarchies. With the rise of anarchism – a pointless, violence-for-its-own-sake creed that sanctioned acts of murder against heads of state – the crowned heads of Europe paid a heavy toll. There were no attacks on the British royal family in Britain itself – an indication of their people's comparative moderation and hatred of extremes – though an attempt had been made to kill King Edward in Brussels in 1900, and George witnessed for himself the agonies undergone by his fellow sovereigns while attending the marriage of his cousin, Princess Ena, to King Alfonso XIII of Spain. On the way to the wedding ceremony through the streets of Madrid in May 1906, a bomb was thrown from the crowd. It failed to kill any royals, but the death-toll included a number of their servants as well as members of the public. The bride's dress was spattered with blood.

George's coronation was held in June 1911 and was followed by a Durbar in India, to acknowledge him as emperor. He used the occasion to announce that the capital would move from Calcutta to a designated site at New Delhi. The vast red sandstone complex, planned and built by the English architect Sir Edwin Lutyens, would prove to be by far the greatest architectural legacy of George's reign, though it would represent British power for an extremely short time.

As king during a time of unpleasant social and political upheaval, George saw his principal role as that of peacemaker between warring factions. He deplored extremes of any sort. Though he disliked the suffragettes for the violence of their protests, he was genuinely horrified by the force-feeding to which hunger-striking members of the movement were subjected in prison. While unsympathetic toward those who caused industrial unrest, he sought nevertheless to promote compromise between management and labour. He also saw it as vital to encourage moderation between the opposing factions in Ireland. He and his wife, now known by her regnal name of Queen Mary, went on a series of visits to the various regions of Britain so that their people could have some sense of personal contact with them, a significant populist gesture that would become habitual with their descendants.

While British society was riven by the bitterest class conflict within living memory, the United Kingdom was in imminent danger of disintegration over the issue of Home Rule for Ireland, which Campbell-Bannerman's Liberal government was hoping to push through during 1912. The threat of rule from Dublin rather than London was enough to cause Irish Protestants to form a paramilitary organization – the Ulster Volunteer Force – which stockpiled arms and trained its members to use them. The nationalists in the southern counties made similar arrangements, and civil war became increasingly likely. While posterity knows that the United Kingdom could survive the division of Ireland and the loss of its twenty-six southern counties, contemporary opinion could not view without alarm the notion that a country that was the centre of a worldwide empire would itself be torn asunder. This was the gravest problem imaginable for a British government.

George's solution was to summon a conference at Buckingham Palace to hear the grievances on both sides. By now it was the summer of 1914 – negotiations began on 21 July. The king would have been hoping for a mutual display of goodwill and compromise but the gathering lasted only three days, for suddenly Ireland was not the most serious difficulty on the horizon. Within a fortnight of the delegates gathering at the Palace, old Europe – the social and political order that had lasted for much of the nineteenth century – would start to unravel.

The European war that was about to begin would be by far the most significant event of George's reign. It started with the assassination of the Austrian Archduke Franz Ferdinand and his wife by Serbian nationalists. Though war had been likely for several years, no one had expected it to start in such an obscure corner of the Continent, and over a matter that seemed at first to have been resolved when Serbia offered an apology. The Habsburgs were one of the few European dynasties with which the British throne had no family connections. Nor was their empire in competition with Britain in any naval or military sphere. Now, because of an internal quarrel within their territory, most of Europe was to be caught up in an Armageddon that would dwarf in size and slaughter any conflict seen before. Because Austria mobilized, Russia did so too. With Russia facing the Austrians, its ally Germany came to its aid. But Germany's plans for a European war assumed that France – which wanted revenge for the *last* European war – would strike at its western border. France must therefore be treated as an enemy and invaded before it could attack. To deal with this threat while avoiding incurring heavy casualties meant invading the country through its 'back door', by crossing through neutral Belgium. Britain, which did not want Germany gaining control of the Channel ports, had guaranteed (by a treaty of 1839) to come to Belgium's aid in such a circumstance. An ultimatum to the German government, demanding withdrawal from Belgium by midnight of 4 August 1914, went unanswered. The war began as British clocks struck eleven on that warm summer night.

George was a cousin of two of the combatants – the German kaiser and the Russian tsar. Could his intervention halt the juggernaut before it ran out of control? The answer was no. Tsar Nicholas had already failed to have the cause of conflict – the Sarajevo assassination – referred to the International Court at The Hague. The mood among the General Staffs was too belligerent for a last-minute climbdown, and no one at the time had any reason to expect a protracted war. Recent European conflicts had been short: the wars fought by Prussia in the 1860s against Denmark and Austria had lasted a matter of a few weeks, while the Franco-Prussian conflict had taken ten months. It was assumed that, with the vast armies and the destructive weaponry available, this new outbreak of hostilities would be a short and violent clash that would bring some decisive result within months at most. The German and Austrian governments even welcomed war as a means of combating left-wing tendencies (the Social Democratic Party) or separatism at home.

For the British government, the outbreak of war diverted attention from the pressing matter of Ireland (many thousands of Irishmen, especially among loyalist Ulstermen, enlisted at once). George gave his consent the following month to a Bill granting Irish Home Rule – no other solution was possible in the end – but it carried the proviso that it would not be enacted until after the war. The issue was shelved for the time being – or so it was assumed. For years it had been received wisdom that a European war would come. Some crisis would provoke it, the spark would be lit and the conflagration begin. It was, however, disappointing that the cause should prove to be events in a small and obscure Balkan country. 'God grant that we may not have a European war thrust upon us, and for such a stupid reason too, no, I don't mean stupid, but to have to go to war on account of tiresome Serbia beggars belief,' Queen Mary wrote to her aunt, the Grand Duchess of Mecklenburg-Strelitz, at the end of July.

The king was naturally grieved by the division of Europe into warring camps that put many of his relatives on the other side. It had always been assumed that the network of relationships among the royal houses would make war between them an impossibility. Though these connections had been important, they were no more than window-dressing, however. The Parliaments or General Staffs that actually ran the different countries could act with no more than nominal reference to them. Even Tsar Nicholas, in theory an autocrat who could take a binding decision to involve his country in the war, was sensitive to public opinion, which was largely in favour of assisting Serbia against the perceived bullying of neighbouring rival powers. The mob-mentality that rapidly grew up throughout Europe was astonishing in view of what was actually to happen. For young Frenchmen, in particular, the outbreak promised an opportunity to wrest back from Germany the provinces of Alsace and Lorraine, lost in the Franco-Prussian War. For almost fifty years schoolchildren had been brought up to hate the country that had stolen this territory from their forefathers. Many gave thanks that they had been born at the right time in history to take part in such a national crusade.

No British sovereign before this had presided over an era of total war. The situation was without precedent, with the country under attack, the mobilization of the entire civilian world necessary to support the war effort, and the need always to work with allies, who could be difficult. George had to make up his role as war-monarch as he went along. He certainly looked the part, and was to feature often in patriotic publications. Though others would naturally be associated with the conflict – Prime Ministers Asquith and Lloyd George, the Cabinet Minister Winston Churchill, Generals French, Kitchener and Haig – the king, who alone among them remained constantly at the head of affairs, became a potent symbol for his armies and his people. His function in the war was, like that of any constitutional sovereign, to be a rallying point for the nation, to attend public events in uniform as Commander-in-Chief of the Forces, to encourage his people through a relentless programme of visits, inspections, speeches, messages.

With his sensitive nature and his highly developed sense of duty, he did this effectively and well. He also set an important example. At the outbreak of war his cousin Nicholas had imposed Prohibition on Russia. In 1915 George was persuaded, reluctantly, to take the more modest step of declaring that the royal cellars would be sealed for the duration of the war

– a move that was aimed at encouraging workers in the munitions industry to follow suit. They were forbidden to drink, on safety grounds. (George in fact thought the gesture pointless and irritating, describing Lloyd George's suggestion as 'a scurvy trick'.) The whole country was aware of the king's abnegation, though it was rumoured he was secretly taking glasses of port regardless. Whatever happened in private, his sense of duty was such that he refused alcohol in public even on occasions such as visits to the Front. He made several such journeys, dressed in Field Marshal's uniform, to inspect the armies, tour the rear areas, confer with Generals. Though as usual surrounded by formalities, he enjoyed the more relaxed atmosphere in France and Flanders. He was flattered by the welcome he received, and gratified that he was sharing the same environment, if not the same dangers, as the fighting men. Hordes of them would follow him about, which he liked. It was on one such visit in October 1915, however, that a sudden burst of cheering frightened his horse, which reared up and then fell on him. The injury was excruciating – his pelvis had broken in two places. It was badly diagnosed, and never properly healed.

In a time of national hardship, the royal family had to be seen to be doing their job, but also to be living as modestly as possible. It had never previously been necessary for the monarchy to seem so ostentatiously ordinary, though this would be something that they would continue to do throughout the coming generations. The king was photographed in shirt-sleeves, tending a vegetable plot in the grounds at Windsor. For much of the war, German U-boats attempted to starve out Britain by sinking shipping around its coast and thus preventing the importing of foodstuffs. With agricultural estates at their disposal at Windsor, Sandringham and Balmoral, the royal family were unlikely to suffer hardship, but the gesture was made and recorded and noticed. While politicians, press and public blamed the war's reverses on the generals and called for their removal, the king publicly maintained loyalty to them. This was most conspicuous in the case of Sir Douglas Haig, who fell from favour as a result of the disastrous losses suffered on the Western Front. Royalty could not indulge itself in the luxury of criticism or disapproval, at least in public.

The king was known to hold humane views on the treatment of prisoners. A fair man in private and in public, he had, as we have seen, created for himself the role of peacemaker and moderator with regard to the domestic politics of the United Kingdom. He showed a similar attitude toward the national enemy. ('Intern me first!' he had cried when the locking up of enemy nationals had first been mooted.) From the moment that German troops invaded Belgium, Britain was awash with refugees who told blood-curdling stories of teutonic barbarity. Civilians had been taken hostage and executed, women had been routinely violated. Much of this was later found to have been exaggerated, but in a climate of wartime hysteria no outrage seemed implausible to the British public. Once the submarines of the German Fleet attempted to starve the country by sinking shipping, public outrage reached a new pitch. George opposed the demand for summary reprisals against captured submariners, and no doubt held the same view toward any airship crews that managed to survive after being shot down. Never by a single remark in public or in private did the king endorse the call for examples to be made of captured Germans. Though sensitive enough to weep over both public outrages and personal slights, he expressed no vindictive or draconian views on the enemy.

As a former naval officer, the king naturally took a detailed interest in the conduct of the war at sea, but this was to be predominantly a land conflict. The British government dispatched its small Expeditionary Force to France and Belgium where, with the armies of those countries, it stopped in its tracks the advance of the enemy The pre-emptive Schlieffen Plan had not worked. The German armies were stuck on the River Marne, east of the French capital, and the war reached a stalemate. With each side unable to push back the other, they dug in where they stood, creating a trench system that ultimately ran all the way from the North Sea to the Swiss frontier, and which would remain substantially unaltered for over four years. The Royal Navy, though it saw action in the South Atlantic, did not play a major role in the conflict nearer to home.

The prelude to war had been characterized by a massive, mutual increase in naval strength – an arms race – in which Britain and Germany had found themselves virtually equal by 1914 in the number of modern Dreadnought-class battleships they possessed. When hostilities broke out the German China Squadron was destroyed in battle off the Falkland Islands at the end of 1914 while another battleship was penned into an East African river estuary until it rusted away. The British Royal Navy commanded the North Sea, and imposed a blockade on the Baltic that at once affected the supply of foodstuffs and raw materials to Germany. The majority of German warships were in harbour in Kiel or Wilhelmshaven, and it would not be until two years into the conflict that they would venture out into battle. The resulting encounter, the Battle of Jutland, fought in May 1916, was indecisive but, though both sides claimed success, it was the Germans whose fleet remained trapped in the Baltic for the rest of the war. The remainder of the German Navy, scattered around the world, was able to do little except mount raids to harass the enemy and tie up resources.

On land, the stalemate on the Western Front was to endure, despite periodic attempts to break through the German lines. The most important of these offensives, along the River Somme in France in July 1916, was touted at the time in the Allied press as a victory, though it represented insignificant gains for the loss of over 600,000 men. The Germans attempted a major offensive against the French fortress of Verdun. This was probably the most horrific fighting of the war, with both sides suffering massive casualties, but the Germans failed

completely to capture the defences. Cavalry, the most prestigious arm of service in European armies, was largely useless in
this type of warfare, and its replacement – the tank, introduced
in 1917 – failed to make more than initial headway. The 'Central Powers' – Germany and its allies – held firm in this war of
attrition despite crippling shortages of food and raw materials at home. When Russia experienced the February Revolutions of 1917 and pulled out of the war in December of that
year, German troops could be transferred to the west. With
this surplus of men, the enemy launched an offensive in March
the following year that drove the Allies back more than thirty
miles and might, had they been more fortunate, have reached
Paris, which they came close enough (seventy-five miles) to
bombard. America had entered the war, however, and in April
began to deploy in the European theatre of conflict.

George bowed to pressure from public opinion. He agreed,
as we have seen, to change his family name, and did so by
Royal Proclamation. (On hearing the new name of the British
royal house, his cousin, Kaiser Wilhelm, remarked drily that
he looked forward to attending a production of Shakespeare's
The Merry Wives of Saxe-Coburg-Gotha.) Though George
personally regarded it as 'petty and undignified' to waste
legislative time on the confiscation of titles, this was carried
out through the Titles Deprivation Act of 1919. Among those
who lost their positions in the British aristocracy were Prince
Ernst August of Hanover, who was also known as Duke of
Cumberland, and Prince Carl Eduard, who as well as being
Duke of Saxe-Coburg and Gotha was also Duke of Albany.
Similarly, British titles were granted to British relatives who
had had to give up their German ones. The Battenberg family
were created Marquesses of Milford Haven.

However, the king would not allow a witch-hunt to be
conducted. He refused point-blank to let the names of the
German kaiser and crown prince be deleted from the Army
List, where they continued to appear as honorary colonels of
regiments. (To this day one unit, the King's Royal Hussars,

continues to wear the black eagle of Prussia as its cap badge.) He was also unwilling to countenance the removal from the stalls in St George's Chapel, Windsor, of the brass plates inscribed with the names of sovereigns who were now in the enemy camp – even though the banners carrying their coats-of-arms were taken down. The plates were, he considered, 'historical records' which should not be destroyed simply because of the feeling of the moment.

There were more serious issues to consider, however. Some sovereigns had begun to suffer loss and harm during the fighting. Queen Marie of Romania, for instance, once the object of George's affection, had championed the Allied cause in her country. As one of the Entente powers, it had been invaded and devastated by the enemy, both the Germans and the Bulgarians. After revolution erupted in Russia in February 1917, the tsar had been forced to abdicate, to be replaced by a moderate Provisional Government that committed itself to keeping Russia in the war (vital as a counterweight to the Western Front). Partly because of this, further upheavals that autumn had replaced the Provisional Government with Bolshevism. The country's new rulers proceeded to get out of the war, on any terms whatever, as soon as it could be managed. They also imposed on members of the imperial family a more stringent confinement than the house arrest they had previously suffered.

The Romanovs were George's cousins, and the relationship between them had been close. The two men were three years apart in age, and of a similar physical appearance. In the manner of royalty in those days, the families met in various countries and on a number of occasions, both official and informal. The last had been in 1913 when they attended, both wearing German military uniform, the wedding of the kaiser's daughter. Nicholas, his wife, four daughters and son were now in considerable danger. Apart from being George's relations they had been allies through the difficult years of war. He offered them asylum in Britain.

He came to rue this decision, however. The Russian Revolution had encouraged socialists in other countries to dream of similar success. This was especially the case if the overthrow of government would lead to abandoning the war at once. Not since the French Revolution had there been such a direct, implacable and serious threat to monarchical rule. Among the British working class there was open admiration for Russia's new government (the tsars, autocratic and despotic, had featured in British demonology since at least the time of the Crimean War). Although the prime minister, David Lloyd George, was sympathetic to the plight of Nicholas and his family, George reconsidered his invitation. It might jeopardize the security of his own throne if he made a show of supporting an absolute monarch. Afterwards it was widely assumed for decades that the prime minister, a Liberal who had no reason to favour autocrats, was the one who was against helping them. The papers of the king's private secretary, however, suggest that it was with George himself that the final decision lay. The offer of asylum was quietly withdrawn. The tsar and his family, imprisoned in the Urals and treated with increasing harshness, were murdered by the Bolsheviks in July 1918.

In view of this, it may be assumed that the king regretted the failure of his own or any other government to protect Russia's imperial family. This has proved to be the darkest stain on his reign, and he has never been forgiven by Russian monarchists. He did not at any rate allow personal doubts to stand in the way of rescuing other royals in danger. He sent a warship, HMS *Marlborough*, to the Crimea to evacuate the tsar's mother and sister. He had the Royal Navy rescue another royal family – the Greeks – when they lost popularity and had to flee (with them was their infant son Philip, who would later marry King George's granddaughter).

After four years, the Central Powers could no longer sustain the burden of war. The first to crack, and to seek peace talks without reference to the others, had been Austria in 1917, though nothing came of this. The following year – on 29 September 1918 – Bulgaria made a separate peace with the Allies. Turkey followed on 30 October, and then Austria–Hungary, the nation which had begun it all, on 3 November. The patriarchal emperor, Franz Joseph I, who had reigned since 1848, had died in 1916. His successor, Emperor Karl I, was young and inexperienced. Though willing to do whatever he could to keep the throne – including approaching the enemy behind the kaiser's back – it was already too late. His armies had been defeated and his realms were disintegrating. Since the war had begun, parts of this empire, notably Hungary and the Czech lands, had been of questionable loyalty. Now that the state was heading for defeat their long-held desire for separation and independence could neither be ignored nor prevented. This was not a violent revolution after the manner of Russia's; the imperial family merely lost their lands and possessions, and were expelled from the country. In this case George V ensured the safe conduct from Austria of Emperor Karl and his dependants by sending his personal representative, Lieutenant Colonel Edward Lisle Strutt, to see them to exile in Switzerland.

The overall peace settlement was to be founded, at America's desire, on the notion of 'self-determination', which meant that subject nations would be encouraged to break away. There was no wish to see Europe clustered into power-blocks as it had been four years earlier. American animosity to the principle of monarchy was also influential. That form of government had failed to keep the peace in Europe, and indeed the rivalries and conflicting claims of the dynasties were likely to be a source of conflict in the future if they were left in positions of power. The era has been seen as one in which thrones were swept away, and of course a great many were, but it is worth remembering that not all countries lost their monarchs – Italy and Romania, for instance, did not because they had both been on the Allied side. Two countries even *became* monarchies in the post-war settlement: Albania and the newly formed Yugoslavia. In the volatile Balkans it was considered possible that the presence of a sovereign would bring stability by providing newly formed nations with a source of pride and national unity on which to build. In the event, neither new monarchy survived for more than a generation.

The 'Great War for Civilization' – as it would be dubbed by its victors – effectively ended with Armistice in November 1918. At Buckingham Palace the wine cellars were reopened in celebration. The king drank brandy that his ancestor George IV had laid down to celebrate the defeat of Napoleon just over a century earlier. Peace was not formally signed until the following year. While German armies had held firm in the west, they could not do so for much longer. They were in retreat, giving up the cities, like Lille and Ghent, that they had occupied since 1914. Crippled by four and a half years of shortages, by the strain of fighting on several fronts and shoring up the efforts of their flagging, increasingly unreliable allies, as well as by the loss of up to four million men (the official figure of two million is thought to be hopelessly optimistic), Germany's public as well as her armies were at breaking point. When the High Command ordered the German Fleet to sail into the North Sea for a final reckoning (actually a suicidal notion that was intended to provide a Wagnerian finale), the sailors mutinied and refused to go. A crippling series of strikes at home undermined the government, as well as military and civilian morale. The country's working class, encouraged by what had happened in Russia, demanded an end to the conflict. All but right-wing nationalists realized that continuing to fight would merely prolong the national agony. Germany therefore sued for an Armistice through the Americans.

It is important to remember that the country was not conceding defeat. They wished for a ceasefire, and this was agreed under certain conditions. Their government was under the impression that all sides in the conflict would be subject to the outcome of an international peace conference, that all would be disarmed and would lose their overseas colonies to international administration. The reality was, of course, very different. The German delegates were simply summoned to the conference at Versailles to be handed the resolutions agreed by the victorious powers. The massive document in which these were contained was not even translated into German, thus setting them the urgent task of first reading and comprehending it in order to sign and accept (any quibbling would result in a resumption of hostilities, they were warned). The terms were draconian in the extreme. It was only the defeated Central Powers that would lose their territories and resources, and would have their armed forces severely reduced. They were also saddled with paying reparations for the damage caused by the war, and even had their national libraries and art galleries rifled to compensate countries whose own cultural treasures had been lost in the fighting. The agreement was finalized in the Hall of Mirrors, the very room in the palace of Louis XIV in which, in January 1871, the German states had proclaimed their empire and thus created a unified nation. In the same place in which they had taken Alsace and Lorraine as part of Germany, they lost them once again to France.

The Treaty of Versailles was signed on 28 June 1919 – five years to the day after the assassination in Sarajevo that had set in motion the whole tragedy. In London, the royal family appeared on the balcony of Buckingham Palace and was greeted with adulation by a huge crowd, just as they would be, less than thirty years later, following another war. The king, moved as ever by the affection of his people, wrote that evening in his diary: 'Please God the dear old Country will now settle down & work in unity.' George's presence, both as a man and as a symbol, had it seemed made an important contribution to victory. One civil servant, Sir Maurice Hankey, cited as the three architects of victory Prime Ministers Asquith and Lloyd George and the king, of whom he wrote that the qualities he had shown were: 'steadfast faith, ceaseless devotion to duty and inspiring leadership'.

In the Treaty, however, the seeds of further strife had already been sown. Germany, a great power with a high sense of mission and of its own importance, had been humiliated and reduced to penury. This was naturally going to cause resentment and the same desire to right historical wrong that the French had experienced over their lost provinces. In order to pay the huge reparations demanded of them, the German government had to devalue its currency to such an extent that the savings of millions became valueless overnight. Throughout the 1920s Germany would lurch from extreme poverty to relative stability (as foreign loans boosted her economy), and then, as global depression struck, back to poverty. The social as well as the political climate – wounded pride, resentment and economic disaster – made the country susceptible to extremism and receptive to a Messiah-figure who promised to lead them out of their difficulties. The Second World War began as a direct result of the First. The two decades between them were simply a breathing space.

Though Britain had no interests to protect in central or eastern Europe, there was to be painful separation for the United Kingdom too. The Irish question had not gone away. In the middle of the war, at Easter 1916, separatist rebels had seized the General Post Office in Dublin and declared Ireland a republic. To prove the strength of their convictions, they had killed several policemen and officials and had holed themselves up in buildings throughout the city. As an attention-getting gesture it succeeded, but in the long term it was doomed to failure. It took two weeks, but the rebels were cleared out of their positions at a cost of some lives and considerable damage to the surrounding area. Booed in the streets, the participants were jailed. When their ringleaders were shot, however, the mood in Ireland turned to one of outrage. The creation of new martyrs fed into a long tradition of Irish heroism and struck a chord with the public. Following the aftermath of Easter 1916, the movement for separation and full independence – as opposed to the already promised

Home Rule – inexorably gained momentum. Ireland promised to be one of the biggest problems to be confronted by
King George's post-war governments, as it had been for their
predecessors.

The war was followed by a redrawing of the map of the
world. Enemy colonies were put in the care of Allied nations,
not only in Africa but as far away as New Guinea. The entire
Middle East had to be reorganized. While the Central Powers
had been defeated – though they would return to destroy the
peace of Europe again within twenty years – there was now an
even greater international menace. Bolshevism had cut off the
vast lands of Russia from the community of civilized nations.
The social and political system that this represented was the
declared enemy of religion and of capitalism – Russia was thus
a neighbour with whom there could be no accommodation –
and its leaders expected it to spread throughout Europe and
the world. Not since the French Revolution had there been
a pariah nation of this sort which, having destroyed its own
government and social order, was intent on helping others do
the same. It marked the beginning of a new world order that
was even more dangerous than the old one.

The conflict had, as might have been expected, led to a general desire for change. With the example of Soviet Russia suggesting that utopia was possible (it was not to be generally
realized how far from the truth this notion was until the thirties) there were serious rumblings elsewhere in Europe. Hungary and Bavaria both had Bolshevik revolutions, though
these were short-lived and easily crushed by right-wing
forces. In defeated countries like these, social and political
chaos made them ripe for such drastic change, but even in victorious Britain there was the threat of trouble too. Glasgow
looked likely, for a brief moment in 1919, to produce a revolution of its own. When the British government, on the initiative of the Minister for War, Winston Churchill, wished to
send troops to Russia to fight the Bolsheviks, public opinion
hostile to the strangling of the Workers' State ensured that

this expedition could be no more than a token gesture. It was the same climate of animosity, already apparent while the war was still going on, that had prevented George V from showing enthusiasm for the scheme to rescue his Russian cousins and bring them to Britain.

Labour relations became as bad as, and then worse than, they had been before the war. The immediate demobilization of a million men from the armed forces meant that widespread unemployment followed almost immediately. The climate was one of imminent class confrontation.

The monarchy, however, was not held responsible for the nation's political ills. The king and queen were popular. Their change of name was a gesture that the public appreciated, and the nominal leadership they had shown through the years of conflict had gained them respect. The Prince of Wales – who would become the first modern 'media celebrity' among royals – would acquire legions of admirers when he undertook an exhaustive series of overseas tours over the following years, and thus reflect further credit on the monarchy. George also decided that in times of economic hardship he and the other members of his family should share the climate of austerity by reducing their expenditure. His desire to cut the allowances from the Civil List on which he and his relations lived was appreciated by his subjects. He was not, in any case, an extravagant ruler, and his plain habits and lifestyle already fitted in with the austere mood of the times.

George was a very conscientious sovereign, willing to take pains over the performance of his duties in a way that his father and his eldest son would not. One instance was the revival of the sovereign's participation in an ancient custom. The distribution of 'Royal Maundy' – the ritualized annual giving of charity to the poor – (instead of clothing and foodstuffs it now took the form of specially minted money, given to as many elderly persons as there were years in the sovereign's age) – still went on, but not since 1685 had the monarch given it out in person. The ceremony was always held at Westminster. Lawrence Tanner, the Keeper of the Muniments there, recorded that: 'After the Maundy Service at the Abbey in 1931, Princess Marie Louise made the suggestion that the sovereign ought once again to make the distributions in person, and added that she felt sure that King George would come if he was asked. The result was that King George and Queen Mary attended the service the following year. The king did the Distribution quite charmingly, with a grave little bow and smile for each recipient. He was taken aback and quite flushed with pleasure when the old people quite spontaneously said: "God bless Your Majesty" or "Long live Your Majesty" as they received the purses.' *The Times* opined that his attendance proved : 'that the Royal Maundy still expresses the will of the sovereign to be the friend and servant of the poor among his people'.

This was a move both populist and popular. It was not of course unique. The washing of the feet of the poor was a custom practised by, among others, the Pope. The immensely dignified Emperor Franz Joseph I of Austria (who reigned from 1848–1916) had performed this act every year. Nevertheless, King George's interest in the event and his willingness to attend – increased by the warmth of the reception for his first appearance – established it as customary, and his descendants have been equally scrupulous in their support. The present queen carries out this duty, in a different cathedral somewhere in Britain, every spring.

From our distant perspective the inter-war decades of George V's reign seem much like those that preceded 1914 – with the same pith-helmeted Britons shooting tigers in India, the same top-hatted cabinet ministers, the same fashionable crowds strolling at Henley or Goodwood. In fact, though, this was an entirely different era. It saw the breakup of the United Kingdom as the counties of southern Ireland formed their own state and, although it was during this reign that the British Empire was to reach its maximum territorial size, it witnessed an increase in momentum toward independence for

India that was ultimately to remove the lynch-pin from the Empire. It saw the consolidation of Bolshevik Russia and thus the beginnings of the Cold War polarization between East and West. It was characterized by the rise of bolshevism's equally ugly nemesis, fascism. In a period of international upheaval and uncertainty it produced extremist, fanatical leaders – Lenin, Stalin, Mussolini, Hitler, Franco – who used naked force and terror to achieve their objectives. This maelstrom of violence and bellicosity abroad must have made Britons grateful to have a gruffly amiable sovereign – a reassuring presence in a world gone mad.

It had been during the pivotal year of 1917 that another change had occurred in the monarchy, one that was significant at the time but soon came to be taken for granted. This was the introduction of a new award that would be available to everyone in society, male or female, regardless of age or social class. Such things were known in other countries – most significantly in France, where Napoleon had established the country's principal decoration, the *Légion d'Honneur*, in 1804. This was an egalitarian, rather than an exclusive, award. It was plentifully bestowed on those who had given routine service to the state rather than conferred in any spirit of elitism.

In Britain it became apparent that there was a need for some similar honour. The Great War was an unprecedented national emergency. Heroism was displayed by women as well as men, by civilians as well as the military. Gallantry awards were naturally not appropriate for those who had organized comfort funds for troops or boosted the output of factories. There needed to be some fitting means of rewarding civilian service that was lengthy or outstandingly diligent, but specifically it was necessary to acknowledge the efforts of the Civil Service in the war effort. It was deemed inappropriate that existing Orders of knighthood should be expanded through more numerous awards, as this would devalue them. The new honour, though this too would be an Order, would confer knighthood only in its higher, and more select, grades.

The notion was the inspiration of Lord Stamfordham, the same man whose stroke of genius had given his master a suitable new name. It had first been mooted at the start of the war, but vague discussion only became properly focused in 1917. It would be called the Order of the British Empire, so that it could be given to all citizens of British territories. There would be five classes. The highest two would confer knighthood (Knight Grand Cross and Knight Commander). The others would be Commander, Officer and Member. Interestingly, at a time when women did not yet have the vote, they were to be able for the first time to earn a title on their own merit and not through that of their husbands. The female equivalent of a knight would be – it was decided after much discussion – a 'dame'. To those like the Foreign Secretary Lord Curzon who had been educated at Eton, this term was taken to refer to the matron or landlady of the boys' boarding houses ('A housemistress!' he exclaimed) and was thus deemed unsuitable. Nevertheless, the term came into use and was quickly accepted.

The Order was to be restricted to civil servants until the war ended, whenever that might be. After that it would be made available to anyone who deserved it, and nominations were invited not only from organizations within Britain but from the governments of the Dominions. Not everyone was willing to cooperate in choosing recipients – some government departments or industries were so big that selecting the most deserving was simply considered too daunting a task to bother with. Nevertheless the medals began to be distributed and the OBE came to dwarf all Britain's other Orders. The Garter had twenty-four members, the Order of Merit one hundred. The OBE was supposedly to be restricted to 1,300 recipients, but Lloyd George, the prime minister who was later to gain notoriety for selling honours, gave 22,000 of them in the first four years of the scheme.

Though the OBE took time to become accepted, it proved to be an immense success. For the first time, ordinary people could not only be publicly recognized by the State for their work or for outstanding service to others, they could also join the Establishment. Thousands every year would be able to feel that royalty had noticed their efforts and appreciated them – even though recipients were in fact decided upon by a committee in Downing Street and not by the Crown. Because presentations were and are made at the Palace, those who receive them are able to visit the monarch's home and receive the attention, and the thanks, of the king or queen in person – an occasion they often regard as a highlight of their life. The Order has proved to be hugely influential in winning the public over to the side of the monarchy, and periodic efforts to abolish, or even rename, it have consistently failed, for despite a name that quickly sounded outdated and uncomfortable, it was an award tailor-made for a meritocratic society and the perfect reflection of the new era in which the monarchy found itself.

After the war, King George and Queen Mary continued living in the modest surroundings of York Cottage, but were struck by tragedy in 1919 when their youngest son Prince John, who suffered from epilepsy, died at the age of thirteen after a short illness. He had not been seen by the general public for some time, and lived in seclusion on the estate. His death caused both his parents tremendous grief.

It was in the immediate post-war years, dominated as they were by a powerful Labour movement, a potentially hostile working class and a wider context of worldwide revolution, that the concept of a more accessible, less remote monarchy took root. The general fear of revolution came afterward to be seen as unfounded. Though there were riots in some British cities (in Glasgow armoured cars had had to be used to suppress public disorder), there was never any serious threat of the overthrow of the State, or real desire for it. George was, like anyone brought up 'in the purple', more at home with the aristocracy and gentry than with the broader mass of his people. Nevertheless he knew that the survival of the constitutional system was vital to the stability and happiness of the British people, and that the best way to ensure this was by making the monarchy as conciliatory toward all parties as possible. No matter with whom he was dealing – and the years would bring confrontation between the British government and some implacable opponents, such as the Irish leader Éamon de Valera or the Indian Mahatma Gandhi – the king would always work on the assumption that some common ground or interest could be found, and that this was probably a mutual desire for peaceful solution. He also acknowledged that there could be no future for a monarchy that was remote, and which could not be seen to be earning its keep. Since the times were bringing new men to power – and Ramsay MacDonald, the first Labour prime minister, the illegitimate son of a farmhand, was the personification of this – he would endeavour to treat them respectfully, to find common ground and to work with them. When the General Strike began in May 1926 and Lord Durham, a wealthy mine-owner, condemned the strikers as 'revolutionaries', George famously snapped at him: 'Try living on their wages before you judge them!'

His determination to make the royal family less aloof was a well-judged measure, eliminating opportunities for public resentment and earning British royalty a goodwill it has never since lost. How did he do this? With more public appearances, including attending events like the FA Cup, a working-class occasion not previously linked with royalty. By voluntarily halving the Civil List, once the Depression began, and by obliging his sons to do the same. He also did it by speaking directly to his subjects through wireless. He did so for the first time in April 1924 when opening the Empire Exhibition in London. Several years later, at Christmas 1932, following a suggestion by Sir John Reith of the BBC, he made a speech by radio to the peoples of the British Empire. Nothing like this had ever before been possible – Queen Victoria had only been able to send simultaneous telegrams to her overseas territories. George was gifted with a beautiful, resonant speaking voice. Heard via wireless sets across the world, it conveyed precisely the right image of pleasant, paternal sympathy. The broadcast proved so popular that he and his descendants have done the same thing almost every year since. Interestingly, not one of them has wished to do so. The three sovereigns involved – George V, George VI and the present queen – have all hated the ordeal of speaking on radio or television, and have only done so because they knew their subjects wanted to hear them. The broadcasts have been of crucial value in familiarizing the public with their activities and personalities, and have greatly helped the image of the monarchy.

Sometimes the populism of the royal family was expressed in everyday gestures, unknown to the public until the appearance, years later, of diaries and memoirs. One of his cousins asked George, as head of the family, whether he felt it would be all right for her to travel by bus. His reply was typical, reflecting the length of the shadow that continued to fall over everything that was done in the royal house: 'What would Grandmama have thought?' However, he conceded that she was 'quite old enough to travel by bus' if she chose to. He then asked her: 'Do you strap-hang?' It was often these simple, taken-for-granted things that monarchs found most intriguing, or even envied, in their subjects. When Queen Mary was a very old lady, at the beginning of the 1950s, she was asked if there was anything she regretted not having done. She thought for a moment and then confessed that she had always had the desire 'to climb over a fence'.

In the meantime there were even more pressing difficulties. Ireland remained an open wound, and three of its provinces remained largely hostile to British rule. When the war ended, the public there voted overwhelmingly for Sinn Féin, the party that advocated breach with the Crown. In rural Ireland officials and policemen were murdered with such frequency that troops had to be sent in to keep order. Continuing attacks led to draconian responses and the deployment of an auxiliary force (nicknamed the Black and Tans for their mismatched

uniforms) that gained a swift and well-deserved reputation
for brutality. Their methods, in a situation that was admittedly unwinnable and deeply provoking, included retaliatory
murder. Politicians sanctioned this – Churchill was one who
thought it effective – but the king was horrified that such
things were being done in his name, and complained to the
prime minister. When a solution was arrived at after negotiations in London – Ulster, with its Protestant majority, would
remain in the United Kingdom while the remaining twenty-
six counties would form a free state that would be part of the
British Empire but not the kingdom – he travelled to Ireland
to open Ulster's new parliament.

By the end of the war the mood in most of Ireland was
implacable. Sinn Féin won overwhelmingly in the General
Election of 1918. There was now open, armed rebellion against
the Crown once again. Though this time no one seized a large
public building, there was gunfire on the streets of Dublin,
and in the countryside maintaining law and order was often
impossible.

George made use of a ceremonial occasion, the opening of
the new Stormont Parliament in Ulster on 21 June 1921. This
was usually a matter of the sovereign presiding and reading
a speech that had been written for him. On this occasion the
king had been advised by General Smuts of South Africa that
he could give a speech of his own, aimed at the whole population of Ireland. The speech was created for him by Smuts
himself, Arthur Balfour, and a civil servant named Edward
Grigg. The king went on to deliver sentences that have been
quoted ever since: 'I appeal to all Irishmen to pause, to stretch
out the hand of forbearance and conciliation, to forgive and
forget and to join in making for the land they love a new era
of peace, contentment and goodwill.'

This was unlikely. Both historical resentment and recent
animosity were too deep-rooted. Irish nationalists saw the
opportunity to end seven hundred years of English domina-
tion and they would not let it pass. Though the speech was

well received it affected neither the determination of Sinn Féin and its allies to end the British connection, nor the determination of loyalists to resist separation, nor the fury of the newspaper-reading British public at terrorist atrocities. The British people were supportive of the tough and uncompromising measures being taken by their government. King George's speech had been a brave – but also a constitutionally dangerous – attempt to intervene in the political process.

In the General Election of January 1924 (there had been one the previous December, but no government had been formed), the Conservatives gained the most votes but the issue turned on support for the prime minister, Stanley Baldwin. Because there was not sufficient confidence in him, the king summoned instead the leader of the less successful Labour Party, Ramsay MacDonald, who became the first-ever Labour prime minister. MacDonald had lived in poverty for much of his early life and was the first Premier to come from such a background. The press made much of his unfamiliarity with protocol, but he found the king not only anxious to put him at ease but pleased to have his service and willing to help him. ('He impressed me very much. He wishes to do the right thing,' said George.) Labour cabinet ministers were suddenly being invited to Buckingham Palace or Windsor, and taking part in occasions at which, a generation earlier, people of their views or background would not have been seen. Some of their supporters derived a certain smug pleasure from seeing them now walking the corridors of power, while others were irritated at the sight of them, dressed – and behaving – like members of the upper classes. MacDonald himself was criticized by members of his party for wearing both Privy Council uniform and a tailcoat, as well as for appearing in photographs dressed in tweeds at the prime ministerial country house, Chequers, for all the world like an aristocrat.

The General Strike of 4–13 May 1926 looms large in British social history. It was prompted by a proposal to reduce working men's wages in keeping with a time of economic downturn. Miners – traditionally the most militant of workers – led the walkout and caused fuel shortages throughout the country. Printers, transport workers and a host of others followed. Though much of the public sympathized with them, large sections of the middle class stepped in to take over their jobs – driving buses and delivery-vans – to keep the country running. Sailors were even brought into Fleet Street to operate the printing-presses and keep newspapers going. Though there was naturally animosity, and class antagonism, there was no real upheaval – no echo of revolution – as some had feared. A team of strikers even played football against their natural opponents, the police. When the Strike collapsed after nine days, George was able to record his pride in the moderation of all classes of his subjects: 'Our old country can well be proud of itself. It shows what a wonderful people we are.'

He himself could not always avoid becoming embroiled in constitutional issues. The onset of the Depression had sent shock-waves through the world, and in 1931 British banks were in imminent danger of collapse. The Labour government could find no viable solutions and its leader, MacDonald, together with his cabinet offered to resign. Informed opinion both inside and outside Parliament favoured Baldwin, perhaps leading a Conservative–Liberal alliance, as successor. King George, after meeting the party leaders, decided however to invite MacDonald to resume power at once as head of a 'National Government' assembled from three parties. MacDonald accepted, without consulting his supporters. Labour was split over the issue. MacDonald lost considerable popularity and the king was blamed for interference. The government was, however, to last until 1945, albeit under changing leadership.

The empire over which the king presided reached its territorial zenith in the early 1930s, though its actual heyday had been in the jingoistic 1890s. It was becoming increasingly difficult, in spite of the common cause shown in the war, to keep it a united, or seemingly united, community. The Dominions were now bent on following their own paths. 'The British Empire has advanced to a new conception of autonomy and freedom, to the idea of a system of British nations, each freely ordering its own individual life, but bound together in unity by allegiance to one Crown and cooperating in all that concerns the common weal.' Though it was not the king but his son Bertie who said these words, in a speech given in 1927, they sum up one of the most profound and significant changes during the reign of George V. In the same way that the Colonies would seek autonomy in the wake of the Second World War, so the Dominions were seeking to separate from dependency on the mother country in the wake of the First. These territories – Canada, Australia, New Zealand, the Union of South Africa, joined by the new Irish Free State – were serving notice that they now considered themselves mature enough to run their own affairs.

Among other things, they wished to decide for themselves who their Governor-General – the *de facto* head of state, representing the sovereign – would be, rather than having individuals imposed on them by the British government. This attitude, which was outlined in the speech above and formalized by the Statute of Westminster in 1931, restructured the British Empire. From now on, although the House of Windsor would continue to provide a ceremonial head, the Dominions would insist on seeing themselves as equal partners in a voluntary enterprise and not as subject nations, or settlement plantations, or 'cadet branches' of the imperial family. The king and his government could do nothing to prevent this trend, even had they wanted to, and their only option was to accept the changes and sound enthusiastic about them. As with so much about the British constitutional structure, the outward forms remained the same – the king continued to be ruler of these territories, but only by the invitation of their peoples. Behind a seemingly changeless façade, significant change was taking place.

The Empire Exhibition at Wembley Stadium in April 1924

was a massive public spectacle – remembered all their lives by those who attended it – and a celebration of the continuing vigour of 'Greater Britain', the association of lands ruled by the King Emperor. There were funfair rides and ice-cream stands, but more importantly there were glimpses of life in places considered to be far-flung: mock-ups of Burmese temples and New Zealand sheep farms, of Canadian ranches and Indian palaces. It naturally instilled a sense of patriotism (Sir Edward Elgar conducted his composition 'Land of Hope and Glory' at the opening ceremony, though by that time he was sick of hearing it and did so on this occasion only at the direct request of the king) and of permanence. For while it was possible that, sometime in the future, the colonies might gain their independence, it was self-evident that the large, white-populated settlements – Australia, New Zealand, South Africa, Canada and Newfoundland – were equal partners in the community. Surely they would have – could have – no reason to leave an alliance to which they belonged as a matter of free choice? The recent war, in which these countries had all taken part even if their own safety and interests were not directly under threat, had proved the soundness of the imperial idea.

It is important to remember that in thus asserting their individuality and their right to go their own way, the Dominions nevertheless chose to retain close links with the Crown, and that King George therefore became sovereign, by invitation, of Canada, Australia, New Zealand and South Africa. The relationship between these countries and the British throne was thus strengthened rather than weakened. When in due course non-white colonies gained independence from Britain, many of them followed the precedent of remaining in the Commonwealth. The king seemed, throughout his reign, to do nothing but concede to the demands of others, yet by being flexible enough to accommodate the forces of change he was able to preserve most of the appearance, and some of the substance, of what had been. The Commonwealth is

George V's monument – this new chapter in the history of the English-speaking world began under his patronage. It was by accepting with good grace what he could not alter that he made possible the successful community of nations it is today.

George did not enjoy sound health. He continued to be affected by the fall from his horse in France, an event that apparently aged him prematurely. In 1928 he suffered a chest abcess that was acutely painful, and afflicted him for almost a year. A heavy smoker, with all that this implies, he suffered from pleurisy, pulmonary disease and septicaemia. His later life was spent in alternating periods of pain and boredom, and he was obliged to take long rests, including recuperation at the seaside town of Bognor (which was then renamed Bognor Regis). His most famous saying, apparently in response to the cheerful suggestion that he would soon be returning there for further rest – 'Bugger Bognor!' – is probably a fabrication, or may have been his reaction when the town asked to restyle itself 'Bognor Regis'. It was an utterance entirely in keeping with his temper and his vocabulary.

He became ill in the winter of 1935, courteously saying to the members of the Privy Council during a meeting: 'Gentlemen, I am so sorry for keeping you all waiting like that. I am unable to concentrate.' In January 1936, at Sandringham, he took to his bed with a cold, and rapidly weakened. There was time to summon his family, the prime minister, and other important people, to his bedside, and to issue one of the most well-known health bulletins in history: 'The king's life is moving peacefully to its close.' Drifting in and out of consciousness, he produced suitably dignified official last words: 'How is the empire?' To which his secretary replied, with equal dignity: 'All is well, sir, with the empire.' It has been confirmed, however, that his actual last words were a good deal more ungracious: 'God damn you,' he muttered at a nurse who was giving him a sedative.

His personal physician, Lord Dawson, admitted in his

diaries – which were not seen until decades afterward – that he had deliberately shortened the life of the monarch, by administering an injection of morphine and cocaine that was strong enough to kill him. The reasons he gave for this action were that the king would have lost coherence and dignity had he lingered. It was also likely that a lengthy death-watch by the bed of a comatose, unconscious man would have been more distressing for his family, who had apparently agreed to the shortening of his life because it would offer him relief from further pain. Most surprising of all, Dawson claimed that with a quicker death the news could be conveyed to Fleet Street in time to be announced in the morning edition of *The Times* rather than the early editions of the evening papers. His wife had already telephoned the offices of the newspaper and asked them to 'hold the front page'.

George had been weary of life. A reign that had begun in political turmoil had become no easier with the passing years. He had presided over the most devastating war in the nation's history, the worst industrial unrest, the upheaval of the suffragette movement and the granting of votes to women, as well as the restructuring of the empire. Yet his greatest worry was the unsuitability of his eldest son to take over his position. 'When I am gone,' he had said, 'the boy will ruin himself within twelve months' – a prediction that was to come true in even less time than that. He died knowing that he had succeeded in doing his duty. He had been a very good king – conscientious, impartial, and highly popular. He had set an edifying moral example and was leaving the monarchy stronger than he had found it. And yet his successor was likely to throw away everything he had achieved. Small wonder that he said: 'I pray to God that my eldest son will never marry and have children and that nothing will stand between Bertie and Lillibet and the throne.' His wife would have the satisfaction of knowing, if he would not, that that was precisely how fate would arrange matters.

Historians, put off by his outward manner, have often

considered him unworthy of serious study. As a result of
his early training and inclination he was always to seem like
a naval officer, ruling the country as if it were a battleship.
Harold Nicolson wrote that the king had the intellectual
capacities of a railway porter, yet admitted that this was a
strength, for he was the common man writ large. His prejudices reflected those of many of his ordinary subjects.

Yet he was far more than the caricatured dullard of popular
myth. He had a sensitivity that was not seen by everyone. He
also possessed a sense of humour that was often delightful, as
when he spoke to Sir Leslie Hoare, the Foreign Secretary, who
had just returned from Paris after negotiating the Hoare–Laval
Pact. George quipped: 'You know what they're all saying? No
more coals to Newcastle, no more Hoares to Paris.' The king
later grumbled that: 'The fellow didn't even laugh.'

He was brusque with his sons, but tender with his granddaughter Elizabeth. Though to describe him as conservative
would be the mildest of understatements, he was sympathetic
toward the poor, and to those who were living on strike pay
during the events of May 1926. His concern, expressed in private, was sincere. Morally, he was beyond reproach. His wife
had expected to be his sister-in-law, a somewhat awkward
start for any romance, yet he and Queen Mary remained happily married for forty-three years. He was ideally suited by
temperament to be the Father of the Nation. His old-fashioned
outlook – expressed in the fact that he wore a Victorian beard
throughout an emphatically clean-shaven era – increased his
air of gravitas in a time of rapid change. To his own surprise
as well as that of many of his subjects, he enjoyed a genuine rapport with Ramsay MacDonald, his Labour premier, as
well as with other socialists. He was self-evidently decent and
well-meaning, to an extent that was unexpected by some of
them. He was to write in his diary, in January 1924: 'Today
23 years ago dear Grandmama died. I wonder what she would
have thought of a Labour government.' Much the same as
he did himself, was the answer. Yet he accommodated this

significant shift in the attitudes of the British electorate, and by doing so he succeeded in becoming a credible modern sovereign, rather than a reactionary stuck in the pre-war world. This tribute – entirely sincere and undoubtedly accurate – was paid him by the Labour leader (and later prime minister) Clement Attlee: 'He knew and understood his people and the age in which they lived, and progressed with them.'

While he could approach political and international issues with tolerance and good judgement and even vision, his views on the details of social behaviour were more narrow and often more pungent. There is something endearing about his determination not to let standards slip and to hold back the tide of modernity that was lapping at the Palace walls. Like his father, who even held views on the appropriate costume in which to visit an art gallery, George believed that clothes summed up a man – or woman. He forbade the queen to shorten her skirts in the twenties, despite the fact that this was by then universal practice even for middle-aged women. He was once so irritated at seeing ladies in short skirts strolling past the walls of Windsor Castle that he yelled at them through a window. He insisted that all women among his family or their staff must have gloves with them at all times, and that ladies must not appear twice in the same dress either at Ascot or at house parties he attended. He despised his eldest son's habit of wearing trousers with turn-ups. 'Are you expecting a flood?' he would enquire sarcastically whenever the young man entered the room. His own trousers looked even more outlandish, for he wore them with the creases at the sides and not at front and back. He once spotted his Private Secretary, Lord Stamfordham, coming up the Mall in plain tweeds rather than in a suit, and berated him for appearing in London in 'ratcatcher' clothes.

It was not only in sartorial matters that his views were inflexible. He had opinions on all aspects of behaviour. (He was to send a telegram to his second son, Bertie, that read: 'Do not embrace me in public, and when you kiss your mother, take your hat off.') When David went to Glasgow to open a trade exhibition, George wrote in surprise: 'I've never heard of a gentleman going to Scotland in January.' He had set views too on the proper dignity necessary for public ceremonial – on one occasion the Bandmaster of a Guards regiment included, in the repertoire that was offered during Changing of the Guard outside Buckingham Palace, a tune from a current musical comedy. Minutes later, a footman appeared from inside and approached him with a salver. The note upon it simply said: 'His Majesty does not know what tune you have been playing but it is never, never to be played again.'

Interestingly, in his emphatic, dogmatic views, George resembled no one so much as his German cousin, Kaiser Wilhelm II who was equally given to making pronouncements on any and every subject. Once he had dismissed the French Impressionists with the statement: 'Unless a painting meets a set of criteria set by me, it cannot be considered art.' George might have said something similar, if he had had sufficient interest in art in the first place. His view of literature was equally forthright: 'People who write books ought to be shut up.' He was equally unimpressed with music, recording in his diary after a visit to Covent Garden: 'We saw *Fidelio*, and damned dull it was.' Nor did he enjoy a game to which his son David was addicted, writing that: 'Golf always makes me so damned angry!' His expressed opinions, though reflecting genuine convictions, often sound utterly comical today. His view of homosexuals, for instance: 'But I thought men like that shot themselves!' sounds as quaint as his comment on the General Strike: 'It was a rotten way to run a revolution. I could have done it better myself.' And the notion of the king in league with those seeking to overthrow the established order was not as far-fetched as it might seem, for he told one Labour politician: 'I tell you, Mr Wheatley, that if I had to live in conditions like that, I would be a revolutionary myself.' He argued that working men could not be expected to keep a family on the wages they were paid.

His pronouncements on many subjects suggest those of some roguish, favourite uncle: sometimes flippant, often reactionary, frequently predictable, but surprisingly sensitive and sensible, and carrying an unmistakable decency. One observer, George Lansbury, called him 'a short-tempered, narrow-minded, out-of-date Tory'. So he was. The surprise was not that he held reactionary views but that he was capable besides of such empathy and ability to see other viewpoints. He was also more self-aware than others perhaps realized. He knew that he was not an exciting personality, and preferred it that way. When H. G. Wells famously criticized Britain's 'alien and uninspiring Court', George retorted: 'I may be uninspiring, but I'm damned if I'm an alien.'

His thoughts on serious issues, however, command respect. Visiting after the Great War a military cemetery in France, he said, with an eloquence that was almost Churchillian: 'I have many times asked myself whether there can be more potent advocates of peace on earth through the years to come than this massed multitude of silent witnesses to the desolation of war.' And in 1935 he told Lloyd George: 'I will not have another war. If there is another and we are threatened with being brought into it, I will go to Trafalgar Square and wave a red flag myself sooner than allow this country to be brought in.' Despite a penchant for colourful language, George read the Bible every day and was more than a purely nominal Christian. The side of his nature, and his behaviour, that gave rise to his noblest acts and utterances was a reflection of that.

He lived to celebrate his Silver Jubilee, in May 1935, though he was to die eight months later. He was genuinely surprised – and not a little moved – by the reception he received as he drove through the streets of London. A modest and reserved man who was well aware that he was perceived as dull, he had not previously realized the extent to which his subjects derived reassurance from this. His personification of the old-fashioned virtues had won him immense public respect, as had his genuine sympathy with the less fortunate of his people. His oft-quoted statement at the jubilee that: 'I had no idea they felt like that about me. I am beginning to think they must really like me for myself', suggests an endearing diffidence on both sides.

George did not fit into the post-war world. Yet ironically it was he who had made the monarchy adapt to the style of the new era. He passionately hated the changes in appearance and behaviour of women in the 1920s. They now smoked in public, wore breeches to ride (and no longer sat side-saddle), shortened their hair and their skirts, drank cocktails, drove about in motor cars, and wore make-up. It is difficult to appreciate, from the perspective of our times, just how completely the way of life of all classes changed as a result of the Great War. Social conventions that had been accepted for generations were suddenly thrown overboard. Showing deference to one's betters was out of fashion, the class structure having been dealt a serious blow by the democracy of the trenches and the success of socialism in Russia. Church-going was out of style; respect for 'the Establishment' – after the fortunes made by war-profiteers and the subsequent ennoblement of many of them – greatly diminished. Nothing seemed certain or stable any longer or worthy of respect. The bewilderment of men of the king's generation was summed up by a fictitious near contemporary – Soames Forsyte – in John Galsworthy's epic *Forsyte Saga*, who surveys with apprehension and disapproval the new era: 'A democratic England – dishevelled, hurried, noisy, and seemingly without an apex ... Gone forever, the close borough of rank and polish! ... Manners, flavour, quality, all gone, engulfed in one vast, ugly, shoulder-rubbing, petrol-smelling Cheerio ... Nothing ever again firm and coherent to look up to ... And when those Labour chaps got power – if they ever did – the worst was yet to come!'

3

EDWARD VIII, 'DAVID', JANUARY–DECEMBER 1936

'I know there is nothing kingly about me, but I have tried to mix with the people and make them think I was one of them.'

King Edward VIII to Prime Minister Stanley Baldwin

'From his childhood onwards this boy will be surrounded by sycophants and flatterers. In due course, following the precedent which has already been set, he will be sent on a tour of the world and probably rumours of a morganatic marriage alliance will follow, and the end of it will be the country will be called upon to pay the bill.'

The man who said this was James Kier Hardie. In this summing up of the future king's likely career, Hardie was uncannily accurate. There were to be three tours for the new king rather than one, and the morganatic marriage was not connected with either of them. Nevertheless the country would indeed 'be called upon to pay the bill', and the monarchy might well not have survived the experience. This second sovereign of the House of Windsor would come to the throne at the age of forty-one. His reign would last less than eleven months.

He was born on 23 June 1894, and burdened with a plethora of Christian names that included a reference to every patron saint in the British Isles: Edward Albert Christian George Andrew Patrick David. He would become known to his family and to intimates by the last of these. His arrival represented the first time in British history that four generations of the royal family had been alive at once, and he was repeatedly photographed with his elders throughout his early childhood. Queen Victoria was extremely fond of him (though afterwards he would scarcely remember her, as she died when he was six), and he was probably rather spoiled. At any rate he developed a sense of entitlement and self-importance – entirely understandable in a position such as his – that was, however, somehow never to be balanced by any notions of duty and obligation, and this would be his lifelong problem. He would expect to receive all the trappings that went with his position – the deference and the loyalty and service of others – yet it did not occur to him that these had to be earned, or that in return he owed his subjects willing service and an ability always to put duty above personal feelings.

He was apparently mistreated in childhood by a nurse, who habitually twisted his arm when he was about to enter his parents' drawing-room, as a means of ensuring good behaviour – a practice not unusual among Victorian nannies. He also suffered a childhood attack of mumps, which would cause him to believe in future years that he was infertile.

Despite this, his upbringing as one of six siblings was affectionate and relatively relaxed by the standards both of royalty and the Victorian era. His childhood home was the same small, uncomfortable house – York Cottage – that his parents had occupied since their marriage. He and his brothers were given lessons in a schoolroom there, and somewhat absurdly he was designated 'head boy' of a form that consisted of only four pupils. At fifteen he followed his father's course of education by going into the Royal Navy and attending Dartmouth, though by this time it had been transferred ashore to become the imposing academy it is today. Joining the Navy required greater commitment than service in the Army would have done. At that time there were still fashionable regiments in which, when slightly older, he could have idled his time away (as his uncle the Duke of Clarence had done), whereas the Navy was a technical Service that required concentrated hard work and genuine ability. It would grant no favours to members of his family, and he would have to earn respect through aptitude alone. On the other hand it could be assumed that he would not, like many of his contemporaries, make a career there, and indeed this quickly became clear. The year after he arrived at Dartmouth his ultimate destiny advanced a significant step closer when his father became king. David was now heir-assumptive, Prince of Wales, and would soon be invested as such.

The Investiture of a Prince of Wales had not previously had any impact on the Principality, because it was carried out at Court in London. In 1911, however, the Home Secretary happened to be the Welshman Lloyd George, and this time the arrangements were to be different. He had persuaded the king to hold the ceremony in Wales itself, and the setting agreed upon was the castle at Caernarfon. The prince could be presented to the people, just as the first such prince had been by King Edward III almost six hundred years earlier. David, who would never see the point of state ceremony, did not undergo the experience willingly, and especially disliked the neo-Tudor costume (a 'preposterous rig' he called it) that he was obliged to wear. In a curious foretaste of the rest of the century in which he would live, the teenager argued with his parents about the clothes he was expected to wear on a formal occasion. Nevertheless he learned to say a few words in Welsh, and to sound sincere when taking the oath.

The ceremony, in effect a tradition invented for the occasion, was acclaimed as a success both in Wales and throughout the empire – a solemn occasion, aspects of which could be shared by the public through photography and film, that brought the royal family closer to their people. It would be a harbinger of the more accessible and inclusive monarchy that was to become the norm within a few generations.

David was to gain great popularity under the title of Prince of Wales. A small, rail-thin man with a face that was described as looking like that of 'a wistful choirboy', he was handsome, well-dressed, and charming when he wanted to be. After his spell in the Navy he had attended Magdalen College, Oxford (he was to describe this as 'a dreary chore'), the snobbish Master of which naturally regarded him as a considerable catch, socially if not academically. 'Bookish he will never be,' lamented his tutor, and with good reason. Under the pseudonym Lord Chester, the Prince of Wales then travelled the Continent to learn something of the places in which he had relatives.

The prince was anything but thoughtful or intellectual. As has been seen, his father was no intellectual either, yet King George possessed a sense of duty that his son would never have. George also had a thoughtful and sensitive nature beneath an often frightening exterior. This enabled him to understand and empathize with others, and to achieve flashes of great wisdom and insight. David lacked any of these qualities. Inherently selfish, he never understood the notion of being a servant of his people, and saw no reason to exert himself in situations that did not arouse his interest, or for which he did not feel in the mood. His tastes never developed beyond mildly strenuous sports or puerile parlour games, and he made no attempt to grasp important issues. Nor did he make any secret of his hatred of official occasions. ('What bally rot these state visits are!' he had said as a young man. 'A waste of time, money and energy.') His outspoken and indiscreet views, which caused embarrassment both to his family and to courtiers, made it obvious that he was simply not suited by temperament to be king. Priding himself on the ease with which he could charm an audience and indeed win over an entire country, he came to think himself more important than the office he would ultimately hold. When one newspaper commented that his easy manner had 'silenced criticism of the monarchy for current lifetimes', it surely uttered one of recent history's greatest misjudgements.

When war broke out in 1914 the Prince of Wales proved to be highly adept at boosting public morale. Genuinely frustrated at being forbidden to serve on the frontline or be exposed to danger anywhere else ('Oh, that I had a job!' he lamented), he was at least able to make official visits to the different fronts. These gave him a more-or-less authentic experience of the war, so that, to himself and to others, he seemed shaped by the same terrible events as the rest of his generation. He went to the Middle East and to Italy, as well as gaining a posting behind the lines in France. From here he made visits to scenes of action once the fighting was over, becoming a familiar sight as he travelled the roads in a staff car or on an egalitarian bicycle. ('A bad shelling always produces the Prince of Wales!' said the soldiers.) On one occasion a 'bad shelling' very nearly killed him. He had gone by car to a sector of the front. He stepped out of the vehicle, and moments later it was hit by a shell. His driver was killed. It is interesting to speculate that if the prince too had died his reputation as a martyr would have ensured him of lasting popularity throughout the empire, and his contribution to history would have been seen as heroic rather than shabby.

Nevertheless with the coming of peace his stock was about to rise. As had happened after the Boer War, it was felt fitting that the overseas territories should be thanked for their contribution to the cause by a visit from royalty. Lloyd George, now prime minister, suggested that the prince should go. The idea proved immensely popular with the public, both at home and in the colonies. One trip took in the Dominion of Canada and the then-separate colony of Newfoundland. On the other he visited India, the Far East, Australia and New Zealand. David had already been portrayed in the illustrated press as a figure of film-star glamour. He was boyishly handsome, smiled often and with a hint of shyness that many found irresistible, and looked very attractive in uniform. In 1915, when a Welsh regiment had been added to the four existing Foot Guard units, he had become its Colonel-in-Chief. His picture appeared everywhere in the khaki service dress of the Welsh Guards, his peaked forage cap with its prominent badge – a leek – tilted at a slight but rakish angle (a major breach of regulations that no one else could have got away with). He wore either this or his naval uniform at ceremonial events. Otherwise, he had a penchant for checked suits in a light grey (this pattern was named Prince of Wales check in his honour) and his trademark suede brogues. These outfits suited his slight, slim figure, and young men everywhere sought to look like him.

His manners were naturally pleasing. He made charming little speeches. He flattered officials, and was grateful for courtesies shown and trouble taken on his behalf. In Canada he shook hands with so many people that he had to stop offering his right hand and use his left instead. In New York – for he visited the USA as well – he received a ticker-tape parade. In Australia his train suffered an accident and he remained calm, which enabled him to be portrayed as heroic. Everywhere vast crowds turned out to see him. His face became what would nowadays be called 'an international icon'. Women, naturally enough, dreamed of marrying him, or at least meeting him, or even just catching a glimpse. One of the popular songs of the era was entitled 'I Danced With a Man Who Danced With a Girl Who Danced With the Prince of Wales'.

Yet he was never quite as agreeable as he seemed. His affability was no more than skin-deep, a veneer that rubbed off very quickly. His charm, which was mentioned by numerous observers, could turn abruptly and without warning to childish petulance, and his thoughtlessness often caused offence.

One lady living at a remote house in Australia held a dance at which he was to be the guest of honour, having invited him and secured his acceptance. The evening wore on without any sign of him and the guests became more and more anxious. Eventually a telephone call from his equerry announced that he was not coming. The road, apparently, was not passable owing to recent rains. The guests, naturally disappointed, set out in their own vehicles to test the road and found it entirely dry. He had obviously decided not to bother attending. This sort of cavalier behaviour – in this case he would have humiliated his poor hostess in front of all her friends – was not forgotten.

Perhaps, however, she was lucky in that she did not actually meet him, for a personal encounter could be worse. A typical instance was seen on a visit he made to his old Oxford College, Magdalen. When he entered the Junior Common Room the assembled undergraduates rose to their feet. Flashing his trademark wry smile, he chided them for being so formal. He had been one of them, he said, and need not be treated with such deference. An hour or more later, having toured the College with the Master, he once again entered the JCR. No one stood up. He stated, with voluble irritation, that when the Prince of Wales came into a room people were expected to get to their feet!

He had few close friends (one of them, Lord Mountbatten, genuinely liked him but later said he would never have made a good king), and did not attract the loyalty of staff, who were often at their wits' end trying to keep up with his changes of mind and mood. The prince was a nightmare to organize. It is incumbent on royalty to plan their activities far in advance. Arrangements must often be timed to the minute so that a multitude of visits, meetings, speeches, ceremonies, can be fitted in. David had the exasperating habit of changing plans at the last minute, and without explanation, throwing into chaos all the hard work of the half-dozen or so people who had expended much time and effort on organizing the occasion.

The prince did not enjoy good relations with his father. It is in fact uncommon for ruler and heir to see eye to eye, and often there is outright hostility between them. King George's utterly conventional nature chafed at the young man's assumed informality in both dress and manner. To the king, it was the business of monarchy to set an example of quiet and unostentatious rectitude, not to follow – or start – trends in clothing. ('You look like a cad, you are a cad!' he was heard to yell at his son on at least one occasion.) A stickler for protocol and etiquette, for these provided the framework within which official life was carried on, the king hated his son's comparative informality, and was genuinely anguished by the prince's failure to marry. Did he not understand that the whole empire was waiting for an heir? But instead of taking anything seriously, David spent his time in nightclubs, or risked his life in steeplechases – a practice that King George forbade him from continuing after a serious fall. Rather than allow a suitable wife to be found for him, the prince carried on affairs with the wives of others – Society women who provided a quasi-maternal presence in his life that he apparently craved. He and his father did not see the world from even remotely the same viewpoint. They were on opposite sides in a generational war, and there could never be concord between them. King George, who simply could not visualize his heir as a reigning monarch, would not allow him access to dispatch boxes or encourage his education in kingship. As a result the Prince of Wales, like his grandfather before he succeeded, was left to a life of largely empty idleness. Lord Stamfordham reported that his parents were grieved by his 'late hours, lack of food, excess of smoking, restlessness and dislike of reading or of any salutary occupation'.

His life was not entirely idle, however. He possessed in full the restless energy and iconoclasm of the post-war world – the desire to seek pleasure, to forget recent trauma in a round of fads and parties and sports. He also, however, devoted energy to the betterment of society, for he became a sincere and consistent patron of ex-servicemen. He toured the poorer parts of his father's realm and was struck by the drabness and misery he found there, yet he uttered no words of private sympathy as King George did, for those on strike in 1926, and indeed lent his chauffeur and his car to deliver copies of Churchill's official newspaper, the *British Gazette*. Nevertheless, he made a difference. He established the Feathers Clubs, their name derived from the three feathers that symbolized the Prince of Wales, as a charity for former servicemen. He also founded King George's Jubilee Trust for Youth. In modern terms he was extremely good at 'fronting' an organization, in being the public face of some deserving cause. Lady Astor, the Member of Parliament, once told him that his charitable instincts and popularity had made 'the way easier for your successors'. He not only looked handsome but spoke easily, and was described as 'a born communicator'. To seek his equal in terms of profile-raising glamour one would only have to think of Princess Diana at the height of her charitable involvement in the 1990s.

David did not accept the teaching of Bagehot, on which other monarchs both before and after him were brought up: the widely accepted belief was that 'letting daylight in on magic' was the fastest way to disaster. Over-familiarity would lose the monarchy the respect of the public and diminish its prestige, it was thought. The Prince of Wales took an approach that was entirely at odds with this. He sought instead to befriend the public by being frequently visible in comparatively informal circumstances. He was depicted in the press more often than any of his predecessors, and was photographed doing ordinary things – or at least ordinary by the standards of the aristocracy – like playing golf, riding in steeplechases, visiting London nightclubs and parties. Though there were plenty of images of him in uniform or in a bowler hat, attending official occasions, he was also frequently shown in photographs dressed in plus-fours, socks and jerseys of outrageous loudness, smoking, chatting, joking with his future subjects in a way that even the genial Edward VII would not have done. It seemed to work. He was as popular as a film star.

He might have become king in 1928, when the sudden illness of his father caused him to cut short an overseas visit and hurry home. Had he done so, two years before meeting the woman he was to marry, he would have been a popular sovereign, though Mrs Simpson might well have caught his attention earlier than she did and events could well have taken the same course. His preference was self-evidently for married women. Frances Donaldson, who wrote a biography of him, said that 'he was actively seeking a dominating, quasi-maternal partner', first in Thelma, Lady Furness, and then in Wallis Simpson. Both women were Americans, from outside the British Establishment, and therefore perhaps more uninhibited about entering into a close friendship with the heir to the throne.

That they had these origins would have made a positive impression on the prince. He had liked America enormously and the affection had been mutual. The United States – the most glamorous country in the world – was to him associated with modernity, informality, comfort and social flexibility. He liked the people, whom he saw as sharing his own impatience with fustian tradition. Both the ladies with whom he was to become seriously involved in Britain had the confidence to dominate him, and in this they clearly fulfilled a need that he probably did not even articulate. Mrs Simpson, in particular, met his emotional needs so exactly that he knew at once she was the partner he wanted. One observer was to remark that he had never seen one human being so utterly and completely possessed by another as the Prince of Wales was by his second American lover. Lady Furness was to be unceremoniously got rid of, entirely eclipsed by his new companion.

Had Mrs Simpson not entered into previous marriages (she had been wed not once but twice, and the second time to a Guards officer – a connection too close to be overlooked), she might just have made a suitable consort. She would at least have given the prince an extremely happy home life. Her second husband, fiercely loyal to the monarchy though himself American in origin, declined to criticize the prince, even when the latter was openly taking holidays with the woman who was still Mrs Simpson, and had a habit of festooning her with jewels. In fact, David and Mrs Simpson made no attempt to keep their friendship secret, and this upset the king, if not Mrs Simpson's lawful spouse. Like many who are smitten with love, the prince did not understand why others should disapprove of his happiness or fail to wish him well. Had he sought to wed before his father's death, it is quite possible that King George would have used the Royal Marriages Act (which allowed the monarch to veto any union among his relatives of which he disapproved) to prevent his son marrying, but the king's health was failing and it was only a matter of time before the prince succeeded. If he could be patient a little while longer, he would need no one's permission.

It might be assumed that the choice of Mrs Simpson as consort to the king of England would be popular in the United States. In fact, many Americans were horrified at the development of this friendship. Had she been a worthier sample of American womanhood – a younger, previously unmarried lady of good family and good character – many citizens of the Great Republic would have felt considerable pride. That she was instead twice-divorced, middle-aged and not strikingly pretty (though men who met her remarked on her considerable magnetism), gave her in the eyes of some compatriots the image of a shop-soiled adventuress. As one American was to comment many years afterward: 'If we had sent over the best we had, it would have been a wonderful act of international friendship. But we felt let down at being represented by her.' Nevertheless, the abdication seemed to others a snub. Decades later, some would still ask if Edward's departure was caused by the fact that his intended wife was a divorcee or because she was American.

After succeeding to the throne on the death of George V on

20 January 1936, Edward – he had decided to take the regnal name of his grandfather – swept into his new role with an impatient gleam in his eye. He created the King's Flight as a modern means of transport. He decreed, somewhat eccentrically perhaps, that Yeomen of the Guard – Beefeaters – need no longer wear beards if they preferred not to. He demanded that his left profile, which was considered his better side, be shown on stamps even though images of sovereigns alternate and he should have been depicted from the right. He continued his father's custom of speaking to his peoples by wireless, and addressed at his coronation an audience of over two million. His modern attitudes were already well known. He disdained formal religion, and so fulfilling his role as head of the Anglican Church and Defender of the Faith was going to be problematic. He had little credibility with Church leaders and his views on divorce were – given his own situation – likely to be unacceptable to the Establishment.

Within the Palace he became both hated and feared. He expected to be waited upon at all hours, making life extremely difficult for footmen, pages and kitchen staff. He instigated cost-cutting measures that largely took the form of sacking staff. A number of these were officials who had faithfully served his father – or even himself. One of them, Admiral Halsey, had been head of his household. Halsey's patience had surely in any case reached its limit, for he had several times had to use his own money to pay the prince's bills. When the Admiral went to say farewell to his employer, the king sat looking at a book and did not even glance at him.

The prime minister, the avuncular Stanley Baldwin, dreaded the prospect of Edward's reign. In his estimation the new king had 'the mind of a child', and Baldwin knew him to be incapable of even pretending interest in the thousands of details of government business that a sovereign must master. He confessed to having secretly hoped ('God forgive me') that a broken neck in the hunting field would deprive the country of its ruler.

While Edward's modernizing zeal could be accepted with resignation, there were more serious issues to contend with. He was, for instance, in the habit of telling Mrs Simpson the details of confidential discussions, held in cabinet or the Privy Council, which she then repeated within her circle of friends. This included the German Ambassador, Ribbentrop, who therefore sometimes proved far more well informed about government affairs than was good for national security. As a result much sensitive information was kept from the king, and he was even under surveillance by his own security service.

It was just as well that he did not have closer dealings with more serious issues of government, for the political views he developed as the thirties progressed were deeply unsettling. He was an admirer of Hitler, and felt it was no business of other countries to criticize the manner in which the Nazis ran their state. Though King George had bluntly told the German Ambassador that his country was the greatest danger to peace and there would be war within a decade, King Edward saw matters differently. He liked Germany for the same reasons that he was impressed by America: he viewed it as aggressively modern, socially flexible and impatient with the past. He also approved of the no-nonsense way in which it had solved the problem of unemployment and had given its workless and its ex-servicemen a new sense of dignity and purpose. The details of how Germany's rising prosperity, social reform and political stability were attained – the stealing of assets, the persecution, imprisonment and murder of anyone the regime did not like – did not interest him. The plight of the country's Jews left him unmoved.

In 1930 he had acquired a home at Fort Belvedere, an eighteenth-century folly in the royal domain near Windsor. It was a fantasy castle surrounded by cannon that had reputedly been used at Culloden. His father had grudgingly made it over to him: 'What could you possibly want that queer old place for?' he had asked. 'Those damned weekends, I suppose.'

He was right. Edward had created for himself an enviable

home there. Gardens replaced the scrub which had formerly surrounded it, cleared away by his own efforts and those of his guests. It had been his headquarters as Prince of Wales, and remained so once he ascended the throne. He had showers and a swimming pool put in, and his weekends there were spent in parlour games and superficial, rather inane conversation over cocktails at the poolside. He often wore a kilt in the house or, as was customary in the royal family, a bearskin while in the gardens, to accustom himself to its weight before a military parade.

While his relaxation there with Mrs Simpson was well out of the public eye, a holiday cruise that he undertook with her aboard the yacht *Nahlin* during the summer of 1936 caused many of his advisers to doubt his sanity, and certainly to worry for his future and theirs. The vessel made a leisurely tour of the Adriatic, and at every landfall the curious could see the British monarch, sometimes casually dressed to the point of near-nakedness, in obviously intimate circumstances with a woman who was quickly identified by the international press. Only in Edward's own country did the newspapers, in a gesture of self-imposed censorship that would seem incredible only a few decades later, agree not to write about his public indiscretion or to publish photographs. As a result, Britons were often bewildered by the innuendo and outright speculation rife among their friends overseas on a subject about which they themselves knew little or nothing.

After his accession the new king's popularity remained considerable with the general public. King Edward at first believed that his affection for Mrs Simpson could be part and parcel of the new era over which he wished to preside. He was determined to be a monarch of his time, in tune with current thinking and fashion – the antithesis of his father, and no doubt a breath of fresh air for his subjects. He took it for granted that his own phenomenal popularity would carry on and would embrace his wife. He believed that the

British people would regard his love-match with a non-royal as a refreshing contrast to the stuffiness of the pre-war years, a milestone in the development of a populist, approachable monarchy. That his wife was American would also be a significant factor in uniting the two most influential countries in the English-speaking world. Anyone who stood in the way of this was simply a reactionary, and the king was confident that public opinion would be on his side.

But the tide of rumour about his private life was rising and it gradually started to dawn on him that he was not going to get his way about marrying Wallis, or at least not without a struggle. It appeared the British populace would not, after all, respond well to a sovereign who was so innovative and modern. He had of course expected opposition from the old guard of Palace advisers, and had had no qualms about getting rid of them, but it seemed that he had underestimated the natural conservatism of the peoples of his empire, and tried their sympathy with too many rapid and radical changes. They might after all, it seemed, prefer a king who was more like his father. If that were so, one of his brothers could take his place. Like the black sheep in any family, he somewhat resented the fact that his brothers were more worthy and conventional. Bertie, with his straightforward private life and his delightful family, would make a highly suitable king if he could somehow be coaxed into developing a more appealing public manner. George, Duke of Kent, was the most handsome of the brothers, and his wife, Princess Marina of Greece, was one of Europe's most beautiful women.

Despite the fact that his entire life had been spent preparing him for the position he now held, Edward clearly saw it as something that could be handed around within the family, and viewed himself as merely one of the possible candidates. Of these, the Duke of Kent was not suited to kingship by temperament, and neither was the other brother, the Duke of Gloucester. Bertie was, in any case, second in line to the throne. He would be summoned, when the moment came, by

fate and by default. Thankfully for history it would prove to
be a most happy choice.

Edward's only really memorable acts as king were the visits he
made to industrial areas blighted by unemployment, and ironically these have proved an enduring – if spurious – symbol of
his reign. At the derelict Dowlais iron and steel works in South
Wales, he made a speech. 'These works', he said, 'brought all
these people here. Something must be done to get them at work
again.' He was also quoted as having said: 'Something must be
done to help the situation in South Wales, and I will do all I
can to assist you.' In its shortened version, 'Something must be
done' became a sort of battle-cry. Long before the 'soundbite'
– the short, pithy quote that could be fitted conveniently into
newspaper or television reports – officially arrived, Edward's
single sentence had become his most memorable saying. At
the time it got him into trouble with the prime minister, Stanley Baldwin, for it represented a publicly expressed political
opinion of a sort the monarch is not allowed to hold. It would
create something of a legend around Edward VIII, suggesting
to multitudes that he was concerned about the plight of the
unemployed, to the extent that decades later a socialist who
knew nothing of recent British history, upon hearing Edward's
name, asked: 'Wasn't he the good one?' What sympathy he had
felt was, however, secondary to his main preoccupation: himself. A month after making this famous statement, Edward
abdicated. Whatever needed to be done, he would not be
around to contribute to it. He showed no further interest in
the matter. One observer, Godfrey Dawson, said that outside
the context of his public tours, the king showed no concern at
all for the social distress of his subjects. His somewhat fleeting
interest in industrial welfare was prompted solely by the desire
to stem the growth of bolshevism.

His marriage plans did not proceed until November 1936,
when Mrs Simpson's divorce from her second husband
became final. It was in that month that the press baron Lord

Beaverbrook was invited to dinner to meet her, and realized that this was not simply a passing affair. She was being seen more and more in public in London, adorned with what looked like the entire contents of a jeweller's shop window. The circle of those who knew, who heard rumours, who realized the danger the monarchy was now in, grew larger. In the House of Commons there was sarcasm and open speculation. It seemed incredible, to the millions who had cheered Edward in the streets and heard him speak on radio, who had shaken his hand on his tours of the empire and who had belonged to the charitable organizations he had set up, that he would desert his post. After all the popularity he had built up, would he seriously opt instead for an empty and uncertain future simply in order to marry a foreign adventuress? The looming crisis was a combination of tragedy and farce.

In the middle of November Prime Minister Baldwin was summoned by Edward to the Palace, and knew in advance what the topic of discussion would be. He answered the king's initial query by confirming that the notion of a divorced woman becoming queen would cause a constitutional crisis. Edward then informed him, succinctly: 'I intend to marry Mrs Simpson as soon as she is free to marry.' He added that, if this proved unacceptable to the cabinet and the public, he was – as he put it – 'prepared to go'. This was naturally devastating news to Baldwin, who in spite of all indications to the contrary had cherished a hope that the king would come to his senses when he saw that his intention caused such general concern. There was no question of this, however. Edward's relationship with Mrs Simpson had scaled new heights of obsession. He was like a small boy who calls the bluff of the grown-ups in an attempt to get what he wants. His innate stubbornness had set in, along with a sort of persecution complex. If he could defy the Establishment – the cabal of old courtiers and churchmen that was intent on bullying him – he could get his way, and would perhaps win even greater esteem in the eyes of his subjects as a man of principle, not dogged by hypocrisy and humbug but willing to put everything at risk for what he believed was right. He saw himself as a martyr.

He was also more than half-resigned to giving up the throne. He did not, in any case, like the job, and would only have been willing to carry it out on his own terms. Despite a lifetime of seeing his predecessors go through the endless routines of official duty, it came as a shock to him to find how unyielding the protocol that surrounded him was. He was visibly impatient with it all, but realized that even as sovereign he could not actually dictate how the Court should be run. He was up against a crushing weight of precedent, established practice, and officials whose own authority and conservatism were insurmountable. In addition Parliament was, to some extent, in a position to tell him what to do. He was not free to make more than minor adjustments. His father might have gone, but his mother remained; a highly influential presence and a formidable personality, she was an important counterweight to the new king's modernizing instincts. He knew, of course, that Queen Mary would not accept Mrs Simpson. Nevertheless if she were his wife (and his mother's sovereign!) time and pragmatism might well soften the old queen's view. He would not know what the reaction of others would be until the deed was done. He also believed – wrongly, it so happens – that the Archbishop of Canterbury, Cosmo Gordon Lang, was plotting against him, stoking the fires of public outrage. Edward fixed on this well-meaning man as the personification of the reactionary, fustian British Establishment.

There was still the possibility of compromise. He could marry Wallis, but morganatically. She would not become queen, and any children born to her would have no place in the succession. Neither Edward nor Mrs Simpson warmed to the idea that she was – as she herself put it – fit for bed but not for throne. He was hypersensitive to any slight on his intended wife, and here was a resounding one. His friends suggested he bide his time. He could not marry until the summer of 1937, because her divorce from Simpson would not become final until April of that year and he was due to be crowned in May. Could he not wait until he had settled in as sovereign and built further popularity with his people – earn their further trust and respect – before he took the plunge matrimonially? In the meantime it was thought advisable that she should stay out of public view, and perhaps travel extensively abroad for a year or so. It was of course hoped by even some of the king's closest intimates that he might forget her – or find some new distraction – in that time. Edward would not hear of this. He could not be parted from her even for a matter of weeks, let alone any longer period, and neither would he allow her to be shut away. He would not, he told Baldwin, consider being crowned 'without Wallis by my side'.

The countries of the Commonwealth were as horrified by his conduct as were the members of his own government – and this indicates that there was no 'plot' within the British Establishment to force his hand. The disquiet his behaviour caused was shared among all the countries of which he was sovereign. The Dominion governments made it clear to Baldwin that they did not wish to see the king married to Mrs Simpson and remaining on the throne. To them a morganatic marriage was simply not to be countenanced. Abdication would at least solve one problem. The king always based his hopes of remaining on appealing to his people over the heads of politicians, but there would never be enough public support for his actions to enable the public to defy their elected or appointed leaders. The 'King's Party' – a notion that his supporters hoped would come to his rescue – was simply not numerous or powerful enough to make any difference. Though backed by a few influential politicians, most notably the then-powerless Winston Churchill, the king was becoming increasingly isolated. While posterity knows that there was not sufficient support for him, contemporaries could only wait and see how divisive the issue would prove to be.

The crisis broke at the beginning of December. The self-censorship of the press had ended, because of an innocent sermon preached by the Bishop of Bradford, Dr Alfred Blunt, who referred to the new king's need for God's grace. Though innocuous enough, the sermon was perceived as a direct reference to Edward's personal life, and reports on it opened the subject to public discussion.

Mrs Simpson decided that she would best serve the king by disappearing from view, as had been hoped she would. She left England and sat out the crisis in the south of France. As the furore increased, she issued a statement – from the villa in Cannes where she was staying – that reiterated an offer she had already made, by telephone, to Edward. She would give him up. She wished to 'withdraw from a situation that was both unhappy and untenable'. It was generous, but the moment had gone. In terms of public relations, the damage was already done. The king, in any case, would not hear of any climbdown. 'But it's too late!' he told her, brightly.

Once the decision was made, he naturally felt relief. The past weeks and months had been grim for everyone, but the stress had been as great for the king as for his prime minister. Now he had got the one thing he wanted, he felt a sense of personal calm that was obvious to all around him. When he held a dinner party at Fort Belvedere, he was in noticeably good spirits. None of his guests shared this euphoria. Baldwin was there. So were his brothers. All of them were deeply saddened by the turn that events had taken. The Duke of York – known by his family as Bertie – horror-struck at the notion of having to take Edward's place, marvelled at his brother's bonhomie and charisma. The king was once again the man who had charmed an empire and whose nature had promised so much. 'Look at him,' said Bertie to George Monckton, the king's solicitor, 'we simply cannot let him go!'

Nevertheless the Abdication Bill was debated in the House of Commons: 403 Members voted for it, 5 voted against. The resulting document – the Instrument of Abdication – was signed by Edward at Fort Belvedere on 11 December. His brother Bertie instantly became king.

There was still a great deal of legal haggling to be got through regarding the ownership of property and the financial settlement that Edward would receive. The new king had effectively to buy Balmoral from the old one, as well as his other houses. Once this process had been put in hand (in the end Edward was to receive considerably less than he had expected), he was willing to depart. He wanted to join Mrs Simpson without delay. On the evening of 11 December he sat before a microphone at Windsor Castle and addressed, through the wireless, the subjects from whom he was now parting:

'I have found it impossible to carry the heavy burden of responsibility and to discharge my duties as king as I would wish to do without the help and support of the woman I love. I now quit altogether public affairs, and I lay down my burden.'

His voice was stiff, formal, strained, and carried the distinctive twang and the Wodehousian drawl ('. . . as I-eeeee would wish to doooo') that had become familiar throughout the world. It was a curious, Anglo-American accent that was unique to him – no one else even within his family talked like this – and was described as 'part Mayfair, part Long Island, part Dickensian cockney'. He had developed it, when young, to make sure he did not sound like his parents. This was to be the last time for decades that the public would hear it.

No longer king, he was introduced to the radio audience as 'Edward Windsor'. He would henceforth take the title Duke of Windsor. His wife would be the duchess. He would be a Royal Highness, she would emphatically not be. His brother, now King George VI, decided that Edward should be a Royal Duke because, if he were not, he would be eligible to sit in Parliament.

The new king at once began the attempt to redeem the monarchy. He had already said to his father's old doctor, Lord Dawson: 'If the worst happens and I have to take over, you can be assured that I will do my best to clear up the inevitable mess, if the whole fabric does not crumble under the shock and strain of it all.'

From our later perspective, King Edward VIII's faults are obvious. Of course at the time less was known about his private life, and among his contemporaries he still enjoyed immense popularity. He was, in fact, much more well liked than his shy and diffident younger brother. As a charismatic ex-king he simply could not be allowed to remain in Britain, distracting public attention – and loyalty – from the man who was embarking upon the difficult task of replacing him. The cabinet agreed that he must be firmly advised to go abroad, at least until the new king had got into his stride. Edward left the day after his abdication, travelling to Austria and then to France.

He left behind him something of a mess. Throughout the empire, stamps and coins and banknotes had been produced bearing his image. Now all of them would have to be destroyed, together with the dyes from which they had been made. The process of minting and printing would have to start again from the beginning for his successor. Only in Britain had stamps bearing Edward's likeness appeared – in his other territories there had not been time to issue them – and these can still be bought from dealers. The Royal Mint melted down virtually all his coinage, and only a few of the new threepenny pieces escaped, to become a treasured find for collectors, as is the 1936 Maundy money. It was not only these government agencies that suffered such immense waste of time and effort, however. Hundreds of private firms had been manufacturing souvenirs for the coronation, and now they too had to cut their losses. One familiar image of the year 1936 is a photograph of workmen in the Staffordshire potteries smashing thousands of commemorative mugs. Despite this setback, there was widespread relief among those who knew the king. One of those who had seen the worse side of his nature, the playwright Noël Coward, commented that statues of Mrs Simpson should be erected in towns all over Britain for the service she had done the nation in saving it from Edward VIII.

The abdication is now familiar to all students of British history, and we take it for granted. It is worth remembering, however, that nothing like it had ever happened before. Edward's departure represented the first time in eleven hundred years that a sovereign had voluntarily abandoned the throne. This happened, moreover, in the midst of an era (the thirties were to be dubbed 'the devil's decade') that was characterized by political extremism and atrocious violence. Had the British been a more volatile people, had there not been a more suitable successor to Edward instantly to hand, there could well have been chaos and anarchy, and even an end to the monarchy itself. This was, without doubt, the institution's worst moment in the twentieth century. It was a graver crisis by far than that which followed the death of Princess Diana in 1997. It was said at the time of the latter event that had the recently elected Labour prime minister not thrown the weight of his influence behind the queen, the royal family would have been abolished in the mood of public and political hostility that prevailed. Though this is a wild exaggeration, it is certainly the case that the atmosphere after Edward's abdication was strained and volatile. It has been estimated that, had the House of Commons voted on the continuation of the monarchy at that time, at least a hundred MPs would have been against it. For the royal family, Edward's betrayal of his heritage was a personal as well as a national disaster. Even a generation later – because several of those most closely affected were so long-lived – the repercussions of the event were still felt throughout the family.

Once Edward had left the throne, humiliation on humiliation was piled upon him. The financial arrangements for his future life, worked out with the Palace, were altered to become less generous, more punitive and more hedged about by conditions, one of which was that he might never return to live in the United Kingdom. His wife would not be accorded the same royal status as he himself was to retain, and no offspring from their marriage would have this style either. No member of the family accepted an invitation to his wedding – which took place the following May at a château outside Paris – including Louis Mountbatten, who had previously agreed to act as best man. It was as if, now that he was safely out of the country and no longer in a position of influence, there was no further need to waste any politeness on him.

In the years that followed, Edward continued to be deprived of any useful role. He might be in exile but he could still embarrass his country, and he made a spectacular gaffe by accepting an invitation to visit Nazi Germany with his wife in 1937. She in particular was fawned upon by the leadership there. 'What a queen she would have made!' Hitler supposedly sighed after meeting the duchess. Their journey was featured in British cinema newsreels, where Edward was seen behaving much as he had at home when king – smiling, shaking hands, inspecting troops. His visit to a coal mine evoked memories of South Wales. Not only was the visit politically ill advised, it also reminded his former subjects of the better side of his nature, the things he had done so much more gracefully than his tongue-tied younger brother. He was thus further damned in the eyes of his family and of the British government. The visit also wrecked, for the time being, the Windsors' relations with America. They had intended to go on there, but had to cancel because of the public odium they had earned through being seen with Hitler. Two years later, when the expected European war broke out, the duke and duchess were evacuated to Britain. Edward asked his brother for some useful war work. He was briefly appointed to the British military mission in France, and held a General's rank, but when that country was overrun he immediately fled to Portugal.

He was eventually got rid of with an appointment as Governor of the Bahamas, a lilliputian territory for an ex-king to rule, far removed from great events or from any chance to do more useful work. The Windsors remained there until the return of peace, and then moved once again to France.

Provided with a house by the City of Paris, they lived there for the rest of their lives, a sybaritic existence that contained little other than golf and dinner parties, gardening and travel to the resorts of Europe and America. There was no full-scale reconciliation with their relatives in Britain (the Queen Mother would not have allowed this, it is believed), although they did return briefly to London in 1953 – not for the coronation, to which they were not invited, but for the unveiling of a memorial to Edward's mother, who died that year. When he himself followed her – he passed away nineteen years later – he was at last brought back to his former realm. He lay in state at Windsor, where hundreds queued to see his coffin. (One of them, a woman interviewed by the BBC, was asked why she was there. She thought for a moment and answered: 'He stuck to his convictions.' There will always, perhaps, be a few romantics who insist on seeing him as a hero.) He was interred in the royal burial ground at Frogmore.

It is worth remembering that Edward lived until 1972. His reign could therefore have lasted thirty-six years. It is very unlikely, however, that he would ever have seen out his life as king. He was such a disaster, and for so many reasons, that had his marriage not caused him to go, something else most probably would have done. It is not difficult to identify another problematic aspect of his life. His Nazi sympathies – unless they could have been played down sufficiently or he had done something to redeem himself – would have made him useless as a British wartime figurehead, and he might even have had to be interned. His Household would, in any case, have been impossible to run, or to rely on, for a head of state who would impulsively cancel long-standing commitments would swiftly have lost any credibility and caused complaints from those taxpayers who had been promised his time and his attention. He would quite likely have made any number of indiscreet, offensive public pronouncements that, reported in the press, would have further undermined respect for the monarchy – and perhaps fatally destroyed its reputation for impartiality.

He would have antagonized every prime minister with whom he dealt (including the long-suffering Winston Churchill, who supported him in 1936), with his hectoring and abrasive manner as well as a marked inability to pay attention to official tasks. His occasional words of sympathy for the unemployed might have continued, but unaccompanied by any practical gestures, respect for him would have dwindled further.

While he was Prince of Wales, the flaws in his nature could just about be covered up or explained away. As king, with his every move observed and reported, he would have been exposed before long as the man he was, and would have been widely disliked. Even had his wife been able to win over public opinion and find acceptance – and that is extremely unlikely, given her own nature – the couple would have attracted odium for their lack of seriousness, their vulgar friends, their expensive tastes, their patent selfishness, and perhaps most importantly for their inability to have children (a fact that was of course not known to the public at the time of their marriage). Had his reign lasted much longer, Edward VIII would have been booed in the streets, savaged in the press, scorned by his own subjects and ridiculed by other nations. The worst and most unpopular monarch since King John, he would almost certainly have abandoned the throne – or perhaps been forced from it by a *coup d'état*, such as had occurred in 1688. His brother George would, in all probability, have had to replace him within a few years, and history would then have proceeded much as it in fact did. It is unlikely, at any rate, that Queen Elizabeth II would have had to wait a further twenty years to ascend the throne.

4

GEORGE VI, 'BERTIE', 1936–52

'How I hate being king! Sometimes at ceremonies I want to stand up and scream and scream.'
George VI, shortly after ascending the throne

Perhaps the most unlikely candidate for kingship of any country in the twentieth century – though one of the most-loved monarchs Britain has had – was Prince Albert, the younger brother of the charismatic but flawed Edward VIII. He became king on the abdication of his brother a few days before his forty-first birthday, and remained on the throne for just over fifteen years until his death at fifty-six. 'Bertie', as he was known to his family, had none of his brother's advantages. Excruciatingly shy, and modest to the point of invisibility, he grew up with a profound feeling of inadequacy. He suffered from a stammer that afflicted him, as all the world learned from the film *The King's Speech*, well into adult life. He was deeply unpromising as a youth, showing little aptitude as a cadet in the Royal Navy (though the time he spent

in the Service gave him wide experience of people and places),
but unlike his elder brother he saw wartime action. He was
also a founder member of the Royal Air Force.

In a technical Service, there was no opportunity to avoid
unpleasant chores or daunting responsibilities. A contemporary photograph shows Bertie, blackened from head to
foot, during the filthy but vital process of 'coaling', when his
ship took on fuel. The Navy also forced him to live at close
quarters with others. This was highly useful training in dealing with all sorts and conditions of men. He was helped by
an excellent memory for names and faces. Decades after his
active career had ended, he was still able to recall former ship-
mates when he met them, not only among officers but ratings
and stokers too.

He was aware of the power of monarchy to cast a spell over
its subjects. He had seen Edward VII and George V, as well as
his elder brother, exercise their different forms of charisma,
and he knew that, whatever his own personal shortcomings,
the institution he represented would exert its usual magic.
He was to tell his daughter Elizabeth that whoever met her
would remember the experience for the rest of their life. He
expected others to recall meeting him and could become furi-
ous (his bad temper and sudden rages, like those of his father,
were legendary) if they did not. During the Second World
War, when visiting the theatre of operations in North Africa,
he shook hands with a number of Generals. He asked one
of them: 'Have we met before?' 'I don't remember,' was the
reply. The king exploded, his stammer returning: 'Well, you
b-b-b-bloody-well *ought* to remember!'

Bertie did not have academic intelligence – a characteristic
he shared with his father and his brother David – but he possessed in full the sense of duty in which Edward had been
lacking. What he would also bring to the role of king was a
thorough, transparent decency that was to win over a number
of those, such as left-wing politicians, or the leaders of independence movements, who had no reason to feel warmly

either toward the monarchy or to Britain. He was naturally obliging and conscientious: or 'dutiful, and rather dull' as he was summed up. This was one of the kinder things said about him. He was variously dismissed as a 'nitwit' (Lloyd George), a 'dull dog' (R. A. Butler), 'a weak character and certainly a stupid one' (Oliver Hardy), a 'very stupid man' (Kenneth Clark), and a 'moron' (Deladier, the French prime minister).

The empire did not need a man of great intelligence or even vision, however. Politicians can provide those things. A monarch needs patience, enthusiasm, and an ability at least to feign interest in what is around them; above all, perhaps, a proper appreciation of history and of their place in it. A sovereign cannot be too imaginative, for the job involves numbing monotony, endless repetition and ceaseless formality. They must also avoid having controversial, publicly expressed views on anything. Prince Albert, when he succeeded to the throne as King George VI, was able to summon these qualities. He sought to model his reign on that of his father. Though in many ways their natures were very different they had a certain amount in common, including the passion for shooting that was almost compulsory among the upper class of that time. Their handwriting was virtually identical, a reassuring symbol for those who yearned for continuity. Such people were not to be disappointed for the new sovereign copied, or simply manifested, the same dedication to duty, tolerance of protocol and irreproachable integrity that George V had done. To his subjects, his accession must have represented a return to reason after the short, turbulent rule of Edward VIII. The new King George was to prove that even a man whose personality and gifts seem unpromising can become an effective and respected sovereign if supported by able officials and sound advice and goodwill.

George VI began his reign in the glow of public favour. People were aware that he did not relish his new role. They knew he had not been trained for it and that he did not feel suited to it by nature. Though he was not regarded as a very exciting individual, the majority sympathized with him and wished him well. The press deliberately built up a positive image of the new king, and helped him further by not giving coverage to his elder brother, who was now beginning a peripatetic life of exile abroad. That George was a family man, married to an eminently suitable wife and with children who at once secured the succession, helped considerably. After months of Edward VIII's furtive love life and his betrayal of his destiny, this wholesome and straightforward family seemed a particular blessing. Its female members – his personable wife and photogenic daughters – provided any glamour that was necessary. Otherwise, his subjects were relieved to have a sovereign who was lacklustre and dutiful.

With his accession there appeared on the national stage someone who was to be more responsible than any other individual for a new era of popularity for the monarchy. This was the new queen, Elizabeth. Her outgoing nature and matchless ability to make small talk hid a will of iron. She would not only bring up her eldest daughter to be a paragon among sovereigns but would make the utmost of the gentle nature and willingness to do his duty that characterized her husband. Her ability to manage what would now be called 'public relations' was unarguable. She presented the world, through the photographs and articles that she allowed visiting journalists to produce, with the image of a devoted, close-knit family, dressed simply and given to uncomplicated pleasures – riding, bicycling, gardening, picnicking. There was no pretence about any of this. The family members were precisely as they were shown. Queen Elizabeth succeeded in presenting them as the nation's first family even before her husband had attained the throne.

At first it seemed Bertie had not been designed by nature to be either a monarch or a wartime figurehead. Born on 14 December 1895 at York Cottage in Sandringham, he was christened Albert Frederick Arthur George (during Queen Victoria's lifetime the name Albert appeared with unrelenting

regularity among the Christian names of her male descendants). From the beginning he lived in the shadow of his more
promising, charming, outgoing elder brother. Bertie was not
only delicate but ill throughout his childhood. He had gastri-
tis in infancy and it was to plague him again once he entered
the Navy. He was also prone to knock knees, a family trait
that is noticeable in pictures of George V, and was obliged to
wear splints to correct this tendency.

At the age of eight he developed his famous stammer. It
has been accounted for by the fact that he was naturally
left-handed but was forced to use his right. His father, who
was affectionate but impatient and certainly not inclined to
mollycoddle, would shout at him: 'Get it out!' if the boy suddenly became stuck over a word, and this naturally made
him worse. There is no question that the royal family of that
era provided a generally supportive environment in which
to grow up. Its members were genuinely fond of each other
and, with a few exceptions, demonstratively so when out of
the public eye. It was also true, however, that the children
were treated with exemplary firmness from the beginning.
The boys must be accustomed to strictness so that they could
cope with serving in the Navy. They could not be indulged,
given the lives of duty they would go on to lead. This, as much
as natural impatience, led their father to shout at them when
occasion demanded. Between the brothers there was a very
strong bond, as might have been expected with those who had
little chance to meet others of their age (Bertie's daughters,
Elizabeth and Margaret, were to have the same close relationship). The common experience of growing up in a unique
family united them, as it tends to do with every generation
of royalty.

Like Eddy and George before them, Bertie and his brother
David were put into the Royal Navy at an early age. As with
the previous generation, it was assumed that this would give
them a sound education. When in 1936 Bertie suddenly found
himself king, he would exclaim anxiously to his cousin, Louis

Mountbatten: 'Dickie, this is absolutely terrible. I'm only a naval officer. It's the only thing I know about!' Mountbatten was to reply smoothly that: 'There is no finer training for a king.' This pronouncement was treated as received wisdom, but it was in fact highly unrealistic. The Service undoubtedly taught some important traits: responsibility, punctuality, respect for authority, and familiarity with the wider world. Yet a naval gunroom was also a place of smug and insular philistinism. The only knowledge required in the Navy was technical. There was no opportunity to develop imagination, creativity or original thought. Character was developed at the expense of individuality or intellectual enquiry, and though some officers might possess these things, they would be seen as odd in an environment where the 'norm' was a bluff distrust of intelligence. The Navy left both princes hopelessly unlettered and uncultured, and with a puerile sense of humour that stayed with them for life. Nevertheless, they both retained a personal loyalty to it, looking back with affection on their time as officers, and they both had a great rapport with servicemen and veterans that served them well as sovereigns.

Since their father's time, a naval school had been set up in the grounds of Osborne House, Queen Victoria's summer home on the Isle of Wight. David, Bertie and their cousin Louis Mountbatten all attended this before going on to Dartmouth. Bertie's performance at the school was dismal. He came 68th out of 68 cadets in order of merit. When he passed out of Dartmouth he managed to stay off the bottom of the class, but here too his performance was unimpressive: 61st out of 67. His career at both establishments was ordinary enough. At the former he was nicknamed 'Bat-lugs' for his protruding ears. At the latter he was punished for horseplay. He became a midshipman in 1913, a member of the world's largest and most powerful navy. He had entered a Service that, at that time, had permanent fleets based in the Mediterranean, the Indian Ocean, and the Far East, and which would thus have enabled him to serve in every part of the globe.

He was to spend four years in the Navy. During that time he was treated like any other junior officer, and was to look back with appreciation on this interlude. He enjoyed life at sea, with its lack of protocol and its frequent challenges. He liked living, on terms of complete equality, with other young men who shared his interests. He appreciated the chance to meet and work with the ratings and petty officers – his only close encounter with the working class, and one that must have exerted a certain fascination. Like his father – and indeed the great Lord Nelson – he became seasick, but this did not prevent him from revelling in his new life. He went on a training voyage to the Caribbean and, because his presence aboard ship was known, crowds gathered in the ports to stare at him. Such was his shyness – and irritation with all this attention – that he got a fellow midshipman of similar build to act as his double.

The era of peace between Britain and the Continental powers, which had lasted almost a hundred years, was about to end with frightening suddenness in the outbreak of the First World War. Bertie was aboard HMS *Collingwood* during the first days of August when the Fleet awaited the opening of hostilities, and stood watch on deck to await conflict. Yet his war was to start badly for him. Within a few weeks appendicitis had put him on an operating table. His recovery was slow, and he chafed at the enforced idleness. A further illness put him out of action for months, though at least during that time he was able to make a visit to France with the Prince of Wales, and to see there the horrific conditions in which the soldiers lived and fought. He rejoined his ship in May 1916, only a few weeks before the showdown with the German Fleet for which the Royal Navy had been waiting throughout almost two years of war. This was to be the clash between two of the world's naval giants, equipped almost equally with state-of-the-art warships – an encounter that in its scale, its weaponry and its consequences would surely be the greatest naval battle of all time. It took place on the afternoon of 31

May 1916, when the German Fleet sailed out of Kiel into the North Sea and met their opponents off the coast of Denmark.

The British called it the Battle of Jutland. To the Germans, it was the Battle of Skagerrak. Both sides claimed they won; neither really did. The British Fleet lost more ships, but their enemy gained nothing. What did happen, however, was that the German Fleet returned to port and did not come out to fight again. Bertie was there, helping to man the guns in 'A' Turret aboard *Collingwood*. It must have been a frantic, frightening, chaotic business, and his ship was fortunate in coming through the battle unscathed, for if a vessel received a direct hit there might well be very few survivors – an entire crew could be lost. Other vessels could be too far away to attempt rescue, and death by burning or drowning would be the result. Bertie would always be rightly proud that he had taken part in this crucial battle. His brother missed it, and so did Louis Mountbatten, who would go on to make a career in the Navy. It was the shy and unpromising member of the family who had gained this distinction.

He had only just been in time, however, because another bout of illness quickly landed him back in hospital. Between sea duty and convalescence he continued to take part in family duties. A photograph from that time shows him, dressed in his naval officer's uniform, pouring tea for wounded soldiers at an event hosted by his parents.

After Jutland he did not return to sea. Instead he was transferred to the Royal Naval Air Service and sent to Cranwell, where he spent the rest of the war in command of a squadron of trainee pilots. He qualified as a pilot himself, beginning the connection between his family and military flying that has been maintained ever since. When in April 1918 the RNAS would amalgamate with the Royal Flying Corps to create the Royal Air Force, Bertie would become the first member of the royal family to wear the uniform of this new service.

He loved his time at Cranwell. He was popular with his youthful charges, who referred to him as 'P.A.' (Prince

Albert). He also made friends among the staff, and one of these, Louis Greig, whose home he visited, introduced him to the pleasures of family life. To see parents and young children living happily together within the cramped confines of a small house filled him with envy. He realized how much he, too, yearned to have his own home and family.

He continued with the RAF once the conflict was over, serving with the Air Ministry in London, a period of useful work in the sense that he saw at first hand a government department and how it functioned. Nothing, however, was allowed to last for long. Though there was no expectation that he would succeed to the throne, he was to be given a taste of several different aspects of national life and his next phase was to be spent at Cambridge. Here, in accordance with family tradition, he did not shine academically, though his personality continued to develop – he lived as far as possible like any other undergraduate, attending debates at the Union, buying a motorcycle, and playing tennis. Mountbatten, his friend and cousin, was there at the same time, and so was Louis Greig. He and the prince became such an effective tennis partnership that in 1920 they won the RAF Doubles. Continuing to play, they would actually make it to Wimbledon in 1928, though they were not successful there.

In this new era Bertie acquired both a title and a purpose. First, his father created him Duke of York. Secondly, he took on the task of wooing the working class. As part of the monarchy's new image, it would be helpful if the poorest section of its people could be shown that royalty was interested in them, through patronage or chairmanship of appropriate organizations, and through visits to industrial plants. This could be seen as a cynical attempt to make the monarchy seem relevant to the masses, and to discourage the spread of socialism. The initiative, however, did not come from the Palace but from the public. Bertie was not designated by his father to undertake this task, he was asked to do it by persons interested in social welfare, and it happened to fit with the monarchy's own inclinations. The royal family had shown an interest in the industrial life of the country for almost a hundred years. When Queen Victoria was a girl she had been taken to visit factories and foundries in the English Midlands as part of her royal training. Her husband Prince Albert had furthered this connection through a genuine enthusiasm for industry and technology, and he had also designed 'model dwellings' – easy-to-build mass housing that could be erected anywhere – in which a workforce could be accommodated. King George V's plan was to make the monarchy more visible to the whole population and more involved in the life of the country, and he could thus draw on precedent. His second son, whose shyness and lack of speaking ability made him an unlikely candidate for a charm offensive, took up the cause of industrial welfare and proved surprisingly successful at it.

It must not be forgotten that he and his father were sincere in their desire to improve the lot of their people. Both of them had a sense of mission, seeing it as their role to conciliate; to encourage unity and moderation and compromise in an era when industrial and class relations threatened to deteriorate drastically. It was a worthwhile task, and Bertie set about it with enthusiasm. He accepted the role of 'industrial duke' (his brothers nicknamed him 'the foreman'), provided he could undertake visits with a minimum of fuss and preparation. 'I'll do it provided there's no damned red carpet,' he said. He founded an organization called the Industrial Welfare Society, on behalf of which he made tours of factories that enabled him to see conditions as they really were. He managed also to have some fun: in 1924, during a visit to Wales, he played a round of golf against the labour leader Frank Hodges on a course in the Rhondda Valley that had been laid out for miners.

His time at Cranwell had given him experience of working with young men, and in 1921 he established a regular summer camp. The boys who attended were to be recruited in equal numbers from public schools and industry, a mixing of classes in which neither side would have the advantage of numbers. It was a highly original and imaginative concept, and it was Bertie's own. The camps were held at Southwold in Suffolk, a beautiful rural corner of England. They lasted a week. The boys, who were nominated by headmasters, local clergymen or employers, were doubtless chosen for their outgoing and confident natures, but the camps might well have failed had there not been a routine of chores and competitive games that required absolute cooperation. Sharing tents, chopping firewood, and then sitting around the resulting blaze in the evenings made for fellow feeling whatever the backgrounds of those involved. The duke himself always attended for part of the camp, and sat for a group photograph with all the participants. Pictures show him wearing tweed jacket, shorts and knee-socks, as informally dressed as any Sunday hiker. He was also depicted joining in the singing of the camps' theme song 'Under the Spreading Chestnut Tree'.

It was an atmosphere of simple camaraderie that was suited to a less cynical generation than our own, and one whose opportunities for leisure were more limited. It marked an important new departure – the chance for representatives of the nation's youth to meet and mingle with royalty in an atmosphere of informality; 'no damned red carpet' indeed. The gatherings continued once Bertie succeeded to the throne. He arrived off the coast aboard the royal yacht, to be rowed to shore by Suffolk fishermen. At 'the King's Camp', it was the head of state who joined in the games and the sing-songs, the notion of 'accessibility' becoming even more pronounced. The camps ceased only because of the war. The king, of course, continued to reign after it had ended and, because the desire for social equality became even more intense in post-war Britain, one wonders why no attempt was made to revive the camps. There seems to be no evidence that they actually did ease relations between the classes, but they were an inspired and sincere attempt to do so, and might have become a lasting memorial to the king whose idealism had made them possible.

Like politicians running for office, the monarchy was seeking to be all things to all people, but to a large extent succeeded. Whatever his drawbacks in terms of shyness, the Duke of York achieved and maintained an impressive level of personal contact with his father's people. Yet it must not be assumed that he was met everywhere with deference or that the public as a whole found him charming. On a visit to London's East End during the Depression, he was heckled with cries of: 'Give us food! We don't want royal parasites!' In an era before the Welfare State and the social safety nets that seek to protect the least well off, it is worth remembering that the poor could face serious malnutrition and actual starvation. Their resentment of the ease and plenty in which others lived was thus more acute and desperate. Bertie's encounters with his people were not, therefore, always a simple matter of smiling and waving. They might have more in common with a present-day visit to a poverty-stricken developing country, and engendered a similar sense of hopelessness and anger.

He entered the 1920s as a bachelor, but at once met Elizabeth Bowes-Lyon, a debutante from an illustrious Scottish family, with whom he fell in love. She was twenty. He was five years older. She was outgoing, spirited and genuinely kind. He was awkward, shy and stammering. They had met once before, as children at a party, when she was five and he was ten. She had given him the cherries off her cake, a kindness he had not forgotten.

He proposed to her, but was unsuccessful. She was unwilling, as other young women have been since, to make the sacrifice of personal freedom that marrying royalty necessitates. It was certainly not a question of dislike on her part, for his shyness and modesty would doubtless have been endearing. He might have been shy, but he was also persistent. She had impressed both of his parents, which was no mean feat, and in fact Queen Mary was as determined as her son was that Elizabeth should have him. The queen had spotted the younger woman's potential and saw in her the best possible antidote to Bertie's reserve and awkwardness. Even the king was said to be 'half in love with her'. The young man was to try again twice more until, in 1923, she at last agreed. Parental endorsement was of crucial importance, for his parents could snuff out any romance of which they disapproved. He had previously set his cap at other women. In the case of one, Helen Baring, to whom he proposed, he received a brusque message from Queen Mary that read: 'On no account will we permit the proposed marriage. Mama.'

Since childhood, Elizabeth had been deputizing for her mother as hostess in a large and hospitable household, and regarded meeting people as a pleasure rather than an ordeal. She was everything the duke was not: sociable, confident, at ease in any company. Beneath an exterior of gracious good manners, she also had a determination that was to stand both of them in good stead in the future. She had been the most popular debutante of the year in which she 'came out', and she had had at least two other serious admirers. Bertie was not an obvious companion for someone of such a sociable disposition, yet he had become passionately fond of her. Even though there was little likelihood, at that time, of the Duke of York inheriting the throne, the prospect of a lifetime of public service was something she had to consider very carefully. Her parents, and his, watched the romance develop with a combination of hope and anxiety. The couple were well suited for the precise reason that they were so different. Others could see that Elizabeth would compensate for his reserved nature and make them an effective team.

This time there could be no question that his mother, and he, had made the right choice. The engagement was immensely popular with the public. The Scots were naturally delighted that a compatriot had won the affection of a prince, and Elizabeth's sunny, unspoiled nature was made much of by the press, which saw her as bringing a new vivacity to the institution of royalty. Despite her aristocratic background the public were, for the first time, able to feel that the wife of a royal was one of their own, and this made a noticeable difference to their enthusiasm for the match. In an emphatically modern, post-war age, this marriage was seen as something new and welcome. Elizabeth would in time become the first native-born queen by marriage since Catherine Parr, who had been one of the wives of King Henry VIII. For the moment, Elizabeth simply offered beauty, refinement and a pleasing nature. As with the adoption of its new name, the royal family had clearly made a change that fitted precisely with the mood of its people.

One reason that family weddings had in the past been small-scale, semi-private affairs had been from the belief that the cost of public celebrations might foster resentment. To make this one a national occasion was an experiment, but one that proved so resoundingly successful it has been repeated at almost every opportunity since. It was decided that the couple would marry in Westminster Abbey. This was by no means the obvious setting that it seems to us now. There had at the time been no royal wedding there since that of Richard II more than five centuries earlier, and the choice of the Abbey was tantamount to issuing a general invitation to the public at large. A marriage in central London meant that many ordinary people would be able to see something of the event, and on the day – 26 April 1923 – over a million turned out. This was the first of the set-piece royal weddings, the great public occasions, that have since become the norm. There was even a request that matters go further by having the proceedings broadcast on wireless, though this was declined by the Chapter of Westminster Abbey.

As it travelled down Whitehall toward the Abbey, the bride's carriage slowed and stopped by the Cenotaph, Britain's national war memorial. Elizabeth, one of whose brothers had been killed in the Great War, leaned out on impulse and placed her bouquet on the memorial, arriving at her wedding without one. It was a touching action, and the more so because it was spontaneous. It also revealed a gift for symbolic gestures that would help greatly to increase the popularity of the monarchy.

The Duke and Duchess of York would have just over thirteen years of semi-private life together before the crisis of December 1936 put Bertie on the throne. They lived in London (at a large town house in Piccadilly, a few minutes from Buckingham Palace) and at Windsor (where a Regency house in the grounds, Royal Lodge, was refurbished for them). Here the restoration and cultivation of the gardens became a passion, a hobby, and – amid the whirl of duty – a means of relaxation for them both. They had other concerns, however. Almost three years to the day after their wedding, on 21 April 1926, a daughter was born to them. She was christened Elizabeth Alexandra Mary. Though not directly in the line of succession, for it was still assumed that her uncle the Prince of Wales would marry and produce children of his own, she was the nearest thing to a royal heir. She delighted the king, who had been waiting impatiently for his eldest son to continue the family line, and she delighted the public for the same reason. General opinion might have preferred a boy, but she was so charming that she became at once a sort of national mascot, feted in the press and extensively photographed. Four years later she was joined by a sister, Margaret Rose, and the Yorks' family was complete. Both girls had been born by Caesarean section, and two such births were the most that medical opinion would condone. There would be no son, and no further daughters.

Elizabeth and Bertie made a lengthy tour to Australia and New Zealand when Elizabeth was less than two years old, leaving her with her grandparents (she herself would leave her own children with the king and queen at a similar age when her husband was serving in Malta). There was also some suggestion that the family would move to Canada because the duke might be appointed Governor-General. This proposal, however, was not acceptable to Canadians, and the position was not the king's to give. The appointment would have had to be approved by the country's government, and this was not done. It might be assumed that a Dominion would welcome the chance to have a member of Britain's royal family resident in Ottawa as a gesture of imperial unity, but Canadians rejected the notion of a royal Governor-General and the man appointed was Lord Willingdon (1866–1941), a highly revered proconsul with extensive experience of India – a professional rather than a symbolic figure. King George was relieved that his son had not been invited. For one thing, he feared that Bertie's shyness and his inability to speak in public without stammering would have made the position a terrible ordeal for him. For another, he did not wish to be separated from his granddaughter Elizabeth, of whom he was extremely fond. There would be enough for the Yorks to do in Britain, and this became even more the case when the king became ill in 1928 and they had to take over more of his duties.

As shown, the economic climate made the cost of royalty potentially controversial. The king reduced his own and his sons' Civil List allowances. David, Prince of Wales, sulked. Bertie was resigned. He could suddenly no longer afford the extensive renovations he was having carried out at Royal Lodge, and had to accustom himself instead to living in a partially dilapidated residence. Worse than that, he was obliged to give up his major leisure interest by parting with his stable of hunters. Those who do not own horses will have difficulty in understanding the extent to which these animals can become friends. It was a terrible wrench for him to sell the horses that had been not only his companions but his hobby. Yet he did. 'I am only doing this,' he said, 'after careful consideration of the facts (damned hard facts).' These economies, in other words, were no mere token but a genuine sacrifice for him.

Despite this, the Yorks led a pleasant and largely untroubled existence. Bertie and Elizabeth were both proving to be useful in the performance of public royal duties, and the attentions of a speech therapist, Lionel Logue, which began in 1926, had considerably lessened for Bertie the stress of his public appearances. He had his good causes, through which he made some impact, and he had a love of sports and out-door life that brought him considerable pleasure – he shot and farmed at Sandringham, continued to play tennis (a left-hand-er, he remains the only member of his family to have reached Wimbledon), and played golf with modest ability. With no apparent desire to travel abroad on holiday, the family went to Balmoral each summer. The girls lived at home – there was no precedent for princesses going away to school – and the four members of the family therefore spent every day togeth-er unless official duties dictated otherwise. Bertie, who had fitted effortlessly into the role of family man, had an enviably happy existence.

All this was widely recorded in books and articles. In the absence of any domestic life around the Prince of Wales, the Yorks became by default the nation's First Family. The public were very interested in their garden, their pets, the girls' hob-bies and accomplishments. The royal family had always been public property – photographs taken of its children at all ages, in both serious and playful moments, had been common in Bertie's own youth. This time there was an added purpose to the exercise – to show their subjects that, in a time of eco-nomic hardship, the family lived a simple and rather ordinary life that was much like other people's. Both before and after he came to the throne, pictures of Bertie showed him cycling, walking, gardening, taking tea with his wife and daughters. Dressed in a tweed suit and brogues, he looked like an agree-able country doctor. The duchess was always stylish. She might have helped her husband to clear the gardens, but she was never photographed in old clothes, and the notion of her being pictured in trousers would have been unthinkable. Similarly, the two princesses were always turned out with emphatic neatness, in sensible shoes and with dresses that matched and looked like those worn by millions of middle-class girls.

The pleasant lives led by Bertie and his family were not interrupted until the death of his father. The jubilee of King George V was celebrated in May 1935, but he died the following January. David became king, as has always been the custom, the instant his father passed away. By this time, however, there were serious doubts about the coming reign. Not only was the new king at loggerheads with many of those around him – he despised the courtiers he had inherited from his father, and abruptly dismissed many of them – he was also preoccupied and agitated, and his relationship with the American divorcee, Mrs Wallis Simpson, was causing serious disquiet. Though the Yorks had met her – she had visited Royal Lodge with David – they had not realized that the king was so intent on marrying her, or that he was seriously considering abdication if he were not allowed to do so while retaining the throne. With typical selfishness, David had not confided his difficulties, or his intentions, to the brother who would have to take over the position he would abandon. The new king was not willing to see his brother or to discuss matters with him, and meanwhile anxiety continued to mount.

Within a matter of days – hours – in December 1936, the storm broke. With a sense of sickening dread, Bertie realized that his taking over the throne was first likely, and then certain. Like others who had come to this position by default he had had no useful training, and felt absolutely no sense of vocation. Fortunately, this was a difficulty that could be overcome. In the same way that an incoming – and by definition inexperienced – government can rely on a permanent Civil Service to keep the country ticking over, a monarch can depend on a long-serving staff of courtiers, Private Secretaries and officials who know exactly how the monarchy functions – the ceremonies and the meetings and the dealing with dispatch boxes. They will normally be the same officials who served the previous sovereign (in Bertie's case his father rather than his brother) and the routine to which they are accustomed will continue until a new monarch has found their feet and developed their own habits. Bertie was not nearly as unprepared as he believed. He had had all around him throughout his life the example of other rulers, a store of remembered impressions, overheard conversations, pieces of advice. He had had half a lifetime of meeting the public, making speeches, opening things, attending parades. He had already carried out many of the tasks that would now take up all his time.

If he felt unprepared for his new role, it was an anxiety that was shared by the courtiers, advisers and Private Secretaries who now surrounded him. Like the 'handlers' who tell an American president what to say and do, they moved swiftly to ensure that he was seen to best advantage. They decided his biggest chance of success was to be as much like his father as possible, but they knew he lacked the gift for simple oratory that George V had possessed. It was decided that there should therefore be no Durbar – he would not journey to India to be proclaimed emperor – and he did not broadcast either at his accession or in the first Christmas of his reign. He must continue to be presented as a family man of simple tastes, and as little as possible of his real personality – the anguish and self-doubt, the rages – must be visible to his subjects.

He was, of course, personally likeable, and did not need to be packaged and sold to the public to the extent that some advisers wished. His athletic ability, his love of dancing, his cheerful philistinism where culture was concerned, his enjoyment of the Crazy Gang – a knockabout group of comedians – all made him seem refreshingly normal. Once the war had begun, he also proved more adept at broadcasting than anyone had expected, making speeches that were both inspiring and memorable. And he had an engaging sense of humour, as well as, on occasion, an endearing self-mockery. When bestowing the first knighthood of his reign, both he and the recipient, Walter Monckton, managed to bungle the operation. 'Well,' quipped the king, 'we did not do that very well, did we? But neither of us has done it before!'

His greatest assets in this new life were both female. He had the backing, the devotion, of two determined women. One was his mother. Queen Mary would never forgive her son David for his behaviour, first in taking up with a foreign adventuress who made him a laughing stock throughout the world, and secondly in throwing away the role for which he had been trained and prepared for the whole of his life, without regard for the consequences to the family, the nation or the empire. She loved Bertie, who had been everything a son and a member of the royal family should be. Knowing the sense of dread with which he viewed the future, she felt immense sympathy for him. The first thing he had done, on the evening of the abdication, was to fall into her arms and sob. She was to help him with advice and support for the rest of his life, and was to outlive him by almost a year.

The second source of strength was, of course, Bertie's wife. Elizabeth had shared his dismay as the events unfolded that led to her brother-in-law's departure from the throne. She, like Queen Mary, was never to forgive him for leaving Bertie in the lurch like this, especially since she was later to believe that the strain of becoming king had shortened his life. The antipathy was mutual, and her hostility was more than somewhat responsible for the ostracism that the Windsors would meet with from the moment of abdication onward. It was dictated not only by personal dislike but by a shrewd understanding of the damage to her husband's effectiveness that would be caused by any further association with Edward. Though Wallis Simpson was not, and never would be, someone with whom the British would feel empathy, her husband remained a threat to the stability of the throne. He had also embarrassed the Establishment and the public. More seriously, he could provide a rallying point for those who favoured appeasing Hitler. This was seen as a real danger as the 1930s came to an end. With war looming, differences would polarize between those who wanted to resist at any cost and those who sought to buy off Germany. The whole country could be divided by this issue, with damaging results.

The new queen, whose name had a stirring resonance for those with a sense of history, had neither sought her role nor expected it when she had married, yet she was as perfectly suited to it as if she had been prepared for it all her life. She was designed by nature to be a public figure and the consort to a head of state, and more especially, to be the consort of *this* head of state. The historian Andrew Roberts has summed her up as: 'Part business manager, part private secretary, part public-relations adviser'. She was accustomed to the protocol and formality involved in royal life, yet she had a sense of humour and of fun that enabled her to find enjoyment in it too. Her natural empathy was the ideal attribute in someone faced with the duties that were now hers. It would take her to heights of popularity that few monarchs of either sex have reached. She would save the credibility of the royal family with remarkable speed following the debacle of the abdication.

Edward had not been crowned. It takes many months to prepare a coronation, and the date had been set for the following year, 12 May 1937. With the Abbey already undergoing conversion and invitations being sent out, it was decided that this date would be adhered to for it would convey a sense of continuity. Bertie would adopt the same name as his father and become King George VI, suggesting that other vital ingredient in constitutional monarchy – stability. The alternative, King Albert, was in any case too Germanic for public taste.

The day itself was a great success. Though a good deal of affection for Edward lingered among the wider public, the new king and queen were popular too and the press worked assiduously to build upon this, informing their readers, among other trivia, that George was a better boxer than Edward. Once the royal party had returned to the Palace and appeared on the balcony, the crowd was enchanted by the sight of the two princesses, attired in miniature coronets and trains. A film of much of the coronation ceremony (excluding the parts, such as the anointing with oil, that were considered too holy to be made public) was produced but not released until careful viewing had been performed by both Church and Palace. Given the king's continuing personal awkwardness (he found the occasion an atrocious ordeal) there had been concern that he would make mistakes. He did not, however, and the resulting footage was a major breakthrough in royal public relations. For the first time since coronations had been staged at the Abbey in 1066, the population at large could see what went on inside, albeit only in retrospect.

The film was shown all over the world. It engendered a similar sense of participation among George's subjects in the Dominions and the empire, and it was widely viewed in the United States. Hollywood, indeed, capitalized on the fascination with kingly ceremonial that this engendered by putting a very elaborate coronation scene into its production of *The Prisoner of Zenda*, which was released later that year. This was perhaps the first time that the splendour of the British monarchy – genuine but modified, updated, re-interpreted and, in part, simply invented – had competed in terms of mass appeal with the manufactured magic of America's film capital. More people watched the *real* coronation. Incidentally, it cost well over half a million pounds to stage (twice as much as George V's), and thus required a budget similar to that of a Hollywood epic.

The Windsors were not without magic of their own. In the interests of national recovery the press was overwhelmingly on their side, and they could rely on positive and almost universally uncritical treatment. Never had Fleet Street stressed so strongly the family's likeable ordinariness – the king's quiet modesty and struggle to do his duty; the charm of both daughters and the endearing earnestness of Elizabeth, the eldest, who was now heir to the throne. Above all the press discovered in George's consort what would vulgarly be termed 'star quality'. A woman of small stature and inclined to dumpiness, she was photographed by Cecil Beaton in a manner that made her seem more statuesque. She was also dressed with an elegance that was to become her hallmark. The inspiration for her wardrobe came from the king. He took her designer, Norman Hartnell, on a tour of the royal portraits and pointed out those of ladies painted by the great German artist Winterhalter. These dated from the 1840s and 50s, the age of the crinoline. The subjects looked wonderfully feminine by the standards that would define the later twentieth century, with their cinched waists, flowing skirts, frills and ribbons. George wanted Hartnell to produce dresses that would be appropriate for the present while conveying a similar sense of style and dignity. The results were to be seen for decades in the gowns and dresses worn by Elizabeth, both as queen and as Queen Mother. Even without such trappings, her personality won her serious and deserved admiration. 'One of the most amazing queens since Cleopatra,' gushed one observer, Harold Nicolson.

The initial priority for the royal family was restoring its credibility in the wake of the abdication – steadying what George called 'a rocking throne'. The tidying up of Edward VIII's financial arrangements proved a lengthy and complicated process, and the king in the end allocated his brother a smaller allowance than had originally been agreed. The issue of how to address the Duchess of Windsor was quickly settled – she would not under any circumstances become an HRH. The impetus for this refusal, which was seen as wanton unkindness by sympathizers with Edward and his wife, would have come from Queen Mary as much as from her daughter-in-law. The king's mother, always a formidable opponent, had lost none of her outrage over the behaviour of her eldest son, and would have vetoed any notion of his wife being treated as equal to those of her family who had done their duty. Further, and decisive, disapproval came from the

Dominion governments, which after all had a perfect right to express views on the monarchy and which made it clear they would not accept her having the status of HRH. It is believed that the king himself did not mind his sister-in-law having the title. Similarly, he did not object to the retaining of a home in Britain by the duke and duchess. Queen Elizabeth, however, refused to countenance this. She wanted Edward and his wife as far away from her husband as possible. Even as an occasional visitor the former king would be newsworthy. His movements would be followed in the press and his physical glamour, still intact, would appeal to a number of those who saw his picture in newspapers or on newsreels. If her husband was to win the complete confidence of his people, there must be no competitors for their loyalty.

There were, however, more serious concerns. The shadow of war was lengthening over Europe. Germany, which had come under the control of Adolf Hitler's National Socialist government in 1933, had cast off the restrictions imposed by the Treaty of Versailles and was now openly re-arming. Conscription, forbidden by the Treaty, was reintroduced, creating at once a large army. The Rhineland, a western region of the country that had been 'de-militarized' by the Allies in 1919 so that France would not have German troops on its border, was now bristling with soldiery. The Western nations – the French themselves, Britain, the United States – took no measures to oppose the alarming resurgence of their former enemy, though it was plain to anyone who listened to Hitler that he was intent upon another European war. In fact he had predicted that it would start in 1936. The only reason it did not was that there was no need – other nations gave way or failed to protest, and he got what he wanted. With each step toward bloodless victory his own and his people's confidence – and bellicosity – increased.

In 1938 Hitler absorbed Austria into the German Reich – a willing junior partner in the state he was creating. He also wanted the Sudetenland, a strategic border area within

Czechoslovakia that had a sizeable German population. Posing as a reasonable man who wanted only to unify the various German communities within the region, he announced that this was his final demand. Readers of his book *Mein Kampf* knew that it was in fact only the beginning, but there was a widespread willingness to believe him, for the alternative was war.

Like many of those who could remember 1914–18, the king desired at any cost to avoid another conflict. The appeasement of Germany, which was to seem in retrospect a shameful chapter in Britain's national life, was largely viewed at the time as a pragmatic response. Nothing could be worse than a return to the horrors of the previous conflict; any efforts to avoid such an outcome were welcome, even if they meant humiliation. When Prime Minister Neville Chamberlain – whom the king and queen liked – returned from Munich in March 1938 with an agreement signed by Hitler to state that the German dictator had no further territorial demands to make, the welcome he received was rapturous. He was met by enthusiastic crowds at the airport. He was cheered under the windows of 10 Downing Street. He went to the Palace and appeared there on the balcony with the king and queen before an even greater throng. The national mood was one of relief and euphoria and gratitude for his statesmanship, and the monarch was as glad as anyone else. The prime minister had saved 'peace in our time', and the preparations for war, which had already begun, could now be discontinued.

By standing on the balcony with Chamberlain, the king was tacitly endorsing a policy of appeasement that many people found shameful and misguided. When Hitler's duplicity was discovered, Chamberlain was not forgiven but the public tactfully forgot George's support of him, a gesture that one historian was to dub 'the biggest constitutional blunder that has been made by any sovereign this century'.

The euphoria surrounding Chamberlain's return from Munich evaporated very quickly. Hitler occupied the remainder of Czechoslovakia, and then set his sights on Poland. It was obvious that he would seek to expand further in the East. His word could not be trusted. All the prime minister had succeeded in doing was buying a little time at the expense of much honour. The more thoughtful among the British public were horrified by his gullibility and at the loss of national integrity. The country resumed its efforts to prepare for all-out war with a renewed sense of determination. When Hitler made a pact with Stalin to divide Poland between them, the pro-communist lobby, especially influential among idealistic young people, felt a sense of betrayal that caused the scales to fall from their eyes. The nation was still not completely united – it would not be even once war had begun, for there was to remain an element that sought to make terms with Hitler when he was poised to invade in the summer of 1940 – but at least now the country and the empire knew how the immediate future would develop.

During the tense months of 1939, the king and queen set about building relations with those who would be their allies in the coming conflict. They exchanged visits with the French Premier. More significantly they made a journey, in May and June, to Canada and the United States. In the former country George was, of course, the head of state. In the latter, he and Elizabeth were simply official visitors, the first British royalty seen by the American public since Edward had been there as Prince of Wales almost twenty years earlier. Their sojourn was brief, lasting less than a week. They visited Niagara Falls, New York and Washington, and the welcome they received was ecstatic. Despite its republican ideals, the United States has always had a fascination with royalty. The American public took to this shy and good-natured man and his pleasant, elegant wife. Surprisingly, perhaps, George and Elizabeth discovered a rapport with President Franklin Roosevelt, who staged for them a supposedly typical 'hot dog picnic' at his home, Hyde Park. Roosevelt, a member of an old Dutch-American family and thus of America's aristocracy, was genuinely friendly, and somewhat paternal, in his relations with the king. George, for his part, responded to this warmth with sincere admiration, and wished his own politicians had more of Roosevelt's personable manner. At home, the visit established George and Elizabeth as what might be called 'players on the world stage'. They were seen to have hit it off with the leader of the world's most powerful nation, winning the affection of the American public and delighting their own subjects in Canada with their interest and enthusiasm. George, it seemed, could charm crowds in other countries just as his brother had done. The public standing of both king and queen measurably increased as a result of their travels. 'That trip made us,' she was later to recall.

They returned home less than three months before the catastrophe. Autumn, when the harvest has been collected, is the traditional time for wars to begin. This one started at 11 a.m. on Sunday 3 September. Hitler had invaded Poland two days earlier, and had ignored a request from Prime Minister Chamberlain to withdraw his troops from a country that Britain had guaranteed to defend. Naturally, nothing could be done to help a nation that was far away on the other side of Germany, but a stand had at least been taken. George, the reluctant and untrained king, now found himself in a situation that few monarchs have faced – that of head of a nation facing absolute disaster. His father had also led the country at the outbreak of war, but the previous one had begun with a sense of optimism, a belief that the conflict would be swift and that Britain was going into it with massive strength. It was now obvious that once again Germany had planned the war for years, though as before its rulers had expected Britain to be willing to stay out of a matter that concerned Continental Europe. The country had acted too late in re-arming and introducing conscription to be a match for the enemy now, especially a Germany bloated by adding Austria and other territories to its human and material resources.

The United Kingdom was, of course, not alone. Between

the British and their enemy lay the whole width of France. Their ally had a huge, largely conscript army, and the seemingly impregnable Maginot Line – a chain of underground fortresses that faced the German frontier (in the event, the attacking Germans simply went round it.) The empire also rallied. Australia and New Zealand both declared war at the same time as Britain. South Africa took a few days longer, for there was an ingrained sympathy for Germany among many Boer citizens and it was their remarkable prime minister, Jan Smuts, who influenced his people to enlist in the Allied camp. Canada, intent on showing that it made its own decisions rather than merely following London's lead, entered the conflict last, its declaration of war signed by the Governor-General, Lord Tweedsmuir. Only one part of the Commonwealth refused to be drawn in. This was the Irish Free State, which had held Dominion status since 1922. For the Irish, the United Kingdom was traditionally the enemy. They had been fighting the British Army less than two decades earlier and, though thousands would enlist as individuals in British units, there was no general desire for involvement in a conflict that put their poverty-stricken country, with its vulnerable coastline, at risk of attack by Germany.

The Phoney War ended with awful suddenness on 9 and 10 May 1940. German armies, in a well-planned and co-ordinated attack, invaded the Low Countries, Denmark and Norway. The same day Neville Chamberlain, whose leadership since the war began had been heavily criticized, resigned. As the chief appeaser, he had naturally lost all credibility when his agreement with the German dictator proved to have been worthless. The king was obliged to summon Winston Churchill, a renegade member of Chamberlain's party who was *de facto* war leader but was at the time First Lord of the Admiralty. The king and queen did not care for Churchill. It is said that his championing of King Edward during the abdication crisis had irritated them, though it is difficult to see why this should be so – after all, if he had persuaded the king to stay on, the Yorks could have kept their cherished private life. Nevertheless, the king acknowledged that Churchill was the sole viable leader. 'There was only one man whom I could send for who had the confidence of the country, and that was Winston,' he wrote.

This was significant for the king would very much have preferred Lord Halifax, an urbane and patrician man who was serving as Foreign Secretary. Halifax, whose health was not sound, knew he did not have the makings of a wartime premier and declined, however. One thing that the king admired about Halifax was his belief in the possibility of a compromise peace with Hitler. George was not the only one in his family who thought this notion sound, if not vital. His mother felt even more strongly on the matter. If war must come, it was surely essential to buy time for further re-armament. Negotiations were preferable to outright hostility, and the German leader had made it clear he had no grudge against Britain. Provided he was left a 'free hand' in Europe, he was willing to leave the country and its empire alone. Was that not evidence of a reasonable attitude?

The appointment of Churchill represented the rejection of any compromise with Hitler. He now had the confidence of both Parliament and people. George had no choice but to set aside his own inclinations and accept his new prime minister's view that it was too late for anything but a military response.

As a prime minister and a personality, Churchill was every-thing his predecessor was not: excitable, unpredictable, rash, over-emotional. The combative Churchill, a warrior since his youth, veteran of three conflicts and various other cam-paigns, had been a voice crying in the wilderness throughout the thirties as he warned of the danger from Germany. He had been proved right, he had the force of character and the temperament to match the direness of the situation, and he knew what must be done.

None of this made him easy to like, or to work with. He was frequently late for audiences with the king, and might simply not show up to dinner when invited to the Palace, though this was hardly surprising considering the other claims on his attention. The queen, accustomed all her life to princely manners, found his rudeness insufferable. The king was unhappy too but, like the rest of the population and the empire, eventually found that Churchill's management of the war effort – granted with some major errors – commanded respect. He and the prime minister knew that they could not allow personal animosity to interfere with the necessity of winning the war and they worked together with increasing confidence, gradually developing a better relationship. Within twelve months, the king was entirely won over, writing in his diary that: 'I could not have a better P.M.'

Unable to speak well in public even after his stammer had been treated, George nevertheless made memorable speeches to his people in these years. During the war – the event that naturally dominated his reign, and which sealed his reputation as one of the most likeable sovereigns ever – his broadcasts could inspire. He did not seek to rouse the public to bellicose determination in the way that his prime minister did. Rather, he had an air of calm reassurance, a measured reasonableness, that was the very antithesis of the posturing and ranting of other speechmakers – such as Hitler and Mussolini – of that time. In September 1940, a week after German bombers had begun their systematic destruction of London, he said: 'It is not the walls that make the city, but the people who live within them. The walls of London may be battered, but the spirit of the Londoner stands resolute and undismayed.'

He was upstaged by his wife, who in the same month uttered one of the great quotations to come out of the conflict. Referring to the fact that bombs had been dropped with near-fatal consequences on Buckingham Palace, she mused that: 'I'm glad we've been bombed. It makes me feel I can look the East End in the face.' The fact that the royal family had refused to leave their people at this fateful time was an immense source of strength to the British public. It also impressed people all over the world.

At Christmas 1939, in the midst of the Phoney War, the king had made the traditional broadcast to the peoples of the empire. It is difficult today to appreciate the power of the spoken word when broadcast across the world. In a pre-television era, when international telephone communications were primitive, the miracle of wireless enabled the king to be present in sitting-rooms throughout the globe. For those subjects who were separated from the Court of St James by thousands of miles of ocean, and who worried about the safety of the mother country, his encouragement would have been a godsend. He did not disappoint them, for he uttered the most famous words he was ever to speak:

> I said to the man who stood at the Gate of the Year,
> 'Give me a light that I may tread safely into the
>   unknown.'
> And he replied: 'Go out into the darkness,
> And put your hand into the Hand of God,
> That shall be better than light, and safer than a known
>   way,
> May that Almighty Hand guide and uphold us all.'

They were not his own. They had been written decades earlier, in 1908, by Minnie Louise Haskins, who was a lecturer at the London School of Economics, and had initially been published under the title 'God Knows'. It was his daughter, Princess Elizabeth, who had given the poem to George. By his use of it, the poem gained popularity throughout the world, and became so associated with the king that after his death the words would be inscribed in his memorial chapel.

In spite of their inspirational statements, the king and queen were not to become the symbol of national will and leadership that might have been expected. The prime minister, it was quite obvious, had been chosen by fate for that role. It was he, as Premier and simultaneously Minister of Defence (he had appointed himself to the role), who wielded power, directed the armies and fleets, and hobnobbed with world leaders. He entirely eclipsed the king as a friend of Roosevelt. The two corresponded continuously, spoke frequently on the telephone, and, once the big conferences of wartime leaders began to be held, met several times in person. Theirs was to be the great partnership that dominated wartime events. The king and queen, nevertheless, occupied a key role as builders of public morale, constantly visiting troops, garrisons, cities and, especially, bombed districts. It was a reprise of the role carried out so effectively by King George and Queen Mary in the previous conflict, and it is something that royalty does well.

When the German armies had invaded western Europe, they saw its royal families as potential hostages to ensure the good behaviour of the populace. These were, almost all of them, highly popular figures in the countries concerned: Denmark, Norway, Belgium, the Netherlands and Luxembourg. If the monarch were under house arrest, anyone planning acts of sabotage would have to weigh up the possible consequences. The Nazis would not hesitate to execute hostages in retaliation for resistance. If their captive were the head of state, the risk was too awful to contemplate. Some sovereigns managed to escape – King Haakon of Norway arrived in Britain by sea. The queen of the Netherlands came by air, having fled The Hague as German paratroops were dropping there, without a change of clothing but with her country's gold reserves. Reaching Buckingham Palace, she apologized to King George for her unexpected arrival, and was put in one of the guest suites.

The British royal family, in other words, knew what their own eventual fate might be if they remained in their country. They had the option of going overseas. Many wealthy Britons had either gone themselves or sent their children to North America, to get them out of harm's way. The grandchildren of the Dutch royal family were in Canada. Should the Windsors, too, not think of going to safety? After all, they could still be an important rallying point for resistance – a government-in-exile – in exactly the way that the other heads of state were becoming in London, speaking to their peoples by radio and gathering around them an expatriate 'Court'. In Canada, they would not even be outside their own realm. If the king decided he wished to stay, could his wife, his teenage daughters, or at the very least his mother, not go somewhere out of danger?

Here again, Queen Elizabeth had a pungent and inspiring retort: 'The girls would not go without me, I would not go without the king, and of course the king would never go.' Even the redoubtable Queen Mary would not leave. Her only compromise was to move out of London, and she was to spend the war years comfortably at Badminton, one of England's grandest country houses. The two princesses were also removed from the capital. They began the war at Balmoral, but moved to an undisclosed location – actually Windsor Castle – where they remained until the return of peace. The king and queen would not have tolerated having their children out of reach. They themselves spent each week at Buckingham Palace, which was twice hit by bombs, and went to Windsor at weekends.

Their courage in remaining in Britain during that terrible summer of 1940 should not be underestimated. They participated fully in Britain's 'finest hour'. Braced for enemy invasion – Hitler had gone so far as to announce that he expected to take the surrender of the country on or about 15 August – they expected to share the fate of their subjects. Both the king and queen – and even Queen Mary! – carried firearms, and practised shooting.

The king and queen made a point of travelling to wherever there had been air raids. They regularly went to the East End, the part of London that bore the brunt of German attacks because of its proximity to the docks. After huddling in an air-raid shelter, people might come out into daylight to find George and Elizabeth waiting for them. Their presence, and their obvious

interest and concern, made a deep impression on the public. It
was during one such walk through a recently blitzed area that
someone called out: 'Thank God for a good king!' George at
once called back: 'And thank God for a good people!' They
naturally went to other cities too, visiting Coventry just after it
had been devastated in a raid. This image of royalty, of the king
and his wife (he was usually dressed in army uniform, she was
in stylish coats and hats, making no attempt to curry favour
by dressing down) among their people, sharing their hardship,
sympathizing with the loss of their homes, was a very powerful
one. It sent the king's popularity soaring and made the couple
part of the heroic legend that the Blitz and the Battle of Britain
inspired.

George appeared in the uniforms of all three Services. He
had served both in the Navy and in the Royal Air Force, in
whose distinctive blue uniform he had been married. He was
Colonel-in-Chief of the Guards regiments too, and held by
virtue of his position the highest rank in each of the armed
forces. He was shown frequently in the press, dressed as an
Admiral of the Fleet or a Field Marshal, emphasizsing the
point that he belonged to the same Services as so many of his
subjects. The queen wore no uniform but their elder daughter
would, by the last year of the conflict, be old enough to enlist
in the ATS (Auxiliary Territorial Service, a female branch of
the Army) and thus to 'do her bit'.

The king awarded medals, and indeed had one named after
him. During 1940 it became very obvious that with the country under attack, civilians, or troops far removed from the
front line, could display heroism – for example, in defusing
bombs or in rescue work – that was just as great as was shown
in battle. An award for gallantry was therefore set up, at the
suggestion of Winston Churchill, and was called the George
Cross. This bore no resemblance to the medal established by
his grandmother. It was of its time, a sleek silver Art Deco-
inspired cross with, in the middle, a medallion of St George
and the dragon. It bore the king's cipher and was hung from

a ribbon of Garter blue. It is arguably the most attractive of British medals. When the colony of Malta withstood successfully a massive and sustained air assault by the Axis powers, the king awarded the medal collectively to the whole island, which he visited in 1943. Malta became independent in 1964 yet the George Cross still features in its national flag.

After the French sued for peace with Hitler, George commented that: 'I feel happier now that we have no Allies to be polite to and pamper.' This was hardly the case. The leaders of several foreign governments were now living on his doorstep. Among this group that turned up in London in need of shelter, resources or encouragement was Charles De Gaulle, a maverick and largely unknown French General. He had written a number of books by then, but was not a recognizable public figure outside France. He claimed to represent the spirit of his home country that had not been destroyed by the German conquest. De Gaulle was a prickly, haughty and almost completely unlikeable man, possessed of a Messianic belief that he was France incarnate and that only he could save his country. Though Churchill regarded him with both suspicion and annoyance, the royal family made him welcome, and he got on well with them on a personal level. Whatever he thought of the rest of the British Establishment – and he was notoriously ungrateful for anything done for him – he always retained a sense of friendship for the Windsors, and was later to acknowledge his debt to them for taking him seriously when others did not.

Buckingham Palace, extremely obvious from the air in its set-piece location facing down the Mall, was targeted by the Luftwaffe. Bombs destroyed the chapel and the swimming pool. On another raid, a bomb failed to explode but detonated the following day, destroying the room in which the king had been working only minutes earlier. Windsor Castle was similarly conspicuous, and over a hundred bombs – both the conventional sort and the remote-control 'doodlebugs' fired from across the Channel during 1944 – landed in its surrounding park. Such was the risk of destruction that the queen commissioned the artist John Piper to make extensive drawings of the Castle, to preserve a record of it.

In the war, as at no other time in recent history, the royal family proved their worth as a national (and indeed international) symbol. While the prime minister was the one who actually inspired the country and galvanized its efforts, the monarchy provided an example of quiet, steady decency that contrasted with the barbarity of the enemy leadership. They were a reminder of old certainties, of a better, pre-war world and – through their children – a better future. The welcome they received when they visited towns and cities was eloquent testimony to this. The king also visited the theatres of war in North Africa, Italy and north-west Europe. He landed in Normandy only ten days after D-Day. Though he could not share the dangers faced by his soldiers, he made efforts to see at first hand the places in which they had recently fought. Because he was accompanied on these trips by a film crew, he was obliged to wear thick theatrical make-up for close shots. Soldiers idling by roadsides who saw him pass were bewildered – and horrified – to see the monarch made up like a pantomime dame.

An unlooked-for and tragic circumstance increased the family's popularity still further. The Duke of Kent, the king's youngest brother, was serving in the Royal Air Force. In August 1942 he was aboard a Sunderland flying boat that was travelling to Iceland, where he would inspect bases. In dense fog, it crashed into a Scottish mountainside. It had been two hundred years since royalty had taken part in battles, and therefore fatalities among them were, in recent history, unheard of. Somehow the death of this handsome young man created a bond between the royal family and the people. They too were subject to the random fortunes of war.

The most enduring image of royalty during wartime is that of the family on the balcony of Buckingham Palace on VE Day, 9 May 1945. The huge crowd that was celebrating the news of

Germany's defeat converged, by instinct (there was no prior arrangement that the family would appear, and it was not clear that they were even in residence), at the end of the Mall. The war was not, of course, over. Japan remained to be invaded – an operation that would, it was thought, cost up to a million Allied lives – but the end of fighting in Europe was nevertheless a moment of national catharsis. Churchill appeared with the royal family. The two leaders, one ceremonial and one political and military, represented the strength of the British constitutional system. The prime minister did not know it yet but he was about to be swept from office by an electorate that wanted radical change from the attitudes and institutions of the past – one which he personified in the post-war era. The empire was about to be dismantled, major industries would be nationalized, education was already being reformed to make it more democratic, and the National Health Service – a utopian concept that would be envied by other countries – was on its way. At no time, however, did these changes threaten the Crown. Even though for a short time the Left in Britain had the chance to put some of their dreams into practice (they considered a Soviet-style medal for productivity by workers, but found that men and women would rather receive monetary rewards), no one thought it possible, or politically advisable, to suggest abolishing the monarchy.

In the new socialist government, George's Foreign Secretary was to be Ernest Bevin, a trade-union veteran and left-winger. They developed a warm and genuine friendship, but this was not the first time that the king had charmed a member of the Labour movement. Both he and his father had been genuinely interested to meet men who had risen from backgrounds so different from their own. Knowing how intimidating the surroundings of the Palace could seem, they went out of their way to put them at ease. For the politicians it came as a surprise to find at the apex of a despised social order men of such modesty and humour. Once both sides had adjusted their expectations there was genuine mutual regard.

The daughter of George VI was to have an equally notable success in winning over Harold Wilson.

The king would reign for a further six and a half years, but the remainder of his life was to be a time of drabness and decline. Despite a few bright moments (in 1947 his daughter Elizabeth was married, and the following year London hosted the Olympic Games), the tone of these years was one of grey austerity and overall poverty. Rationing of some commodities continued until after his death, so that when Elizabeth married she had to be allocated additional clothing coupons for her dress, and food rations had to be arranged for all the foreign royals who were to stay at the Palace. India, which not for nothing was known as the 'jewel in the crown' of the British Empire, became independent in August 1947, a year earlier than had been envisaged by the government.

To anyone who had grown up in the reign of Victoria and her successors this loss would have seemed immense, though the departure of the sub-continent was not unexpected. India had been increasingly difficult to govern since the end of the previous war. It was too big, and now too politically aware, willingly to remain a vassal of another nation, and because of the war the whole climate of international feeling was in favour of self-determination for Europe's colonies. The Holocaust had produced an outpouring of sympathy for subjugated peoples, and the victories of the Japanese over the British, Americans and Dutch in the Pacific had shown that Westerners were not invulnerable. Now the two superpowers, the United States and Russia, were both opposed to colonialism, and in any case the colonial masters were impoverished by the war. In Gandhi's famous words to a British official: 'It is time you left.'

This was the feeling throughout much of Asia and Africa in the post-war decade, and as one territory after another gained independence the momentum, and the clamour, picked up. Churchill, in another famous phrase, had said that he 'did

not become prime minister to preside over the dismember-
ment of the British Empire', but that appeared to be precisely
what George VI would have to do. The king, perhaps having
learned greater wisdom after mistakenly siding with Chamberlain, made a point of not showing any regret at the loss of
India, since the issue was a political one in Britain.

In fact he was deeply attached to his overseas territories,
and resented enormously the new Labour administration's
willingness to get rid of them. 'What bits of my empire have
you given away today?' he irritably asked one of them, Lord
Stansgate, when it became plain Britain's new government
could not afford both to keep the empire and to pay for the
National Health Service that was one of their key objectives.
Trivial though it may seem, George hated losing the title of
emperor and the practice of signing himself 'GRI' (George
Rex Imperator), for from now on he would merely be 'GR'.
His mother shared this sentiment in full, cherishing the last
missives he wrote her with his imperial title on the letterhead.
She also added Louis Mountbatten (who as the last Viceroy
had been the one to grant independence to India, and who
had carried out the process with surprising speed) to the list
of those she would never forgive.

One especially painful severance was very close to home.
The Irish Free State had for decades held Dominion status
and had distanced itself, consistently and deliberately, from
the United Kingdom. It had remained neutral during the war,
and without having undergone that experience was separated
by something of a gulf from the rest of the Commonwealth.
In 1949 the Eire government completed the process of estab-
lishing a Republic, with a president at its head instead of a
Governor-General acting – however nominally – on behalf of
the Crown. Indeed they had abolished the position of Governor-General even before the war. The drift to separation was
unstoppable, and Ireland was to relinquish its membership.

With Ireland there had, of course, been a violent, sometimes horrific, past. The country's War of Independence had

indeed been a war, albeit a guerilla one. Though fighting had been bitter, most of the separation of Ireland from Britain was to be a matter of legislation carried out by Eire's parliament, yet there was considerable regret on the mainland that a country whose history was so bound up with Britain's, and whose common interests ought to have made for friendship, should so completely have left the fold.

Though the king was in no sense involved in the politics of this matter, he asked John Dulanty, the Irish High Commissioner (who was about to lose this status), '*Must* you leave the family?' The king and queen were both genuinely fond of Ireland, and had had hopes of visiting the country. When the moment came to part, the British government drafted a message for the king to deliver, but he amended it to express his own thoughts more clearly. It read in part: 'I send you my good wishes on this day, being well aware of the neighbourly links which hold the people of the Republic of Ireland in close association with my subjects in the United Kingdom. I hold in most grateful memory the services and sacrifices of the men and women of your country who rendered gallant assistance to our cause in the recent war, and who made a notable contribution to our victory. I pray that every blessing may be with you today and in the future.'

To modern ears this may sound like a mere exercise in bland officialese, but many in the Republic were deeply touched by this personal message of farewell. Seven hundred years of resistance to what nationalists portrayed as draconian, repressive foreign occupation had ended with a friendly greeting from a pleasant, quiet and well-meaning man who was known to love their country, and who genuinely wished them well for the future. This was not how they had expected the struggle for independence to reach fulfilment. Sean T. O'Kelly, one of the most committed supporters of the Republic, was so impressed by the message that he wrote that: 'It was a most generous and imaginative act on the part of the king and its sensitive and moving terms had been deeply valued. When the English did a thing,' he concluded, 'they did it sensitively and well.'

The real dismantling would not come, however, until the reign of the king's daughter. For the moment India, Ceylon and Burma departed, while the African nations remained for a further generation. While the king lost the title of emperor of India (in a touching gesture, he awarded both his daughters the Order of the Indian Empire just before it was abolished), he became the first Head of the Commonwealth. Though Burma refused to join this organization, George remained nominal head of state for many millions of those whom he had formerly ruled as subjects. It was a smooth transition from outright colonial rule to something the modern world found – and still finds – more palatable. No other colonial power had so high a success rate in turning vassals into partners and then colleagues. The Dutch were to fight a bloody and unsuccessful war in the forties to retain their East Indies territories. The French would suffer a similar fate in Indochina and Algeria in the fifties, the Belgians would lose the Congo in the sixties, and the Portuguese Empire would descend into chaos in the seventies. Though Britain's decolonization, in Palestine, Kenya, Cyprus, Aden and Ireland, would by no means be without bloodshed and horror, it was at least without the virtual civil war at home that plagued other powers.

One thing that member countries were supposed to have in common was an expressed loyalty to the British Crown. India became a Republic, yet wanted to remain within the organization. After considerable discussion it was agreed that the rules could be bent to allow it to do so, and this opened the way for other countries to belong while retaining their preferred form of government. This flexibility meant that more nations were happy – indeed eager – to join, and made the Commonwealth stronger.

The king presided over the beginnings of this decolonization with apparent equanimity, but then it was not obvious at first what a landslide it was to become. In his reign Kenya was still recruiting white settlers with the promise of lifelong access to fertile farmland, and young men were joining the Colonial Service expecting to make a career in overseas administration. King George, his wife and daughters made an official visit to South Africa – the first of what were expected to be several such tours of British territories – to thank the country for its help during the war. Here too they were immensely popular. The king's modesty, as well as the queen's gift for engaging with those she met (she famously charmed a Boer whose hatred of Britain was undiminished almost fifty years after the South African War by saying: 'I know just how you feel. In Scotland that is how we regard the English!'), made the tour a triumph. The two princesses were now young adults – Elizabeth was to celebrate her twenty-first birthday while in the country – and they too won many hearts. Perhaps the most appreciated gesture by the family during this visit was the return – by the king to General Smuts – of the Bible owned by President Kruger, which British troops had captured during the Boer War.

The king, however, was unwell, and this was to be the last overseas tour he would make. The war had been a serious strain on his health, and complications caused by his heavy smoking began to tax what vitality remained to him. He continued to fulfil royal duties – the notion of soldiering on regardless of ill health is something bred into the royal family through generations – but he found it increasingly tiring. At that time the family was so much smaller than it later became that there was not the same opportunity to delegate. Apart from Queen Mary, who was more or less in retirement, there were only the king and queen and the two princesses, who had to cover all official business between them. Princess Elizabeth added another member by marrying Philip Mountbatten, but he was a career naval officer who had neither the time nor, so far, the experience to take on much of the workload. When he was posted to Malta in 1949 the king encouraged Elizabeth to go with him, despite the fact that the couple by now had one child and were soon to have another. Their departure meant that Prince Charles, between the ages of one and four, lived with his grandparents. He would always be grateful for the opportunity this gave to acquire at least some memories of King George.

George's health declined so fast in the years after the war that even by 1949 – two years after the South African visit – he was visibly ailing. He appeared at Trooping the Colour that year in a carriage because he was unable to ride, but then he had had a major operation only three months earlier and the amputation of his right leg had only just been avoided. He was found to have Buerger's Disease, which attacks the arteries, as well as having bronchial carcinoma. His health had been undermined by the strain of the war, and his lifelong habit of heavy smoking had of course not helped. He had to have an operation in September 1951 that removed one of his lungs, and his recovery was slow.

Princess Elizabeth was obliged to return several times to Britain to deputize for her father, and in 1951 she and Philip had to undertake an entire official visit for him, spending a month in Canada. The following year they were asked to undergo another tour. On this occasion it was to be a lengthier and more exhausting itinerary that would take in East Africa, Ceylon, Australia and New Zealand. The princess and her husband were to depart by air, and her family went to see them off. Newspaper images showed King George standing on the runway, hunched against the wintry chill, bare-headed and haggard. He looked a decade or more older than his fifty-six years. Nevertheless his family believed his health was improving, and there seemed no reason to think he would not be on the same tarmac to meet his daughter on her return in six months' time. 'Look out for yourselves,' he said on parting.

That was on 31 January 1952. Just days later the princess and her husband were in Kenya, staying in a tree-house on a game reserve. The royal family was at Sandringham, where this was the last day of shooting. The king went out with the gamekeepers to clear up what birds were left, and much enjoyed himself. He dined with the queen and Princess Margaret, and once again his spirits were high. He retired to bed and, sometime in the night of 5–6 February, he died.

His health and appearance had been so bad that his death was not the shock to the public that it might have been, but his family were naturally grief-stricken. The most immediate problem was to find and inform the new sovereign, who was somewhere in the African bush. The code for George's death – 'Hyde Park Corner' – was sent but not received, perhaps because the telegraph operator mistook it for the address. It was hours before Elizabeth discovered that she was now queen. A journalist contacted her Private Secretary, who told her husband, who broke the news. The king had died of thrombosis.

George VI lay in state in the church at Sandringham, guarded by tweed-suited gamekeepers – the very men who had spent with him his last day alive. His body was then conveyed by train to London. Crowds stood by the trackside to watch it pass, the men doffing their hats. After lying in state once again, in Westminster Hall, he was buried in St George's Chapel, Windsor, in an attractive little side-chapel. His wife, who was to have a longer and more remarkable career as a dowager than she had had as a consort, would join him there just over half a century later.

5

ELIZABETH II, 1952–PRESENT

'Voluntary change is the life-blood of the Crown.'

Prince Philip

Queen Elizabeth II is within a few years of becoming the longest-reigning monarch in British history. The daughter of a long-lived mother (who was almost 102 when she died), she may well continue to rule for some time yet. Her presence has dominated almost the entire post-war era in Britain, so that to many of her subjects the notion of the country without Queen Elizabeth at its head is difficult to grasp.

She came to the throne, suddenly and largely unexpectedly, in the late winter of 1952. She was twenty-five, the wife of a serving naval officer and the mother of two very young children. In the decades since then, British society has undergone massive changes, yet she has remained astonishingly consistent in outlook, tastes and habits throughout that time. She may seem like a gentle old lady, and she is, but the firmness of her views is legendary and there are within her qualities of self-discipline, determination and devotion to duty that match any of her predecessors'. Because she has been by far the longest-serving sovereign of the House of Windsor, it may well be her reign, and her personality, that will come to dominate its history.

Christened Elizabeth Alexandra Mary, she was named after three generations of her female ancestors, not quite in reverse chronological order. Elizabeth was her mother, Alexandra her great-grandmother and Mary her grandmother. Like so many successful monarchs, she came to the throne by accident of circumstances. When she was born, on 21 April 1926, her father was the Duke of York and second in line to the throne. His elder brother was young, athletic, vigorous and widely popular, especially with women. It was unthinkable that he would not marry, and highly likely that he would have children – indeed the pressure to do so would be overwhelming. It looked then as if Elizabeth's future would go in one of two directions. The first possibility was that she would spend her life as a second-rank royal, a cousin of the immediate royal family. She would perhaps marry a member of the British aristocracy as her aunt had done (Princess Mary, her father's sister, had become Viscountess Lascelles). Thereafter, if there were enough members of her uncle's family to cover the necessary range of public duties, she would fade from sight to live a quiet life on her husband's estates as a duchess or countess. Catching a glimpse of her now and again among the royals at some state event, people might ask: 'Now, which one's that?'

Alternatively, she might go abroad. Though as we have seen the age of dynastic marriages had ended, the princess would still have been considered a considerable catch by members of other royal houses. The First World War did not entirely bring an end to the Age of Kings. Parvenu sovereigns would have welcomed an alliance with a dynasty as ancient and prestigious as Britain's, as would families who had lost their thrones. The idea of Princess Elizabeth as consort in a Balkan country is not as fanciful as it first seems, for in the event she was to marry a member of the Greek royal family.

Whether she was destined for a life of public duty or comparative obscurity, Elizabeth was brought up in an atmosphere of formality. Her grandfather was king. He was surrounded by splendour and protocol, and had to be treated with deference even though he was openly affectionate and indulgent with her. Her father and mother were often involved in official duties. She saw from her earliest years the respectful manner in which visitors to their home would speak to them. She herself was saluted by sentries whenever she passed them, and was bowed to by people to whom she was introduced. She was treated throughout her childhood as if she were an honorary adult – not a person to be ignored, patronized or scolded, but one who was respected, taken seriously, and her sayings or foibles filed away in memory. In addition, there could be no ignoring the attention she received from all over the world. When her parents went on a tour of Australasia, they brought back more than three tons of toys that had been given her (most were donated to hospitals). Her image – she had appealing golden curls – appeared on a Canadian stamp and on the cover of the American magazine *Time*, and a section of Antarctica was named after her. Not the kind of things that happen to ordinary children.

As a result, she grew up with a precocious seriousness. She had few playmates of her own age, and was never to go to school. She would have become accustomed, as she walked in Hyde Park with her nanny or rode her bicycle in the little garden behind her parents' London home, to being stared at and photographed. She was acutely aware of a gulf between herself and other children of her age, for she was not allowed to meet or talk to those she saw when out in public. It was made clear to her that, because of her parents' – and more significantly her grandfather's – position, she must always act with dignity. She was continually being noticed, watched and judged. Her behaviour was more important than that of other children. When a sister, Margaret Rose, was added to the family in 1930, Elizabeth began to develop a sense of responsibility for her younger sibling that further increased her natural earnestness. The girls became extremely close, and would remain so all their lives. The fact that they had few experiences of the outside world meant that they would always have more in common with each other than with anyone else. Added to this was the fact that their parents preferred their company to that of any outsiders. The family was thus extremely – unusually – close.

The girls' lives were not, of course, an imprisonment, either physically or emotionally. They were constantly meeting people of importance – prime ministers, archbishops, senior figures in Church and State – either at their parents' homes or at the residences of their grandfather. They had the run of Buckingham Palace gardens, which were just across the road. They also had the gardens of Royal Lodge, Sandringham and Balmoral to explore while staying there, and their home provided a secure, extremely loving environment. Both parents adored them and, though they lived in a top-floor nursery, as was customary for the children of upper-class families, there was no question of their being banished from sight or left in the impersonal care of servants. The family always had meals together. The duke and duchess, who did not like Society and spent as much time at home as possible, saw the girls for hours every day and took the closest interest in their activities. They deliberately set out to give their daughters the happiest possible childhood. Their mother ensured that they read the same books she had loved as a girl, and that there were picnics and games and frequent outings.

The duchess also organized their schooling, teaching them some subjects herself. A young Scotswoman, Marion Crawford, was engaged in 1933 to superintend their general studies, because their parents never considered sending them away to school. 'Crawfie' became a vital component in the girls' education. She planned their lessons and taught them in the schoolrooms at the big town house in Piccadilly or – because they worked on Saturday mornings too – at Royal Lodge in Windsor. Sometimes history was taught in the Royal Library at Windsor Castle, which was the former bedroom of Queen Elizabeth, and objects could be summoned from the Royal Collections to illustrate particular subjects. Elizabeth found this enchanting, and had already developed a fascination with the two great female sovereigns from England's past: Elizabeth I and Queen Victoria.

It was Queen Mary who devised the curriculum that the girls were taught. She and their mother saw no point in wasting time on subjects that would be of no practical use to them, so that arithmetic received scant attention. They had lessons in French but not in other languages. They were required to be familiar with current events, and therefore subscribed to the *Children's Newspaper*. They had to learn copious amounts of history, and to study the Bible. They must also learn poetry, since this helped train the memory and gave them a feeling for the sound and rhythm of words. The school day was deliberately kept short. Each lesson lasted only thirty minutes, and there were none in the afternoons. There were no examinations, or any other measures of progress. It was a very limited education that would not have equipped them for any career in the wider world. Many years afterward, when Elizabeth's children were entering higher education, Margaret said to her: 'You and I would never have got into university.'

Miss Crawford also took them on walks and accompanied them – sometimes with Queen Mary, an authority on art and furniture – on expeditions to museums or galleries. On one such outing they travelled by Underground to Tottenham Court Road and had tea at the YWCA, the only time during their childhood that the princesses needed to hand over money to pay for something. Though they undoubtedly found this chance to live an ordinary life for a few hours fascinating, they were recognized on the return journey and so crowded in on by curious onlookers that they had to be rescued by their detective.

By nature, Elizabeth (she was called 'Lilibet' in the family – a name that is still in use – owing to attempts in infancy to pronounce her own name) was obsessively correct and meticulously tidy. Miss Crawford later told stories (and was ostracized by the family for betrayal of confidence) of the princess neatly folding the paper in which presents had been wrapped, and getting up again after being put to bed to ensure that her shoes were properly arranged beneath it. These are doubtless true, but she also had an engaging sense of fun. Nevertheless, she was always 'the serious one'. While Margaret was from the beginning comical, mischievous and spoiled – for her father admired her rambunctious and confident nature, which contrasted so much with his own – Elizabeth always displayed a highly developed sense of responsibility.

She acquired very early the passion that was to dominate her life. She loved horses. She and Margaret had a collection of toy ones, but there were many opportunities for the girls to become familiar with the real thing. They visited the Royal Mews in London and the stables at Windsor. When she was little more than four the king instructed his stud-groom, Owen, to teach his granddaughter to ride. Knowing the English to be a horse-loving people, he saw it as useful for the members of his family to be associated with them. Elizabeth responded with immediate fascination and an enthusiasm that has never lapsed. She began with a pony before progressing to larger mounts. She was to be remembered as saying that, when she grew up, she wanted to marry a farmer so that she could 'live in the country and have lots of horses and dogs'. She also acquired a lasting affection for corgis and the family obtained its first one – Dookie – when she was seven.

The princesses learned to swim at the Bath Club in Mayfair, and a troop of Guides was founded at Buckingham Palace. (Margaret, at first too young to be a Guide, was a Brownie.) The members of the troop were a mix of upper-class daughters of their parents' friends, and the children of Palace staff. Margaret, the less shy of the princesses, enjoyed the communal aspect of their activities; Elizabeth was more aloof. When the troop went camping at Windsor, she found an excuse to sleep on her own elsewhere.

As was the case with their parents, the girls led a placidly enjoyable life until the abdication of their uncle in 1936. They were aware of the stress that their parents were undergoing but did not grasp the seriousness of the situation until the day itself. Elizabeth saw a letter that had been left in the hall of their town house, addressed to 'Her Majesty the queen'. 'That's Mummy now, isn't it?' she asked. Both sisters went on to realize the further implication of this. 'Does that mean,' Margaret asked her sister, 'that you'll be the next queen?' 'Yes,' was the answer, 'some day.' 'Poor you,' replied Margaret.

From then on Elizabeth's life took a new direction. There could be no possibility now of a country life spent among dogs and horses, or of marrying into another country's ruling dynasty in a subordinate role. She represented the future of her own country. She had already grown up to be familiar with courtly protocol and good manners – her grandmother had seen to that – but now she was to be trained specifically for the task ahead. Ten might seem a little young for such an education, but her father's coronation provided a useful opportunity. The king made sure that she learned the meaning of every part of the service, as well as the names and functions of all the officials who took part. The entire event was then, of course, brought to life before her eyes on the day itself. Even as children, Elizabeth and Margaret were already accustomed to appearing in public and waving from balconies and carriages. Some aspects of being royal did not need to be specifically taught. They could be learned just by watching and copying those around them.

The princesses were still too young to play much of a part in state occasions, though Elizabeth made a speech in French to welcome René Coty, France's representative at the coronation. Her education advanced considerably when it was arranged that she should have lessons with Henry Marten, Vice-Provost of Eton, to learn more about the subjects that would be important to her: geography, constitutional history and law. If she were in London or Balmoral she would take her lessons by post, writing essays and sending them to him. When at Windsor – for she lived at the Castle for the duration of the war – she travelled twice a week, accompanied by Miss Crawford, to the School to have lessons with Marten where she sat in his book-filled study, writing notes while he lectured. She was also required to write essays which, if they were not satisfactory, he would mark with an 'N' for nonsense. These tutorials were as valuable for Elizabeth as a course at university would have been. It must be emphasized that she was a diligent and extremely willing pupil. She had never rebelled against her destiny, or been – like her father – panic-stricken at the thought of succeeding to the throne. All her life she had been willing to learn, to take advice, and to profit from the opportunities given her. She wanted to be queen and she wanted to do well at it. She was as eager to learn her job as others were to teach her. If we are ever tempted to see her as lacking in formal 'book learning', we must remember that she received from Marten the best education of its kind available to anyone in Britain, and that it was specifically tailored to her needs and personality.

On the cusp of the Second World War, in June 1939, Elizabeth and Margaret accompanied their parents on a visit to Dartmouth Naval College. Present there was the king's second cousin, Louis Mountbatten, who made a point of introducing his nephew Philip, a cadet. There can be little doubt that Mountbatten, a man of considerable ambition both for himself and for his family, put his handsome nephew on display in the hope that Elizabeth would be impressed. If so, he succeeded beyond his highest hopes. Philip himself was detailed to entertain the girls, a task he did not relish. He did so by showing off on a tennis court and then eating more shrimps than anyone else at tea. When the royal party took its leave, sailing out of Dartmouth harbour in the royal yacht, a number of the young men accompanied them in smaller boats. As the yacht gained the open sea, the smaller craft turned back – except for one, which ploughed on. It was Philip's. The king thought him a fool for carrying on into dangerous waters, but his daughter, it seems, thought the gesture wonderful.

With the outbreak of war, the girls were 'evacuated', though this merely meant they were sent to live at Windsor Castle. The cellars were an effective air-raid shelter, and they continued with their routine of lessons and leisure, albeit with the addition of wartime activities like collecting scrap and knitting for the troops. Elizabeth made a broadcast to the children of the empire on the BBC programme *Children's Hour*. An appeal to youthful listeners throughout the world to keep their spirits up, it moved some adult listeners to tears.

The king and queen remained in London but travelled to Windsor at weekends. On the first night that the air-raid siren sounded, the girls were reprimanded for taking too long to dress before going to the shelter. Their mother was to make a point of dressing slowly, to show that she would not be hurried by mere bombs, and after a few alerts decided that, in fact, she would not go down at all, as it was too much bother.

At sixteen Princess Elizabeth, who longed to do something for the war effort, was appointed Colonel of the Grenadier Guards. She might have been young but she took the post with utmost seriousness, showing such strictness in her first inspection that she had to be asked to be more merciful. In April 1944 she reached the age of eighteen, and was obliged like every young woman to register for war work. At first her father would not let her enlist in the Forces, considering her royal duties sufficient national service, but he allowed himself to be persuaded. She joined the ATS (Auxiliary Territorial Service), an organization with considerably less glamour than the Navy or Air Force could offer women. She was to train as a motor-mechanic. The king stipulated that she must live at home, and so she did – driven to the camp each day. She did not mix with the other junior officers, who had to address her as 'Ma'am', and who stood to attention when she entered a room. She did, however, wear overalls as they did, and learn the mysteries of the car engine. She passed her driving test after successfully taking her commanding officer from Aldershot to Buckingham Palace, via Piccadilly Circus. Shortly afterward – the European conflict ended in May 1945 – Elizabeth wore her uniform to appear on the Palace balcony with her parents. By her next such appearance, when Japan surrendered in August, she was in a print dress.

Throughout the war her friendship with Philip Mountbatten had deepened into serious affection. They had become better acquainted during visits he had made to Windsor, and had written to each other every week. It was clear that Elizabeth's liking for him was no mere schoolgirl infatuation. Neither he nor she has ever talked publicly about their feelings for each other, but their attraction was mutual and genuine, despite the zeal and energy – indeed interference – with which Mountbatten was pushing his nephew toward marriage. Elizabeth's parents were unsure about this potential son-in-law. He was personally likeable, his overwhelming confidence a stark contrast to the king's – and Elizabeth's – shyness. He was a member of Greece's royal family, which made him more or less socially suitable. He had been educated in Britain and had served in the Royal Navy. Nevertheless he was seen by courtiers as bumptious and disrespectful. Extremely handsome, he was popular with women, and it was feared he might not prove to be a faithful husband. His foreign connections could pose difficulties, for the recent practice of royalty choosing their spouses from within the United Kingdom had proved so popular that to depart from it might risk arousing public hostility. (In fact the one foreign marriage made by the family since 1917 had also been with Greece, when the Duke of Kent had married Princess Marina.) Far more seriously,

Philip's sisters were all married to Germans, some of whom had very tainted recent pasts.

The British people did not at first take to Philip. His friendship with their princess had been an open secret for years, to the extent that their marriage was considered extremely likely, if not certain. When he appeared with her at a Mountbatten wedding it provoked a frenzy of speculation. An opinion poll showed 40 per cent of respondents as being opposed to him, on the grounds that he was foreign. He was known to be virtually penniless, and indeed homeless, spending his leaves from duty staying with relatives. The only clothing he seemed to own was his uniform. A wartime photograph of him in a naval cap but sporting a full beard, which the princess had treasured, was published to howls of derision. He looked like the mate off a tramp steamer.

The Palace made numerous denials, and the king tried to interest his daughter in other men. Dukes who happen to be both young and single are a rare species, but she was given the chance to meet those that could be assembled. Her preference for Philip did not waver. Indeed, they became secretly engaged at Balmoral during the autumn of 1946. It was decided that no announcement should be made until after the forthcoming royal tour of South Africa. Elizabeth was to celebrate her twenty-first birthday while they were there, and that was considered enough of an event for the moment.

She marked the occasion with another radio broadcast, this time to all her father's peoples. In a speech that she had written and rehearsed exhaustively, she pledged her life to their service in an address that was simple and sincere and gracious. Once again, listeners felt the sting of tears. On her return, the engagement was announced. Elizabeth, obedient and sensible by nature and inclination, had had the single disagreement of her life with her parents over the issue of when she might marry Philip. Her determination to do so was never in doubt, and once her father gave his permission she forgave him for causing the delay. The wedding took place at Westminster Abbey, as was now the custom, on 20 November 1947.

Whatever the public's view of Philip, they longed for a great royal occasion. There had been no colour in their lives since the coronation a decade before, and the wedding represented the first time that state coaches and scarlet uniforms had been seen on the streets since then. The bride and groom received over a thousand wedding presents, some of which have been in storage ever since.

The first years of their marriage were to represent the only comparatively carefree interlude they would have. Philip remained a serving naval officer, but he was either at the Admiralty in Whitehall – a ten-minute walk from the Palace, in which the couple were living – or at the Naval College in Greenwich, and thus they were together every day. (Elizabeth would look out of the Palace window in early evening to see him return.) Clarence House, an historic royal property beside St James's Palace, was renovated to be their family home, and a country residence was rented for them. Almost exactly a year after their wedding, on 14 November 1948, their first child, Prince Charles, was born.

Philip was then posted to the Mediterranean Fleet based in Malta. As a career officer he was naturally delighted to undertake sea-duty, and the delightful and historical island was as pleasant a posting as could be found. His uncle Mountbatten was commander of a cruiser squadron there. It was decided that Princess Elizabeth would accompany her husband but that Charles should stay behind, for the climate could be difficult for an infant. Though an affectionate mother, Elizabeth was always guided by an overwhelming sense of duty. If her husband was overseas, it was her place to be with him.

In Malta she lived the life of an officer's wife – after a fashion. She was not in the least anonymous – she was after all the daughter of the island's king – and she was accompanied by a detective, as well as a dresser and a footman. She brought with her forty cases of clothes, and she lived in the Mountbattens' villa. She was often asked to perform official functions, but was frequently able to find time for shopping, sightseeing, visits to the cinema or the hairdresser, as well as for watching numerous polo matches, since this was her husband's new passion. He soon acquired another when he was given command of a frigate, HMS *Magpie*. The ship was tasked to cruise the Mediterranean on goodwill visits. In August 1950 the young couple's second child, Anne, was born, though this meant that Elizabeth had to return home for several months.

Their lives on the island were in any case increasingly interrupted by the illness of the king. The princess had to fly home and deputize for him by hosting two state visits, and at the end of 1950 she and Philip went in his stead on a month-long visit to Canada. The vivacious young couple made a good impression there, as they did on President Truman on a sidetrip to Washington. The king was pleased enough with them to request that they stand in for him again the following year on a royal tour of several countries. They would go to Australia and New Zealand via Kenya and Ceylon. It would take six months. Once again, their children would be left behind.

They set off by air on 31 January 1952, to return far sooner than anyone had imagined they would. As before, there was an official party waiting to receive them, but this time everyone was dressed in mourning. The king had died while Elizabeth and her husband were staying at a Kenyan game reserve. They had to return at once, by the shortest air route and without their luggage, which had already started for Ceylon. With the sleight of hand at which royal aides are so accomplished, black clothes for them were spirited aboard the aircraft just after it touched down, so that queen and consort could emerge suitably dressed.

Elizabeth's new role was abruptly assumed, but she was already very well versed in her duties. Having received no training himself, King George VI had seen to it that his daughter was given a thorough grounding in the everyday tasks of a sovereign. She had watched him work through his dispatch boxes, and was to prove adept at doing so herself. Courtiers were impressed by her quick grasp of essentials. She could deal with business in half the time it had taken George, and she could remember more. She was, as always, surrounded by advisers who kept in motion the smooth flow of routine. All she had to do, until she found her feet, was follow precedent.

Her coronation took place more than a year after her accession, in June 1953. The climate of austerity that had cast such gloom over the post-war years was still evident, and once again the chance for a national celebration was welcome. After a good deal of discussion, it was decided that the service could be televised – thus bringing to fulfilment the concept introduced with her father's wedding thirty years earlier, that the wider public could participate in the occasion. People responded in their hundreds of thousands by buying or renting television sets. This was not the first time it had been possible to experience a state event without leaving home – the previous coronation had been relayed by wireless – but it was certainly the first opportunity to share in the visual splendour of the ceremony. Sitting-rooms across the country were crowded with families, friends and droppers-in who watched – often in respectful silence – the long hours of ceremonial. Many gatherings stood to attention on hearing the National Anthem.

The queen herself endured the long service with equanimity. Such was her veneration of her father and her determination to do things in the same manner that she refused to have the crown made smaller to suit her woman's head. She bore the same seven-pound burden that he had.

She was queen of a realm that expected her reign to be a golden age. The fact that she shared a name with – and was the same age at her accession as – one of England's greatest monarchs was seen as a good omen, an indication that there would be a return to greatness for a country that was physically and financially exhausted by the war. The phrase 'new Elizabethan' was everywhere in use. It was mere hyperbole, and in time would mean that the coming era could only be viewed as a disappointment by those whose expectations had been raised too high.

The first crisis she faced was within the queen's own family. Princess Margaret had fallen in love with one of her father's equerries. Group Captain Peter Townsend was a hero straight out of *The Boy's Own Paper*. A former Battle of Britain fighter pilot, he was handsome, urbane and charming. He was also divorced, though he had been the injured party. Margaret had developed a girlish infatuation with him that became mutual when they discovered they shared the same interests and sense of humour. They wished to marry, though they knew there would be disapproval. As the sister of the Head of the Anglican Church, Margaret could not marry a divorced man. The queen had in any case, under the Royal Marriages Act, the power to veto any union involving a member of her family. Whatever the queen privately thought of Townsend (she and her mother would probably both have disapproved of him for forming this friendship), Philip did not like him, and was able to influence his wife. If Margaret married Townsend she would lose her royal status and the privileges that went with it. For a while the relationship was kept secret. At the coronation, however, Margaret made a serious mistake. Outside the Abbey after the service she was seen by a reporter to reach up and brush something from the uniform of an RAF officer. It was a gesture that is only made between intimates and the journalist in question, Audrey Whiting, at once guessed the situation. The man was soon named, and the story was out.

The public was fascinated. After decades of dull and worthy royals, here was a scandal that allowed people to take sides, to pry into the personal lives of the family and to criticize the attitudes or behaviour – depending on whom they supported – of their rulers. The reaction to the last royal scandal – the abdication – had in general been muted because the press had published so little information. Now there were to be no such constraints.

Townsend, who was severely criticized by courtiers for having allowed such a relationship to develop, was appointed Air Attaché at an overseas embassy to take him off the scene, but this was only in Brussels, well within telephoning distance of London, and he and the princess remained in contact. His posting ended after two years and he returned home, where the question of their future was reopened. Matters had now reached such a pitch that it seemed they must finally decide between marriage or duty.

They chose the latter course. Margaret made a statement in which she told the public that she had decided not to marry him, and that was that. It was like the abdication all over again, but with the opposite outcome. It was a noble gesture on Margaret's part, for she was a woman perfectly capable of selfishness, but the simple fact was that she could never have been happy without the status, the trappings and the wealth that went with royalty. It was these things she had opted to keep. A few years later she would find at least initial happiness in marriage to a less suitable but more acceptable man. As for the public, a number of them would never again be quite so deferential in their attitude to the monarchy.

If the Townsend business represented any sort of milestone it was this: until that time, the modern monarchy had been revered as a matter of course. Since the House of Windsor had begun, there had been no overt mockery of its members. George V had been left alone by newspaper cartoonists because he was considered too dull and too dutiful to caricature. Edward VIII had been a popular idol to some, while those who knew his faults did not talk about them in public. George VI represented such a return to 'dull worthiness' that, again, there was no scope for satire. Elizabeth II had, all her life, been a model of rectitude, and she too was seen as being above reproach. The only discomfort she had experienced with the popular media had been speculation about her engagement to Philip, and a certain amount of criticism when she left her children behind while abroad on official business. Within recent memory, the royal family had known nothing but respect, and with the coronation this had reached new heights. Those of a more cynical bent felt stifled by the atmosphere of what they considered to be fawning reverence around the family. But they were about to have their day.

The post-war decades were a time of conspicuous change. The war had undermined moral standards through an increase in casual sex and illegitimate births. Divorce had become widespread as wartime marriages foundered and, because it affected the upper classes as much as the rest of society, a great deal of the stigma that had formerly been attached to it was lost. The years of conflict had created an impetus towards much greater social equality, and this had been furthered by the Labour government that came to power in 1945. In the fifties and sixties levels of prosperity increased, with more money in people's pockets and more things available on which to spend it. Travel became easier so that foreign holidays became possible for millions. The university population vastly increased as new campuses sprang up across the country. The finer things of life were now within reach of those who had never previously felt entitled to them. 'You've never had it so good,' the prime minister, Harold Macmillan, was paraphrased as saying. With this unprecedented sharing of material well-being, small wonder that the habit of unquestioning deference to supposed superiors went into decline.

Two men publicly criticized the royal family in print. One was Malcolm Muggeridge, a journalist who made his reputation by taking up contrarian stances. In 1955 he wrote a satirical article entitled 'Royal Soap Opera'. Two years later, before a visit by the queen to Washington, an expanded version appeared in the US publication the *Saturday Evening Post* under the title 'Does England Really Need a Queen?' and was much more widely read. There was outrage in Britain. Two of his employers, Beaverbrook Newspapers and the BBC, sacked him, and Muggeridge was hounded by hostile, threatening letters. He went on, incidentally, to be equally rude about another national icon – the Beatles.

John Grigg was not a journalist. As Lord Altrincham, he was a member of the Establishment. When – also in 1957 – he too wrote an article in which he commented on the queen's public presence, he intended his remarks to be read as constructive criticism, aimed not at Her Majesty but at those who were responsible for her image. Her manner, he complained, was that of 'a priggish schoolgirl, captain of the hockey team, a prefect and recent candidate for Confirmation'. He also took a swipe at her accent, which carried the tones of a girls' public school even though she had never attended one. It was, he said, 'a pain in the neck', while her public speeches, often filled with wholesome moralizing and usually written by others, were 'prim little sermons'. He too was vilified for his article, and indeed physically attacked as a consequence of it. Nevertheless his shafts hit home. There was, of course, no official riposte but the queen's voice, which one sympathizer described as 'cruelly easy to caricature', became steadily less shrill and girlish. The message was received even if the messenger earned no thanks.

The monarchy, perceived by critics as stuffy and backward-looking, was actually undergoing many changes during this decade. Some were small and to a large extent insignificant, such as the moving of Trooping the Colour from Thursday to Saturday so that it would interfere less with the capital's traffic, but they showed that a process of continual adjustment was being made to accommodate the mood and outlook of a new generation. All of these changes came voluntarily from within rather than being imposed, or advised, from outside. 'Presentation at Court' – the ritual in which upper-class young women processed past the monarch and dropped a curtsey as their names were announced – ended in 1958, to be replaced by a charity ball that was privately organized. To replace it in the Court calendar there was an increase (from two to three, as well as another held in Edinburgh) in the number of royal garden parties held each summer. These had previously been for members of Society only. Now they were for representatives of the wider public. Invitations were allocated to businesses, school and college staffs, government departments, military units, charity organizations, the law, medicine, the Church, and so on. Anyone belonging to one of these institutions over a period of years was likely to receive an invitation at some point – to have the chance to walk through the Palace gates, stroll in the gardens (which were never normally open) and enjoy the queen's hospitality in the form of sandwiches provided by Lyons the caterers. Though only a fraction of those attending ever met Her Majesty, they could enjoy the sense of occasion and the knowledge that they and their spouses had 'been there'.

The participants today are overwhelmingly middle-class – professionals who are eligible because they hold senior posts in their profession – but a significant minority are not. The garden parties, each attended by about 8,000 people, have proved to be a thoroughly welcome innovation and have increased, as nothing has done since the advent of the OBE, the feeling that the general public can have access to the Establishment.

At the same time, the Palace instituted the custom of staging regular lunches for groups of prominent people. Chosen for their contribution to national life, they might typically include the director of a high-street bank, the mayor of a large city, a painter, a professor from a redbrick university, and a theatre producer. These were originally intended to be evening gatherings, but it proved too difficult to find dates on which the queen and her husband were both free. Though the people invited were, and are, successful and important, these occasions represent another opportunity for the monarchy and its people to meet. The atmosphere, despite the setting, is surprisingly informal.

The queen agreed that the Christmas broadcast could be delivered on television rather than by radio. This was a major concession on her part, for she disliked intensely this annual ordeal. She is aware that she has no gift as a speaker. She is unable to relax in front of a microphone, and knows that her voice sounds stilted, cold and formal. This is a matter of personality – she simply does not like addressing audiences – rather than training, for her diction is always clear and her timing perfect. (She is, of course, being directed off-camera.) However she felt, and still feels, about this event, her appearance on screen since televization of the speech began in 1957, has increased immensely both audience numbers and appreciation of the broadcast. Ten years later, as a means of making the event more visually interesting, film-clips began to be used that showed her travels, visits and other experiences over the past twelve months. The programme, instead of being recorded live (and thus ruining her Christmas Day, since she could not relax until it was over), was taped in advance.

One thing that brought monarchy and the nation's youth together very effectively was the Duke of Edinburgh's Award Scheme, which began in 1956. The duke did not devise it. It was the brainchild of his old headmaster, Kurt Hahn, and was based on a prize awarded at Gordonstoun. What Prince Philip did was to assume the chairmanship of the body that regulated this programme of activities, lending it, through his name and his continuous patronage, the prestige associated with royalty. The scheme, which builds confidence and broadens experience, was originally only for boys aged under eighteen, but within two years girls were also participating, and the upper age-limit rose to twenty-five. So popular has it been that it has spread all over the world, though many countries call it something else (The President's Award, for instance). A successor to the Duke of York's Camps of the inter-war years, it is perhaps one of the most resoundingly successful gestures ever made in the name of royalty, and will in the future provide a lasting memorial to the reign.

Two further additions were made to the family as the queen approached middle age. Andrew was born in 1960, and was followed by Edward four years later, creating two distinct generations of children. Charles and Anne had been brought up with less formality than their royal predecessors – attending schools instead of having private tutors and, in the case of an operation that Anne had to undergo, being treated in hospital rather than having medical facilities set up in the Palace. All the royal children were naturally of interest to the press, but an attempt to shield a younger one from publicity backfired – Andrew did not appear in public until several weeks after he was born, and this provoked speculation that he was physically or mentally impaired.

The sixties were a difficult time for the monarchy, as for all established institutions. Though the Suez crisis was now a memory, Britain was rocked by the revelation that young men of good background – Philby, Burgess and Maclean – had been betraying national secrets to the Soviets. A fourth man, Anthony Blunt, was actually employed inside the royal household as Surveyor of the Queen's Pictures. Though his complicity was not revealed, and he was not disgraced, until many years later, the queen had known of his guilt since the other three were first discovered, and had somehow remained courteous in her dealings with him. The Profumo scandal, in which a senior government minister was found to have compromised national security through a relationship with a call-girl, was another blow to those who advocated the Establishment status quo. These events caused a major lapse in public confidence and an increasingly cynical outlook among a younger generation that had already lost faith in the world view of their elders. These were, of course, the years that saw the rise of the Beatles, the Rolling Stones, and the whole pop music 'scene' that, almost overnight, added a new dimension to popular culture and made staid and class-ridden Britain – or at least its capital, 'Swinging London' – the most fashionable place on earth.

Though the appeal of this culture was lost on Charles, his sister was to some extent identified with it, wearing a miniskirt and attending a performance of the hippy musical *Hair*.

Princess Margaret, who in 1960 had married a photographer called Antony Armstrong-Jones (he was ennobled as Earl of Snowdon), was more a part of contemporary culture than any other royal. Always the family rebel (unlike her sister, she smoked), she enjoyed the raffish, bohemian world in which her husband moved, and the company of film stars and pop singers. While this did not endear the monarchy to the younger generation – they were too caught up in their own diversions to notice. Rather, it gave Margaret a reputation among the older generation for self-indulgence and for choosing her friends unwisely.

The Palace was besieged by photographers when the Beatles, on the recommendation of Labour Prime Minister Harold Wilson, received the MBE for services to British export. Though this may briefly have made the Establishment seem in tune with the nation's youth, the gesture was deplored in some quarters. Those who had been given the same award for more onerous services – such as enduring years in a Japanese prisoner-of-war camp – were horrified by its trivialization, and several people sent their medals back in protest.

The demands of an information-hungry, televisual age became increasingly strident and the Palace, after long years of regarding the press as a nuisance to be avoided, suddenly changed tack. The catalyst was the replacement as Press Officer in 1968 of Commander Colville, a gruff ex-naval officer, with an Australian called William Heseltine. Colville had made no secret of his dislike of journalists, and had seen it as his primary function to protect the privacy of his employers. Heseltine, a young and outgoing man who was untainted by the conservatism of older courtiers, decided to befriend the press instead. He was pleasant when answering the phone, and as helpful as possible – checking facts, providing quotes, and confirming or denying stories with a refreshing lack of obfuscation. Though there could never be complete amity between the royals and the Fourth Estate, Heseltine, who remained at his post for over a decade, significantly eased relations.

There was another attempt to woo public opinion, through the medium of television. Lord Mountbatten, now an elder statesman among royals, had been the subject of a biographical television series directed by his son-in-law, Lord Brabourne. It had been very successful, and he persuaded the queen that television could also benefit the public image of her family. She agreed to 'host' a documentary called *The Royal Palaces of Britain*. Shown in 1966, it offered an overview of the royal homes. The aspect that most interested viewers, though, was the incidental, behind-the-scenes insight it gave into her family and their lives. This led to a further, bolder suggestion: that another documentary be made, about the family themselves this time rather than their houses. The result was shown three years later. *Royal Family* (or *Corgi and Beth*, as it was nicknamed) ran for sixty minutes. It showed the queen, her husband and their children lunching at Sandringham, relaxing at Windsor, barbecuing at Balmoral. It was pleasantly spontaneous, without the feel of having been staged (a string on Prince Charles's cello broke and hit his brother Edward), and genuinely informative. The Windsors were seen on holiday in pullovers and headscarves, looking just like any other family. The screening created such overwhelming interest that an estimated 68 per cent of Britons – almost two-thirds of the population – stayed in to watch it in June 1969.

Though it made television history – and £120,000 in profits – it was a step that the Palace clearly regretted. It had, it was felt by traditionalists (and by the family), let too much daylight in on magic. Though it had enchanted viewers to see the queen buying sweets for Prince Edward in a village shop, it had set a new threshold for intrusiveness, and in consequence the public expected the same degree of access from then on. The programme rapidly disappeared. Her Majesty owned the copyright as well as the actual reels of film, so that it could not be shown again without her permission. This has never been given, and only short extracts have been seen since. It was, as those who saw it can confirm, both innocuous and endearing, and tame by the standards of accessibility that exist today. Nevertheless it is unlikely to be seen again during the lifetime of Elizabeth II.

Only two weeks after it appeared there was another televisual airing for the royal family. The Investiture of Charles as Prince of Wales was staged at Caernarfon Castle. This was not an ancient ceremony. Only one such event had been held before, in 1911, but what did that matter? Pageantry can capture the imagination even if it has only just been dreamed up, and this event was beautifully staged. Lord Snowdon, the queen's brother-in-law, had designed the backdrop – medieval trappings like the stage-set for a school Shakespeare production – for use with the imposing castle ruins. There was a throne of Welsh slate, a specially made modern crown, and a transparent canopy that would allow cameras to show proceedings while still keeping the rain off. It was the biggest royal event since the coronation sixteen years earlier, and fully maintained Britain's reputation for simple yet impressive ceremonial.

The same year saw the beginning of a new era when terrorism came to both Northern Ireland and mainland Britain. What began in Ulster as a civil rights movement to end discrimination against Catholics, was hijacked by the IRA and turned into a campaign of violence to secure British withdrawal. The royal family became potential targets for assassination in a way that they had never been before, and faced danger that had not been encountered since George VI and Queen Elizabeth had remained in London during the Blitz. In spite of this, the next set-piece state event – the marriage of Princess Anne – went ahead in November 1973 as if nothing had changed. The queen, as a matter of principle, would not allow the threat of terrorism to disrupt or prevent any public event. The annual pageantry of Trooping the Colour and the state opening of Parliament went on as usual. The Metropolitan Police, and other responsible agencies, simply had to become expert at managing these occasions – searching the route, scanning the crowds, maintaining an unobtrusive but vigilant presence. That they have done these things ever since without causing major disruption to these events is a tribute to the level of professionalism they have achieved. Even an almost-successful kidnap attempt on Princess Anne, carried out within yards of the Palace and resulting in the shooting (fortunately not fatal) of her detective, failed to prevent the regular public appearances of the family. Since time immemorial, monarchs have used such appearances in two ways: to reinforce their authority and to allow their subjects a limited level of access and thus increase public interest and loyalty. This approach is as relevant today as it ever has been, and is something the present monarch will not abandon.

Ironically the same decade that produced the greatest recent threat to the safety of the Windsors was also the one that brought them closest to their people – the single biggest stride forward made by 'popular monarchy' since 1917. This was the advent of the 'walkabout'. The term can be defined as an informal stroll, by members of the family, along a street or crush-barrier, with stops to talk to the public. These are now commonplace, but they were unheard-of until a generation ago. People had always been willing to stand for hours at roadsides to see the royals pass, but the most they had expected to see was a swiftly moving vehicle or a waving hand. As a kindness to the crowds, royals would often have the collapsible roof of a car put down, even in pouring rain, to give a clearer view.

In March 1970 the family made a visit to Wellington, New Zealand. The queen, Prince Philip, Charles and Anne were to attend a function at the town hall. It had been suggested by their hosts that, instead of simply arriving at the entrance by car, they should disembark on the other side of the square and walk across it, greeting the crowds on the way. They did so, and the effect was magical. For the first time members of the public could have brief conversations with, and take close-up pictures of, the royal family in the setting of their own streets. The walkabout had taken considerable planning, but it gave the impression of spontaneity. It was repeated in the UK, in Coventry, some months later, and met with the same enthusiasm. In 1977, the queen's walkabouts were to be perhaps the most cherished aspect of her jubilee celebrations.

The seventies was an era of economic gloom, industrial anarchy and social unrest. The Silver Jubilee – the twenty-fifth anniversary of the queen's accession – fell in February 1977, though the celebrations were to be held in June. There was at first little enthusiasm for this event. The country, it was felt, would be preoccupied with its troubles, the risk of terrorism was likely to be great, and the cost of the national party would attract potentially damaging criticism. When the plans were made, by a committee chaired by Prince Charles, it was assumed that they would have to be kept modest.

In fact, it was precisely because of such pervasive gloom that the populace at large wanted a party. Britain was shown on television screens across the world as a country paralysed by strikes, financially unstable, choked with uncollected rubbish, and with its youth represented by snarling, foul-mouthed punks. Knowing that no other nation could match them at staging a celebration, however, the British wanted to show the world – and themselves – that there were some things in which they still effortlessly dominated. The jubilee – with the service at St Paul's in London, the series of tours that Her Majesty made of Britain and the Commonwealth, and the innumerable village fetes and ox-roasts and street-parties – was a triumph. 'An older Britain briefly re-awoke,' as one commentator put it, though in truth that older Britain is always there, awaiting such opportunities. If the monarchy cannot cure the ills of society, it can at least provide colourful diversions and a sense of pride. So it proved in 1977.

This success was repeated, in even greater measure, four years later when Prince Charles was married in St Paul's Cathedral. His continuing bachelorhood was causing concern to his parents, but like a previous Prince of Wales he seemed content to put off matrimony indefinitely. He was by no means uninterested in women, and had had friendships with several who might have made suitable consorts. What the public did not know was that his affections were already committed to a woman, Camilla Shand, whom he had met when she was single but who was now married to an army officer. Charles needed, for dynastic reasons, to marry, but his wife must be suited to the role that she would expect to inherit. This meant in effect that she must not have 'a past', and must be sufficiently well drilled in duty and politeness to win the approval of the family's older generation.

Lady Diana Spencer, the sister of one of Charles's former girlfriends, seemed a perfect candidate: very young – at nineteen she was twelve years his junior – and from an aristocratic family. Her grandmother and his were friends. Lady Diana had lived on the Sandringham Estate, and appeared to take pleasure in the country pursuits that formed an essential part of the royal family's lifestyle. She was not overly bright, but was obviously good with children (she was working at the time as a nursery assistant), and possessed qualities of kindness and modesty (she blushed easily) that won the affection of the public as soon as they began to see her in photographs.

She and Charles seemed very happy together. On the day of their wedding – 29 July 1981 – an estimated 600,000 people lined the streets to witness the event, and some 750 million watched on television. This time there had been no doubting the public enthusiasm beforehand. The populace had shown willing from the moment the engagement was announced. Television coverage was all-encompassing; souvenir manufacturers were in ecstasies. Once again, celebrations were mounted on village greens and at street parties throughout the country. As during the jubilee, Britons felt that the whole world was watching them with envy, and they enjoyed this further moment of national glory.

This new spirit of nationalism was unexpectedly put to the test the following year. The Falkland Islands, a British dependency off the coast of South America, was invaded without warning by Argentinian forces. Argentina had always claimed the islands, which had been populated by British settlers since 1833. Since the Falklanders refused to consider abandoning their British identity, no government in London would even discuss the matter with Buenos Aires, let alone concede ownership. Sudden military occupation was the result. Could Britain, 8,000 miles to the north, do anything about this? Were there the resources – was there the will? The answer was yes. The indomitable British prime minister, Margaret Thatcher, immediately ordered a taskforce to be assembled. The journey was too long to make by air, and the expedition had to sail to the Falklands, warships accompanied by commandeered merchant and passenger vessels filled with troops. The voyage lasted three weeks, the campaign almost three months. At a cost of 258 British fatalities Argentinian forces surrendered on 14 June 1982, and eventually the taskforce returned to Britain. Waiting for them in Portsmouth were the queen and Prince Philip, for one of their number was Prince Andrew, a naval helicopter pilot who had faced a degree of personal danger during the fighting. His craft had been used as a decoy for deadly Exocet missiles, and he had also flown anti-submarine patrols.

His specialist skills had been required in the conflict, but because of his position there had naturally been reluctance to deploy him. It would have been understandable if he had been kept away from the 'sharp end'. In fact, it was the queen herself who had insisted that he be sent. 'No, he's a serving officer,' her chaplain later quoted her as saying, 'he must take his turn with the rest.' He is her favourite, and she would naturally have been deeply anxious about the outcome, but she wanted her son to take the same risks as his comrades. He was the first member of his family to serve in active combat since his father took part in the Battle of Cape Matapan in 1942. As in previous wars, equality of service – and perhaps sacrifice – strengthened the bond between monarchy and people.

Courage is always impressive, and this was shown by the

queen herself on two separate occasions. At Trooping the Colour in 1981 she was shot at – with blanks, as it transpired – while she rode along the Mall toward the parade. After calming her horse she coolly rode on, and the ceremony proceeded as usual. The next year she awoke one morning to find a stranger in her bedroom, and managed to keep him distracted until help arrived.

Apart from these events it was her children who claimed the lion's share of the attention. Andrew was married, in the summer of 1986, to Sarah Ferguson. She was an exuberant, confident young woman whose boisterous sense of humour matched his own. As with Diana, who was a friend (and had brought her and Andrew together), Miss Ferguson seemed a highly promising addition to the family. The daughter of Prince Charles's polo manager, she had known the family since childhood, and therefore understood the environment she was entering. Her sheer jolliness was seen as refreshing. The public expected to warm to her.

They didn't. Remarkably quickly, she irritated them. She proved to be clumsy, boorish, undignified and selfish. She made too much noise, and she was a liability rather than an asset. She also proved to be greedy, and went on seemingly endless expensive holidays. 'She was having too much fun,' said one critic, adding that the public like the notion that, when royals are on holiday, they spend their time shivering at Balmoral rather than going somewhere nice. Sarah Ferguson took advantage of every privilege her position offered, and still wanted more. The nadir was perhaps reached when she produced a children's book – *Budgie the Little Helicopter* – and pocketed the proceeds instead of making them over to charity.

Prince Edward, the only one of the siblings still unmarried, was also in trouble. He had made two decisions regarding his future. One was to attend Cambridge University, the other to join the Royal Marines. He was accepted by Jesus College, but it was obvious that he owed this to his position rather than any innate ability. There were protests, and a good deal of public derision. He survived three years there, however, and received a degree. His fees had been paid by the Marines – the sponsoring of officer recruits is usual – and afterwards he had to start the notoriously tough training course. Though he was making good progress, the few weeks he spent with the Corps convinced him that his ambitions lay elsewhere. He pulled out of training, bringing further opprobrium on himself and his family.

He sought a career in the theatre, and was willing to start at the bottom as a general dogsbody in a production company, provoking yet more sneers. Having begun with this, he aspired to be a producer himself. Using his connections, he arranged a television spectacular that would raise money for charity while giving him national exposure. *It's a Royal Knockout*, modelled on a much-loved television programme, used teams led by members of his family (Princess Anne, Sarah Ferguson) and filled with celebrities (Jackie Stewart, Cliff Richard, John Travolta) to compete in a series of comical races, while dressed in historical costume. It was not a success. In fact it was regarded as painful, and Edward's sulking, when he discovered that the press had been unimpressed, compounded his misfortune. The queen disapproved, and those who wish the monarchy well have tried to forget it. Young people are allowed to make mistakes, it is how they learn, but in the case of royalty the media is always there to record and preserve such lapses.

The royal family was by now the subject of widespread ridicule, and it was not simply the mistakes of the younger generation that were the cause.

Throughout the earlier half of the twentieth century other countries had experienced a trend towards satirical humour: the cabarets of Paris or inter-war Berlin, for instance. From the 1950s, however, the United Kingdom saw a fashion for increasingly zany humour – often incomprehensible and bewildering to foreigners – that manifested no respect for

anything. *The Goon Show*, which appeared on radio throughout the fifties, was followed by *That Was The Week That
Was*, a political lampoon. *Private Eye*, a magazine that poked
disrespectful fun at the Establishment, began publication in
1961. Other programmes followed, most famously *Monty
Python's Flying Circus*. All of them had one thing in common
– they were the work of young people. It was in the sixties
that youth took over the media. Ludicrously inexperienced
men and women still in their twenties – David Frost, Joan
Bakewell, Simon Dee – were given access to their own television platform, and used it to lecture their elders. The chief
targets of ridicule were the caste of patrician Tory politicians
personified by Harold Macmillan, but the satirists also took a
swipe at many other aspects of the Establishment.

In view of this, the monarchy got off lightly for a very long
time. Writing in 1977 the foreword to a book about cartoon
images of the royal family – an historical survey that covered
centuries – Prince Charles was to remark that, compared with
their predecessors, his family had been treated kindly. This
was true up to that point, but it was not to last. The satirical
shows had introduced a climate of ridicule that made abuse
a generally accepted part of entertainment. The increasing
vulgarity of tabloid journalism was a further blow, and this
would become worse when the anti-monarchist Australian
Rupert Murdoch became proprietor of one of them.

It was in the eighties, with the advent of the ground-breaking
television programme *Spitting Image*, that any deference to
public figures was to vanish without trace. The programme
used cruelly exaggerated, life-sized latex puppets to lampoon the world's leaders: Mrs Thatcher, John Major, President Reagan, François Mitterrand. The creators, Peter Fluck
and Roger Law, were both former newspaper cartoonists
whose irreverence certainly did not spare the members of the
Labour Party, but whose strongly-held left-wing convictions
meant that anyone who represented the established order was
unlikely to be treated gently. The queen, Prince Philip, the

Queen Mother, Charles and Diana, were all depicted with varying degrees of disrespect. Only when the series spawned a book did the Palace take exception. This depicted Prince Andrew in a nude centrefold, suggestively draped with a string of sausages. There was no outright objection from the royal family, but the Prince of Wales abruptly cancelled a contract with the book's publisher, for whom he had been producing a volume of his own. When the Post Office produced, some time later, a series of stamps that celebrated British cartoonists, it included a design by Roger Law. All stamps must be approved by the queen, and it seems she simply refused to do so in this case. The story is probably true, though the Post Office Archives cannot confirm it. There are subtle but effective ways in which the monarch can express disapproval.

Satire comes in waves as styles go in and out of fashion, and *Spitting Image*, which ran on television for no less than twelve years, has not been followed by anything as pointedly cruel. Humour of a much gentler kind has been found in Sue Townsend's novel *The Queen and I*, which was published in 1992 and subsequently made into a stage production. This is set during the general election of that year, and imagines the consequences of a victory by the People's Republican Party.

The Windsors are stripped of their properties and titles, and sent to live on a council estate in Leicester (Miss Townsend's home town), in order to experience ordinary life. The older generation are pensioners, the younger members have to find something to do. The humour comes from imagining how the various family members cope with their change of lifestyle. Prince Philip, despite a real-life reputation for no-nonsense pragmatism, cannot make the adjustment. He takes to bed and effectively goes on hunger-strike; Princess Margaret complains endlessly; the Queen Mother befriends an elderly West Indian widow and enjoys long afternoons reminiscing with her about their respective families (she later dies and is buried with her new neighbours in attendance). Charles becomes not only an enthusiastic gardener but a political activist, jailed for a crime he did not commit – punching a policeman. He asks Diana to look after the plants in their modest garden, but she is more interested in forming a close friendship with a successful black accountant. William and Harry attend the local primary school and quickly slough off any signs of 'poshness', learning to talk in ungrammatical slang for protective colouring. Princess Anne, displaying the tough practicality for which she is known, drives her own removal van to the small cul-de-sac (Hell Close) in which the family have been settled. She immediately sets to work on repairing the plumbing with the aid of a household manual, and later takes up with a shy and unpersonable local handyman. Prince Andrew features only incidentally. He is at sea on a submarine. And neither does Prince Edward who, in his capacity as a production assistant in the theatre, is touring New Zealand with a musical called *Sheep!*

As for the queen herself, she does remarkably well. She has, after all, been described as 'riddled with common sense', and would probably deal with such a change of lifestyle in much the way that is described in the story. She is shown as a much stronger character than her husband, and emerges as something of a heroine. She has been assigned a social worker to help her adjust, but is exasperated by the woman's jargon-heavy and patronizing counselling, and shuts her out of the house. When, in the dramatized version of the novel, she berates a local government official in the manner of any outraged housewife, the audience cheers.

Meanwhile the republican government has broken its electoral promises, run out of money and sold the United Kingdom to Japan. One component of the deal is that Prince Edward will marry the Japanese emperor's daughter. The story ends with the queen waking up to find that the whole situation has simply been a nightmare and that the Conservatives have won the election after all. Despite this, a sequel was written nearly fifteen years later. Queen Camilla continues the original plot, with the royal family still living on their council estate, but it has not had the same success as the original.

Meanwhile, in reality, the family was living through its most difficult years since the abdication crisis.

The queen's forty years on the throne were celebrated in a 1992 documentary, *Elizabeth R*. It was well made, and widely watched. It concentrated on her work, its purpose being to show how busy she is, how well she does her job, and what a pleasant personality she has. It was, however, a book rather than a film about royalty that was to make this year memorable. Andrew Morton, a journalist with some experience of covering the royals, published a book entitled *Diana: Her True Story*. It revealed to an astonished readership that the Princess of Wales was desperately unhappy in her marriage to Charles who was still seeing his former ladyfriend, Camilla. His family were portrayed as uncaring and unsympathetic towards Diana, who suffered from bulimia, an eating disorder, and had even attempted suicide.

It was later discovered that these revelations, attributed to friends, had come from the princess herself. She and Charles had reached the end of their marriage. They had never had anything in common. He had no patience with her vacuous cultural tastes and lack of serious thought. She was tired of his friends, his family, his courtiers, and above all his mistress. She briefed Morton because she was sick of living a lie. She wanted to hurt her husband, and she had found a way to do so.

Unfortunately she hurt others too. The queen, whose discretion had prevented her from prying into the lives of the couple, was as horrified by the revelations as she was by Diana's trumpeting them in the media. She summoned them both and asked them to give their marriage one more try, though it was obvious to intimates that matters had gone too far.

This turned out only to be the beginning. Andrew and Sarah announced that their marriage, too, was over, and they were followed by Anne and her husband Mark, though in this case the couple had already been separated for years. Yet another blow came in August, while the family were at Balmoral. The *Daily Mirror* had on its front page a photograph of the Duchess of York having her toes sucked beside a swimming pool, by a man identified as her 'financial adviser'. Her daughters were shown nearby. And then the dam burst: another newspaper revealed transcripts of telephone conversations that seemed to be between Diana and a man, James Gilbey, with whom she was clearly intimate. His pet name for her caused the scandal to be known as 'Squidgygate'. There were even more revelations to follow concerning Charles and Camilla, whose private telephone conversations were now published for all the world to read ('Camillagate'). It seemed impossible that so much could have gone wrong so quickly – that such disaster could befall almost an entire generation at once. The year ended with one final tragedy: Windsor Castle caught fire on 20 November. The blaze was ferocious, caused initially by a light bulb coming into contact with a curtain. By a miracle the flames were put out before they spread to the Royal Library, and equally fortunately the rooms gutted, which included the great St George's Hall, were largely empty because redecoration was going on. Nevertheless, the queen was clearly utterly dejected.

Her mood was not improved when the prime minister announced that taxpayers' money would fund the restoration – the cost would be £37 million – and the news was greeted with a chorus of outrage. She was the world's richest woman, said the press, why was she expecting her people to pay? 'When the Castle stands it is theirs,' wrote one journalist, 'but when it burns down it is ours.' The queen was shocked by the hostility shown toward her over this issue. It was the more painful for being so unexpected. In the end she paid most of the bill, but the opening to the public of Buckingham Palace for a few weeks each autumn, commencing the following year, was begun to help cover the cost. The queen also announced that she and Charles would in future pay income tax. That they did not had been a source of continuing resentment, and she had been in the process of arranging to do so. Now she appeared to have been stampeded into the decision to assuage public opinion, which was humiliating.

Only four days after the fire she made a speech at the Guildhall that summed up, with gentle self-mockery, the awful twelve months she had endured: 'This is not a year on which I will look back with undiluted pleasure,' she said. She went on: 'No institution, including the monarchy, should expect to be free from scrutiny. It can be just as effective if it is made with a touch of gentleness and understanding.' For a stoical and self-contained woman to make such a plea is an indication of the level to which her spirits had sunk.

The troubles of Charles and Diana would continue for several years. There were more cruel and disturbing revelations – both in turn were interviewed on television and Diana revealed much, not only about her own recent past but about Charles's fitness to rule. As soon as the programme was released, the queen gave up any hope of a reconciliation between them and asked that they divorce to save further damage. They did so, but the public had already taken sides in the matter and the mud-slinging simply went on. Charles returned to Camilla; Diana took up with a man many considered appallingly unsuitable.

And with him she died, on an August night in Paris. Pursued by photographers, their car crashed into the side of an underpass. The royal family were at Balmoral, where Charles had to break the news to his two sons. In the world beyond the estate walls, grieving was ostentatious and widespread. Diana's gifts of empathy and compassion had been an enormous benefit to the monarchy. She had been able to reach out to people – especially the dispossessed and vulnerable – in a way that the Windsors could not. For a few months she would be treated like a saint, though after that the magic would start to wear off.

Her husband's family, meanwhile, had done their griev-ing in private. Because they were not on view, people thought them callous, and even glad, that Diana had gone, and there was a stirring of public anger when the queen did not appear in London to share in the general mourning. Eventually she did return, and broadcast to the nation. The queen had, for the second time in a matter of years, misjudged the mood of her people. It was later suggested that general hostility was so intense that the monarchy might have fallen, but that is the wildest of exaggerations. When she returned to London, she was forgiven within hours, even minutes, for her absence. The death of Diana was a body-blow to the nation, but it was not a crisis severe enough to threaten the constitutional system.

By the start of the twenty-first century, these difficulties already seemed distant. The millennium began with a cele-bration of the Queen Mother's hundredth birthday, and two years later there would be the queen's Golden Jubilee. In the months before this, however, both the Queen Mother and Princess Margaret died, bringing a sudden end to the affec-tionate and tightly knit family circle in which the queen had spent her whole life. Margaret, who had not been revered by the public for decades owing to her self-indulgent lifestyle and unsuitable friends, had in any case been out of sight, suf-fering from illness, for some time. Her mother, who had car-ried on with undiminished lucidity if with waning energy, had just seen her great-grandson off to university, with the request that if there were any good parties he was to let her know. She had never, in the whole of her long life of service, known anything but the adoration of the British people. She was mourned by a million on the streets of London.

The Golden Jubilee was much like its predecessor a quar-ter of a century earlier, and like the Diamond Jubilee would be a decade later. There were the same tours of Britain, the same chain of bonfires, the same service of thanksgiving at St Paul's. The royal family now included Camilla, married to Charles and created Duchess of Cornwall, as well as Sophie

Rhys-Jones, Countess of Wessex and wife of Prince Edward. Much attention focused on Charles's two sons, William and Harry. New generations, new personalities. The monarchy is constantly renewing itself. That is why it remains strong.

The populism of the monarchy can produce some surprising moments. The queen took part in the opening ceremony for the 2012 Olympics by appearing in a film sequence with the James Bond actor Daniel Craig. She did this without any loss of dignity, though some courtiers must have thought that the situation would be touch and go. In the film she was called upon at the Palace by 007, and then accompanied him to a waiting helicopter, from which both of them, apparently, parachuted into the Olympic Stadium. The pink dress she had been wearing was clearly visible to the thousands below, who could not initially be sure that this falling figure was not Her Majesty rather than a (very masculine) stuntman. Minutes after the landing, the queen herself appeared and took her seat. Endearingly, she was later to ask the Mayor of London, Boris Johnson, what the public reaction had been. The answer is that, in the context of the occasion and the whole atmosphere of the Games, it worked – though it might not have done. A Japanese commentator, apparently believing the monarch had actually made the parachute jump, remarked that the emperor would never have been persuaded to take part in such an event. The image will surely be one of the best-remembered of her reign, and certainly one of the most important royal photographs of the year. Since she volunteered to take part in the event, might it be hoped that this will banish forever the popular misconception that Queen Elizabeth II has no sense of humour?

6

CHARLES, PRINCE OF WALES

'All the time I feel I have to justify my existence.'
Prince Charles, musing on his role

*'Like all the best families, we have our share of
eccentricities, of impetuous and wayward youngsters and of
family disagreements.'*
Queen Elizabeth II, quoted in the *Daily Mail*,
19 October 1989

Charles was born 14 November 1948 at Buckingham Palace.
His birth, like the marriage of his parents a year earlier, was
seen as part of the national recovery that followed the Second
World War. An heir to the throne was important for national
morale and for that sense of continuity that the British people
prize so greatly, and so, like his mother, he was to be the
object of considerable public affection in his earliest years.
Throughout this time he would be surrounded by flattery
and indulgence (among other things he would be voted the
Best Dressed Man in Europe – at the age of five), yet he would

not have things all his own way. His sister Anne, born two years after him, grew into a self-confident tomboy with an aggressive, no-nonsense approach to life that was inherited straight from their father the Duke of Edinburgh.

Charles was a somewhat timid, indecisive child, and seen as lacking toughness. His father certainly saw him in those terms, and was strict with him. Edmund Murray, Winston Churchill's police bodyguard, recalled once being in the courtyard of Buckingham Palace and seeing a car pull up. Out of it got Prince Philip – pulling Charles by the ear. Faced with a role model of such towering presence and personality, Charles made repeated attempts to win his father's approval, but he could not measure up. His thoughtful, reflective, introverted nature was simply too different. His mother was affectionate but left all matters concerning the children's upbringing to her husband, and she was in any case often too preoccupied with affairs of state to pay much heed to his emotional development. It was unfortunate that his infant years coincided with his father's posting as a naval officer to Malta (his mother therefore left him for months at a time to go there) and with her succession to the throne. She was so busy adjusting to her new role that, once again, his needs were forced to come second.

Nevertheless, his mother's absence during his early years meant that he was brought up in the household of his grandparents. He began, at this time, the very close relationship with his grandmother that was to last for the rest of her life. She recognized his shyness as perhaps a characteristic inherited from her husband, and provided a refuge for him from both his mother's preoccupation and his father's strictness. Like most royal children he learned gradually that he was different from others. (It was his sister who was to ask their nanny: 'Why do people keep waving at us?') He noticed that sentries would present arms when he or Anne walked past them. She, as Princess Margaret had done as a child, would strut past just to see them go through this ritual. He, like his mother at a similar age, showed an instinctive consideration by not doing so.

Charles and Anne were to be educated not at home by private tutors, as had been the case with their mother, but at schools. This was seen as a new departure for the royal family, though in fact its more minor members had been shipped off to boarding school for generations. The various male Kent and Gloucester cousins had all gone – or would go – to Eton, and as far back as the reign of Victoria one of her grandsons had been at Wellington. Nevertheless, it was unprecedented for the heir to the throne to sit in a classroom with a chance collection of other boys, and Charles's first day at Hill House Preparatory School in Knightsbridge was much reported in the press.

This was not, in any sense, an ordinary school. It was not an ancient foundation, having been set up in London only five years before the heir to the throne went there in November 1956. It was founded by an English couple living abroad, Colonel and Mrs Townend. (The Colonel would serve as headmaster for fifty-one years until his death, at which point his son took over.) The school's distinctive – some would say hideous – uniform of mustard yellow jersey and rust-coloured corduroy knee-breeches was adapted from Colonel Townend's mountaineering clothes. Mrs Townend believed that, as she put it, 'a grey uniform produces grey minds'. The connection with mountaineering was not coincidental, for the school had been founded in Switzerland and has retained premises there to this day, teaching in two countries simultaneously. This expresses its founder's commitment to promoting an international, cosmopolitan outlook. Whatever the idealism that launched it, its setting in a very upmarket part of London ensured that it was as associated with the socially privileged as a major public school. Charles was photographed, looking somewhat frightened, in the flat cap and blazer that was the school's more formal dress.

From Hill House he passed to a country prep school, Cheam, that had educated Prince Philip before him. This was a far more traditional English establishment, situated on the border between Hampshire and Berkshire, and with a pedigree – extremely unusual for a prep school, since most are Victorian – that went back to 1645. Here he encountered for the first time the bullying that would follow him throughout his schooldays. Boys would be unkind to him to ensure that they were not seen to be toadying, and anyone who was seen being pleasant would be subjected to a sucking sound. Charles was also now in direct competition with his father, who had excelled at the school. While Philip had had a natural ability to play cricket, Charles had neither a flair for the game nor any great interest in it.

From Cheam he went to face an even harsher test. Gordonstoun School is in the north-east of Scotland, not an old foundation at the time but as spartan a place as its bleak surroundings might suggest. It was considered a democratic place because Charles's fellow pupils came from a wider variety of backgrounds than would have been the case at a more traditional public school. He would, it was assumed, be sharing a classroom with the sons of shopkeepers and farmers as well as members of the gentry. This proved to be less the case than had been expected – it was still a very expensive private school, after all. It was, for several reasons, entirely the wrong place for Charles, though it had the single advantage that it was far removed from Fleet Street and the attentions of journalists. Prince Philip, who had been a star cricketer and had become Keeper – the school's term for its head boy – had loved it. Gordonstoun had perfectly suited his extrovert and uncomplicated temperament. He knew that Charles had a very different nature from his own, but believed his son needed the toughening that the school would provide – an escape from the somewhat feminine atmosphere in which the boy had been living at home.

Gordonstoun is housed in a former country house. This, and its outbuildings, form the nucleus of the establishment. Comfort was not a priority when arranging the pupils' accommodation, and the dormitories were unheated. There were compulsory early-morning runs in the depths of the Scottish winter, and a great deal of emphasis placed on sport, sailing and the outdoors, as would be expected of a school whose major asset was its surrounding landscape and the adjacent North Sea. Because the founder had believed the school should be fully involved in the local area, the boys were responsible for running units of the Fire Brigade and mountain rescue, and for lifesaving on the nearby coast. There was no tradition of academic endeavour and significantly Philip, its archetypal successful pupil, had not gone to university. Charles was expected to respond to the environment by becoming less thoughtful and sensitive, yet also by doing well enough academically to gain more-or-less plausible admission to an elite university (Trinity College, Cambridge was chosen on the recommendation of Robin Woods, who was at that time Dean of Windsor and had been there).

One good thing about Gordonstoun, at least, was that its pupils – dressed in casual pullovers, and bare-kneed in shorts or kilts – were not as instantly recognizable as privileged individuals as were the inmates of Eton, for instance, whose tail-coats so infuriate the proponents of equality. The choice of Gordonstoun could be seen as a gesture toward the new, more egalitarian era into which society had supposedly progressed. It was a brilliant, inspired deflection of any criticism that the royals enjoyed a pampered existence. At the time Charles entered the school, in 1962, it received a good deal of coverage in the media. Though Morayshire is a tranquil and beautiful place, and though the Gordonstoun buildings are gracious, television images made it look as bleak and remote as Dartmoor Prison. Few young people of his age, as they trudged to their comprehensives, would have wanted to change places with Charles, or considered him to be wallowing in privilege.

The expectations placed on him were a very tall order and Charles was, from the first, unhappy at the school. It is remembered that he was always reluctant to return there at the start of term, just as countless public schoolboys have been before and since. When the car was due to leave he would often be difficult to find, and would delay his departure with lengthy farewells for as long as he could. He found it difficult to make friends and suffered, as he already had at his prep school, from bullying. He was especially vulnerable on the rugby field, where others could knock him down and get away with it. His father would not have been sympathetic to any complaint and his mother, who of course adored her husband, trusted his judgement and regarded the notion of Charles being formed into a second Philip as a happy – and perhaps necessary – outcome.

In the midst of this, Charles found temporary refuge in Australia. He was sent to Geelong Grammar School for two terms, to sample education in a Commonwealth country. The school was a relaxed place and the climate was naturally less rigorous than that of Morayshire. The attitude of his schoolmates was also far more sympathetic. He was reputedly almost at once called a 'pommy bastard', which can be seen as a token of familiarity and affection. The boys – and Geelong, like all his schools, was entirely male – were curious about him but also friendly. Australians are a talkative people who automatically assume a sense of equality with whoever they meet. To Charles this must have been a godsend. He delighted in the lack of protocol, just as he appreciated the chance to 'be himself' without the need to compete with his father's or with a host of other expectations. He was also to a large extent left alone by the press. Small wonder that he was to retain very happy associations with Australia and to enjoy his future visits there. Small wonder, too, that the experiment was to be repeated, after a fashion, with his two younger brothers – Andrew would go for a term to Lakefield College in Canada while Edward, seen for some years as the most academic of the queen's children, would spend a term not as a pupil but as an assistant master at a highly prestigious boys' school in Christchurch, New Zealand.

Returning to Gordonstoun, Charles had some share in the glory that often comes to those who are at the top of a school. Like his father, he took part in a production of *Macbeth* and played the title role. Like Philip, he too became Keeper. Unlike his father, he would not be an enthusiastic old boy and he certainly never considered sending his own sons to the school – he later referred to it as 'Colditz in kilts' – although Prince Harry would undoubtedly have thrived there in the atmosphere of high spirits, athletic competition and more modest academic expectations. Andrew and Edward seemed to have had far happier experiences of Gordonstoun than their brother did, though by the time the youngest of the boys arrived there were not only heated rooms but female pupils. The family connection did not die when this generation had passed through the school, for Princess Anne – always her father's daughter – sent her own children there.

Charles went to Cambridge, in the autumn of 1967, not through personal choice and certainly not through having demonstrated the requisite academic ability (he achieved two A-levels: a B in history and a C in French). He read history, archeology and anthropology. His education was planned by a committee, chaired by his mother and including Prime Minister Harold Wilson and the Archbishop of Canterbury. It was, however, a good choice. It gave him the chance to live in a civilized academic community and, for the first time, to make his own friends – or so it seemed. One contemporary recalled that: 'He was very nice but his friends were chosen for him – and they were not [nice].' This time, it seems that his colleagues were not afraid to be seen speaking to him, and one of his neighbours interested him in joining the University Labour Club (courtiers advised him not to). He lived in ordinary rooms in college and not, as his grandfather and other forebears had done, isolated in a distant building with only tutors for company. In fact, when asked for his impressions of living in Trinity, he mentioned the novelty of being awoken in the mornings by the arrival of the dust cart. At the end of three years he was to graduate with a 2:2, and have the distinction of being the first heir apparent to have earned a university degree. Like all holders of a Cambridge BA, he was entitled to style himself MA six years after completing his first term.

Charles was never intended to be an ordinary undergraduate, or to have to the full the experience his contemporaries were enjoying. He had other perspectives and priorities. His studies in archeology were a personal hobby (and one which he still maintains) but, while he had no future to worry about and no career to plan or to compete for, he still had a good deal to do. He undertook flying lessons with the Cambridge University Air Training Squadron, and left Cambridge for a term during his second year to attend the University of Wales at Aberystwyth, taking a crash course in Welsh and Welsh history. This was the first time that any part of a Prince of Wales's training had been undertaken in Wales. He was, of course, to be formally initiated as Prince of Wales, and it would be a politic gesture to say some words in the Welsh language. (Nationalists, needless to say, resented his status as an imposed and alien presence in the Principality.)

Charles did not look like an undergraduate of his generation. With his short hair, ties and tweed jackets, and his beetle-crusher shoes, he seemed more like an old-fashioned prep school master than a product of the sixties. At Cambridge, a traditional university, there were other young men who dressed in this manner, and doubtless this was true at Aberystwyth too, but the sheer neatness of the prince and those around him made them stand out like the proverbial sore thumb. His police detectives were especially conspicuous. When his protection officers tried to behave like students their police footwear, as well as their bearing and manner and – in this small town – their unfamiliar faces, gave them away at once in pubs and cafes, and they would often be greeted with mocking exclamations of 'Evening, officer!'

Charles's stay in Wales did nothing to endear him to the

more extreme nationalists, but it did please many others among the Welsh. Older people, in particular ladies, would look out for him in the streets and the tea shops, and would go home delighted if they had seen him. He did not make any close friends at Aberystwyth, though to be fair there was little opportunity to do so, but as a self-confessed 'incurable romantic' he was highly susceptible to the beauty of the language and the strength of the Welsh national identity. He takes seriously his connection with Wales. He has bought a property in Carmarthenshire, which is rented out when he is not using it, and he employs a personal harpist whose instrument can be seen by visitors to Clarence House.

He had held the title Prince of Wales since 1958, but was not officially invested until he had come of age. The outdoor ceremony, held at Caernarfon Castle in July 1969, was a triumph. It brought worldwide attention to Wales, boosted the local economy, and proved to be the usual happy hunting ground for the manufacturers of souvenirs. The setting was almost too romantic – the looming grey walls of the medieval fortress brightened by banners and uniforms, the dais designed by Lord Snowdon with its slate thrones and slanting, transparent canopy, the beautiful, specially designed princely crown which his mother placed upon his head. Instead of the pseudo-Elizabethan foppery that had so appalled his great-uncle David at the same ceremony in 1911, Charles was dressed in the dark blue uniform of the Royal Regiment of Wales – the first of many colonelcies he would hold and of the numerous military uniforms he would wear. His speech was partly in Welsh. This was the royal event of the decade, a spectacle not to be surpassed until his mother's Silver Jubilee some eight years later, and it was a successful beginning to his public life.

Anne, meanwhile, had had an unremarkable school career at Benenden, a top-drawer girls' boarding school in Kent. Untroubled by academic concerns, she spent her schooldays happily, developing the interest in equestrian sports that was to take her, ultimately, to the Olympics and to marriage with a fellow eventer. Charles, too, had hopes of competing in the Olympics, but failed to make selection for the British polo team, just as he had failed to get a Blue in the sport at Cambridge. Despite these disappointments he was a devoted player until the nineties, when advancing age obliged him to participate less often. He still does so occasionally if irregularly. Inheriting the passion from his father and great-uncle, he has passed on this enthusiasm in turn to both his sons.

He was typically described, in his early twenties, as 'dreamy and artistic'. He played the cello, and painted in watercolours. The public had an impression of him as serious, earnest, yet with a sense of humour that was schoolboyish and inoffensive. The fact that he liked The Goons and The Goodies, and could recite sketches by the former, endeared him to many.

After university he went into the armed forces. He had already had flying training at university, but now took this a stage further at the RAF College at Cranwell, earning his pilot's wings. He then went straight to another Service academy and underwent officer training all over again. This time he attended Dartmouth, as his father and grandfather had done. He was to make the Navy a more-or-less full-time commitment for the next five years, serving as a junior officer at sea on a destroyer, on frigates, and on the aircraft carrier *Hermes* – for he qualified as a helicopter pilot. In 1976, his final year in the Senior Service, he was given his own command, captaining the minesweeper HMS *Bronington* – a minesweeper so given to pitching and tossing that, according to her crew, she would 'roll on wet grass'. For several years the media would be filled with pictures of him in a variety of military uniforms: in RAF blue, being presented with his 'wings'; in a naval pullover and cap aboard ship; undertaking parachute training with the Army; crossing a river by rope during a training exercise. The press dubbed him 'Action Man' at this time, and he deserved the title. He was obliged, as future Commander-in-Chief of the Forces, to gain credibility and respect in advance by undergoing certain rites of passage.

He became Colonel-in-Chief of the Parachute Regiment, for instance, the good opinion of whose members is not easily won. It is not especially easy to pilot an aircraft, and jumping out of one – even with a parachute – is not something everyone is willing to do. There is no doubt that Charles pushed himself to gain these qualifications, and that he deserves respect for having done so.

His brother Andrew followed him into the Navy as a career officer, becoming a successful helicopter pilot and seeing action in the Falklands campaign. Their younger sibling Prince Edward also opted for military service, but his choice of the most difficult branch of the forces – the Royal Marines – was unfortunate. When Charles left the Navy it was to chair a committee that planned events for the Silver Jubilee of 1977. From that time on he has devoted himself full-time to royal duties and to the numerous charities he has set up.

From his university days onward he was increasingly guided by his great-uncle, Lord Mountbatten. It is difficult to overestimate the influence of the older man upon the younger. An indulgent, avuncular figure during Charles's boyhood, a naval hero and a man who had held high office in both war and peace (as Supreme Commander South East Asia and as Viceroy of India), he was what Charles aspired to be – supremely confident but without Philip's brash and sometimes offensive manner. His urbanity, his wide interests, even his implausibly left-wing views (which may have given Charles a certain liberal bent), made him mentor of choice for the prince. At his funeral in 1979, Charles's wreath bore a handwritten message: 'To my HGF [Honorary Grandfather] and GU [Great-Uncle] from his loving and devoted HGS and GN Charles.'

Mountbatten had indeed occupied the place in Charles's life that had been left empty by the early death of his grandfather, but ironically he was nothing at all like George VI. Notoriously, overwhelmingly vain, he had none of the late king's innate modesty, and was characterized by a restless ambition that kings do not need to possess. He was also far more intelligent, and more worldly, than Charles's actual grandfather had been. King George, for instance, would never have advised Charles, as Mountbatten did, that: 'In a case like yours, the man should sow his wild oats and have as many affairs as he can before settling down.' Charles was to follow this advice, though he always sought to be discreet. There is no doubt that he enjoyed a number of close friendships while single. Lucia Santa Cruz, the daughter of the Chilean Ambassador, was the first whose name was bandied around by the press, while he was at Cambridge. Some of these relationships were serious enough to heighten speculation, but upper-class young women such as Anna Wallace or Lady Jane Wellesley did not relish the thought of life in the royal family, and though countless girls have dreamed of marrying a prince it is worth remembering that some of those who have been in a position to do so have rejected the fairy tale out of hand. They know that beyond the glitter of the wedding awaits a lifetime of routine and formality and intrusion by the media. Spirited young women who are used to being independent naturally find this an unwelcome prospect, as did Elizabeth Bowes-Lyon two generations earlier.

Modern women were also likely to have a 'past'. After advising his nephew to sow some wild oats, Lord Mountbatten had gone on to say that for a wife he should 'choose a suitable, attractive, and sweet-charactered girl before she had met anyone else she might fall for'. Mountbatten had already engineered one of the most successful marriages in royal history by bringing Elizabeth and Philip together, and now had in mind a candidate for Charles. This was Amanda Knatchbull, his granddaughter. Critics saw this, as they had seen the previous wedding, as an attempt to raise the standing of his own family. ('The House of Mountbatten reigns!' he had boasted when his nephew became consort to the monarch.) Charles, moreover, genuinely liked the young lady. Respectful of his uncle's judgement, he actually proposed to her in 1979, but

the death of Mountbatten himself – as well as her grandmother and youngest brother – in a terrorist attack that summer is
likely to have caused her to reconsider her future. After such
a personal tragedy, the notion of life in a high-profile family
may well have seemed too daunting.

Charles, in any case, was always more attracted by mature
women. The most important friendships he developed were
with two women who were already married. Dale Tryon was
the Australian wife of a businessman. Charles, who gave her
the nickname 'Kanga', delighted in her irreverent sense of
humour. The other woman was Camilla Parker Bowles. He
had first met her while she was single and they had found a
mutual empathy that promised well. Charles had been a serving naval officer at the time and, preoccupied with his duties,
had not pursued the relationship – or at least not fast enough
to prevent her from marrying elsewhere. Her husband was
an officer in the Household Cavalry and, in the value system
that still applies within the world of the mess, the greatest sin
that an officer can commit is to steal the wife of a colleague.
Given his innate decency and desire to please, as well as his
awareness of the scandal that could result from any such liai-
son, it can be assumed that the prince agonized over this relationship for years. The friendship was sometimes chaste and
sometimes not, but they developed a rapport that was likely
to make for a successful marriage, and which spoiled him for
any other woman. The public was largely unaware of these
two relationships though *Private Eye*, the satirical magazine,
reported them all along.

When Charles had reached the age of thirty without marrying, both his family and the nation at large became increasingly impatient. There must be no echoes of Edward VIII,
and an heir to the throne who remained steadfastly single
suggested a lack of seriousness that was not acceptable. The
public would wink at a certain amount of philandering while
a prince was young, but they expected him to settle down
soon and not have too much fun. The privileges the royal

family enjoy have to be seen to be balanced by the observance of routine, duty and formality if public resentment is to be avoided.

The young woman who became his wife was actually the sister of a former girlfriend, Lady Sarah Spencer. They met at a shoot held on the Spencer family's estate, Althorp. Charles was drawn to her girlish shyness, her sense of humour, sympathetic nature and love of country pursuits. There was no question of his being struck by instant passion. He developed a fondness for her, while she was overwhelmed by him. His greater age – there was twelve years between them – as well as his position were somewhat awe-inspiring for a schoolgirl, even one who belonged to the aristocracy. Lady Diana Spencer was unacademic, athletic, and of a classic English beauty that was just beginning to ripen as she emerged from adolescence. Her lack of education (she was later to describe herself as being 'as thick as a plank') was compensated for by a natural charm and winsomeness that instantly won people over. Despite her upper-class credentials she seemed to be precisely what the public wanted – an ordinary girl, chosen almost by chance from among their daughters, modest enough to be a dutiful wife and mother. It was Elizabeth Bowes-Lyon all over again.

Charles proposed, she accepted. The engagement was announced at the beginning of 1981 and the wedding – the greatest royal spectacular since the coronation – took place in July. 'This is the stuff of fairy tales' announced Robert Runcie, the Archbishop of Canterbury, who conducted the service. No one was to remember, until much later, that when interviewed for television and asked if they were in love, Diana had gushed: 'Of course!' while her fiancé had said, with apparent cynicism: 'Whatever "in love" means.'

Though they were visibly happy at the beginning, the affection soon wore thin. They had so little in common. Charles's earnest desire to do good was something his wife could appreciate – she was to give notable service to charities herself – but their attitudes toward this, as to everything else, were very different. She proved not to be shy at all. Instead she was strong-willed, demanding and confrontational. Their rows became legendary. He saw her, increasingly, as tiresome and juvenile. She did not share his cultural interests, or like his friends, and he was irritated that the media – enchanted by her glamour and accessibility, which contrasted strongly with the formal aloofness of her husband's family – increasingly showed more interest in her than in him. Though the couple had two sons, and were united by affection for them, their approaches as parents were as different as everything else about them. She wanted the boys to grow up amid as much normality as possible. She dressed them casually, took them unannounced on visits to public places, and involved them in charity work so that they could see another side of life. Charles got them interested in polo and shooting. As they grew up they came to look more and more like him, dressing in the same way in charcoal-grey suits and slip-on shoes.

There was little affection left in the Waleses' marriage by the beginning of the 1990s. The simple fact was that Charles had not given up his friendship with Mrs Parker Bowles, and would not do so. She was, apart from any other status she had had in his life, an old personal friend, and he would not think of doing without her company. Diana had known all along that this would be so, and was to confess that she had been obsessed even at her wedding by the thought of this rival. She and Charles, equally stubborn, clashed head on over this issue, which was never resolved. She in any case found she hated the gilded cage in which his family lived. She sought distraction not only in the philanthropy that brought her such a wealth of public affection but in romantic friendships of her own.

The 'war of the Waleses' broke out in 1992 with the pub-lication of a book: *Diana: Her True Story*, by the journal-ist Andrew Morton. This made public what had been half known and hinted at for years – that the marriage was at an acrimonious stalemate. It also revealed that Diana's 'fairy tale' had been such a sham that she had actually attempted suicide. She depicted her husband in a particularly unflattering light: as a man who was uncaring, unsympathetic, and preoccupied with someone else. The sources from which this narrative was assembled were supposedly friends of the princess who had been authorized to speak for her. Only later did it transpire that she herself had given extensive interviews to Morton; Diana was the source.

The next few years were a time that monarchists would like to forget. It was revealed that Diana had had at least two extramarital relationships and that Charles's friendship with Camilla was intensive and intimate. Though Diana was able to win a good deal of public sympathy as a wronged wife, no one emerged from these revelations with any credit. Matters simply went from bad to worse as the prince, in an interview with Jonathan Dimbleby, allowed himself, like a defendant being cross-examined in court, to be cornered into admitting adultery. Diana responded with an interview of her own – a stage-managed soul-baring in which she too conceded unfaithfulness, but within the context of a loveless marriage. She threw in for good measure the observation that she thought her husband would not make a good king. Though Charles did not want to put his side with the same directness, he fired back a few salvos through his friends. He had initially held back, in part, because of the effect of this squabbling on his sons. The public was appalled, and well-wishers of both parties were braced for an ugly confrontation that might last the rest of the couple's lives. Given that Anne and Andrew both divorced in 1992, the royal family's previous air of rigorous respectability was badly compromised. While the queen remained above criticism, the press now seized on their chance to comment freely on the younger generation of royals to whom they did not feel obliged to show any deference. So spectacular was the damage done by the family to itself that the press lost all restraint. The Waleses announced their separation in 1992, and on 28 August 1996 they divorced. One year later, Diana was dead.

Whatever the rights and wrongs of the situation, death brought her almost instant sanctity, while Charles endured an opprobrium such as he had never known. As he followed her coffin down The Mall, he could feel the hostility in the crowds and hear the shouts of: 'You didn't deserve her!' No one could be sure his standing would ever recover, or whether public opinion would allow him the future for which he was destined.

Yet he kept his head down, carried on with his work and his official duties – and continued his friendship with Camilla. He remained stubbornly determined throughout that this would remain the case no matter what it cost him in terms of popularity. And gradually he won. The relationship was eventually accepted by the queen and the public. The fact that Camilla never openly uttered a word about her part in the affair was helpful, as was the fact that she took to royal duties effortlessly and with genuine flair. As time passed, people grew accustomed to his new consort and their marriage, at Windsor Guildhall in 2005, while not a national celebration, was at least seen as putting the family back on a normal footing. It can now be seen that Camilla is the companion he should have had all along, and that there is in their marriage a contentment that would never have been attainable between Charles and Diana. The war of the Waleses was bruising and traumatic for the people of Britain and the Commonwealth as well as for the participants. Most are simply relieved it is now over.

There is much to like and admire about Charles. His genuinely caring attitude to social ills is something he developed for himself. He could easily have spent his life making bland, forgettable speeches that avoided controversy. Instead he has chosen to join the fray over issues he believes in, to risk causing outrage and to court criticism that is often shrill to the point of hysteria. Having been an undergraduate in the rebellious sixties without reflecting any of the concern for social change that preoccupied many young people at that time, he became precisely that sort of ideological crusader in middle age (he has described himself as a 'dissident'), while his contemporaries were settling down into complacency.

He has wonderfully wide interests. He is not only a qualified pilot but a useful polo player and a watercolourist of some talent. He is also an author. His book about architecture and the environment – *A Vision of Britain* – was a bestseller in the 1980s, and a newer book, *Harmony* (2010), brings together his views on religion, medicine, agriculture and pollution. A children's book, *The Old Man of Lochnagar* (a story he invented for his younger siblings when they were children), was made into a musical. He is a member of the Magic Circle, that highly secretive association of conjurers, admission to which can only be gained by proven skill in magic. One evening, as television viewers watched a concert by the Bach Choir in London, a camera panned along the rows of singing faces and passed that of Prince Charles, whose presence in their midst was not even referred to by the commentator. He skis and fishes and takes part in archeological digs. He has followed a variety of personal interests and used the opportunities offered by his position to experience a wider spectrum of life than most people realize or give him credit for. And he has a deeply spiritual side. His friendship with the South African writer Laurens van der Post (a godfather to Prince William), whom the press dubbed Charles's 'spiritual guru', reflected a serious preoccupation with metaphysics, as do his visits to the spiritual home of Greek Orthodoxy, Mount Athos.

One aspect of his work that has received little publicity is his interest in Islamic art. He is a patron of the Oxford Centre for Islamic Studies, and knows so much about the subject that he was involved in setting up this institution. He established the Prince's School of Traditional Arts originally to preserve and pass on Islamic design skills that were being lost in the lands in which they had been developed. Though the idea of offering postgraduate courses in this field was not his – it was introduced at the Royal College of Art – Charles gave it a permanent home and lent his influence to further it. As a member of staff explained: 'Skills that you can no longer learn in parts of the Middle East are actually still available here – they have survived in the unlikely setting of Shoreditch!' The school's remit has now broadened to include the preservation of *any* artistic tradition that is under threat. There is no other institution that provides such high-level qualifications (the M.Phil and PhD) in this subject.

He is also a prominent agriculturalist, running his estate at Highgrove according to the principles of organic farming to which he is committed. He has created a business empire through the foods marketed under the name Duchy Originals, an enterprise that has made healthy profits, which are ploughed back into the charities he supports. He is also possessed of strong opinions on alternative medicine that can infuriate members of the medical profession (he has suggested that GPs offer homeopathic remedies as well as traditional ones) and, typically, he has set up yet another official body – this time the Prince's Foundation for Integrated Health – to further his beliefs. Though he may lack a qualified doctor's years of study and practical training, no one can doubt his sincerity when he makes pronouncements on medical matters, or question the fact that his opinions are the result of deep thought and reflection.

What Charles has brought to the role of Prince of Wales is a good deal of imagination. He has not only fulfilled the normal duties of the post – deputizing for his mother in opening ceremonies, conferring honours, visiting regions, cities, towns, serving as titular head of military units – he has also found ways to affect agricultural, architectural and social policy. His influence is unofficial but immense, as can be seen in the manner in which he prevented two high-profile building projects from being carried out. One was the proposed extension to the National Gallery in Trafalgar Square, memorably described by the prince in a speech as being like 'a monstrous carbuncle on the face of an old and much-loved friend'. The other was the former Chelsea Barracks, scheduled for redevelopment as luxury housing. Though a less conspicuous site, this too was architecturally sensitive, and a well-placed letter from the prince to the owner of the land, the Sultan of Qatar, stopped work almost immediately.

Naturally, the prince is highly unpopular with certain members of the architectural profession, as well as with many others. Nothing could be more calculated to infuriate those of a 'progressive' bent than the notion of an unelected public figure, lacking any professional training in the fields in which he voices strident views, undoing the work of others in the name of aesthetics. His preference for craftsmanship and beauty draw predictable sneers from those who think he is trying to recreate a cosy – as well as mythical – bucolic past through the building projects he encourages (the new town of Poundbury, built on land owned by him in Dorset, is an example). Architects naturally want to produce work that is original and individual, enabling them to set their own stamp on the age; pastiches of established styles allow them little scope to do so. Though of course there are members of the profession who specialize in traditional forms, many take the view that now technology enables them to build higher, more daring and innovative structures, they do not wish to be confined to the more modest scale and unadventurous design of the past, whose buildings are all around us anyway. They also resent the way in which, though their names and reputations can be made by a successful building, they can also be ruined overnight by the negative publicity following a single comment by the prince. His concern for the harmony of the built environment is seen as unacceptable interference, and even bullying. Nevertheless a surprising number of people agree with him. Architects are seen as arrogant, cocksure and uninterested in what the populace actually likes. There are many among his future subjects who applaud his views, however outspoken they may be.

Royals are naturally expected to take up charitable patronage. They usually do it well, and can become seriously engaged with the causes they officially represent, as has been seen with Princess Anne's work for Save the Children. Their involvement brings a considerable increase in media interest and funding to the campaigns or organizations they support, and this aspect is a very strong argument in favour of monarchy. There are enough members of the family – seventeen of them at present – undertaking this sort of work to cover a very wide range of organizations, and once connected with a charity they tend to remain its champion for a long time.

Contrast this with the situation in the United States. The First Lady is the traditional, high-profile charitable patron, the only American with a social standing comparable to that of royalty. Once her husband is elected, she chooses a cause – or perhaps one major cause and several minor ones – that she will make her own. Barbara Bush, as is well known, selected child literacy. The trouble is that a president's wife is only there for four years, or perhaps eight. When she leaves, all her power to raise awareness, to generate funds and attention and prestige, goes with her. Her successor, naturally wanting to make her own mark, will choose something entirely different. With the British royals the charitable connection, and the vital publicity that it brings, is there for their lifetime, and after that they may well be replaced by another family member.

This promise of long-term commitment is seen very obviously in the case of Charles. So far, he has founded seventeen philanthropic organizations, known collectively as the Prince's Charities. He is also patron of some 350 additional ones throughout the Commonwealth. He established the Prince's Trust in 1976, aimed at helping young people – aged between eighteen and thirty – with backgrounds as truants or petty criminals, or who had been in care or were long-term unemployed. It is run by a council chaired by the prince, and best known for giving grants to individuals to start their own business or to develop particular ideas. It also provides business mentoring and valuable work experience for young people. It is able to do this because it raises money through events (several high-profile rock concerts have helped to fund its work) and donations from notable benefactors, including Bill Gates. While its royal origins give it prestige – the queen granted it a charter – it is the business community that provides the all-important financial backing.

Through this and other charitable endeavours, Charles is brought into contact with a world of celebrity glitter in which he would not perhaps be expected to feel at home. In fact, he is quite comfortable in the company of film stars and rock musicians – he is on bantering terms with many of them – though perhaps not as much on their wavelength as newspaper pictures occasionally make him seem. Once, upon entering a room full of media personalities he mentioned, *sotto voce*, that since he never watches television he had no idea who any of them were. It is also authoritatively stated that he wears ear-plugs when attending rock concerts. Hardly surprising, perhaps, for a man whose taste is so firmly entrenched in high culture. He is patron of the Royal Opera and the English and Welsh National Operas as well as president of the Royal Shakespeare Company.

He has by no means confined his interests to his own country or the Commonwealth. As a representative of the British monarchy, his presence can be valuable elsewhere in the world. When, in 1986, Harvard University celebrated its 350th anniversary, it sought a guest speaker who would be suited to the dignity of the occasion. The obvious choice, President Ronald Reagan, apparently could not be asked because his presence would be viewed as 'political'. Prince Charles was invited instead – as an articulate, interested member of a revered institution – proving perhaps the power of the monarchy to meet all situations and smooth over all differences.

His interest often lies deeper than mere speech-making, however. His Trust has made possible the saving of damaged and endangered literary manuscripts in St Petersburg. His architecture students, as a summer school project, planned the restoration and re-design of Potsdam in Germany, a town – it is the Prussian equivalent of Windsor – that was destroyed by RAF bombers in 1945 and then badly rebuilt by communist planners. He has taken an interest in the heritage of Romania ever since the reign of Nicolae Ceauşescu, whose megalomania was responsible for the wholesale destruction of monasteries and churches there. Charles, a member of whose family (Queen Marie) is buried in a Romanian church, has visited the country and become patron of a conservation project there. As if this is not enough, he has bought two houses there, one of them (it seems extraordinary!) in Transylvania. Small wonder that he has been, according to rumour, invited to become king of the country by local monarchists.

That offer may be the nearest he gets to a throne for some time to come. If his mother lives as long as *her* mother did, he will be seventy-nine when he succeeds. There was a notion, during Australia's bicentennial year in 1988, that he might become Governor-General of the country. He would have been delighted, and would have done the job very well. As we have seen, however, it was made clear as early as the 1920s that Dominions would not have such officials foisted on them by London, and Australian prime ministers have been adamant that not even the country's future ruler can be given a post that is intended only for one of its own citizens.

Nevertheless, the prince has found a multitude of ways to make himself useful. It would have been very easy to lead a life of mild duty and predominant personal pleasure, as did his predecessor in the twenties and thirties. He could have been a nondescript figure whose opinions no one would have bothered to read in newspapers. Instead he has taken up a host of issues, often stirring a hornet's nest of controversy in doing so. He has created debate, forced people to think, focused attention on unpopular causes, and often proved himself to be ahead of the trend in doing so. Whether or not people agree with his views or hate them, he is doing valuable work for the country, the Commonwealth and the world. In the popular parlance, giving 'value for money' in terms of hard work and dedication.

A paragon among previous Princes of Wales was Prince Henry, the son of King James I, who may be considered the perfect pattern of an heir to the throne: a Renaissance figure, wise beyond his years, an athlete, a would-be military hero, and – more importantly – the founder of the national and royal collections that have graced the country ever since. Henry died in 1612 as a result of a typhoid fever, all his glorious potential laid waste by his early death. Given a much longer life in which to be useful, has Charles done better than Henry, or any other of his princely predecessors in terms of his commitment, industry, breadth and depth of vision, devotion to duty, imagination, care for the people of the realms over which the British monarch rules? Is he, therefore, the best Prince of Wales there has ever been?

Yes.

7

PRINCE WILLIAM, DUKE OF CAMBRIDGE, 'WILLS'

'I don't deliberately select my friends because of their background. If I enjoy someone's company, then that's all that counts. I have many different friends who aren't from the same background as me and we get on really well ... it's brilliant.'

Prince William, in interview

Prince William is, naturally, the prospect for the future that monarchists most cherish. Not only does he offer the physical guarantee that the House of Windsor will continue through another generation, but the hope that a line will eventually be drawn under the unfortunate matter of his parents' broken marriage. Descended both from Charles and the sainted Diana, he unites both sides of a quarrel that still reverberates.

He was born on 21 June 1982, and has naturally been the subject of close public interest ever since. Just as he is the product of a home in which two such different people tried to live together, so his background and nature represent a blend of the two cultures – the traditional and the modern, the old and the new – to which he was exposed. Shortly after his parents divorced, an American magazine commented that a glance at the clothes worn by the two boys would indicate which of their parents had had custody of them that day. With their father they wore tweeds, or blazers, and ties, while with Diana they were dressed in baseball caps and sweatshirts. While with him they went to shoots and to the Guards Polo Club; she took them to have hamburgers at Ed's Diner in the King's Road and on funfair rides at Alton Towers. However much this may cause traditionalists to shake their heads, it looks as if she succeeded in giving them a hefty dose of normal childhood experiences. In addition she ensured that they learned about the other side of life by, for instance, having them accompany her on night-time visits to the rough sleepers on the Embankment. She gave both her sons a sense of duty toward the less fortunate that has later been manifested in the charity work they undertake.

She also enabled them to suffer the occasional frustrations of ordinary life. To cite one example out of many, she took the boys on an unscheduled visit to the Imperial War Museum in London. One of the attractions there is The Blitz Experience, a simulated Second World War air raid. Visitors sit crammed into a shelter while appropriate sound effects can be heard outside. The ground shakes, and there is the smell of cordite and of burning. It is realistic and popular. When Diana and the boys arrived, museum staff explained that there was a lengthy queue for the shelter but offered to take them straight in. Diana refused to inconvenience people who had waited their turn, and the boys went home without seeing it. This too can have done them nothing but good.

In the 'culture war' between tradition and modernity it was always going to be the former that won. William had from the beginning a strong sense of duty and this was nurtured by the influence of the queen (who regularly invited him to tea at Windsor while he was at school across the river), Prince Philip, Prince Charles and the Queen Mother. His *own* mother, whatever her views on the rest of her husband's family, also wanted him to be a good king. He has, all his life, had access to good advice and good example. The surroundings in which he has grown up are the kind that stir the imagination and impart a sense of history and duty and of privilege that must be earned. He has responded to this, as has his brother, by choosing a career of service, and in both cases this has won the approval of the public. If, instead, he had wanted to be a craftsman and furniture designer like Viscount Linley, would it have made much difference? Probably not. The important thing is that he is a decent young man seeking to earn his way, and to achieve a sense of personal worth through what he does before his future catches up with him.

William is nothing like his father was at a similar age, but he is comfortable in a world of tradition and ceremonial and conservative, guards-officer values. He pursues hobbies – the polo and shooting to which he was introduced by Charles have become his passions too – that are typical of the class to which his mother belonged. He looks relaxed in tweeds and suits and uniforms. He loves the armed forces and, having been in all three of them, has had intensive experience in two. It has always been obvious, too, that his involvement is more than merely cosmetic. He relishes the chance to know and to work with members of other classes. Significantly the Service in which William feels most at home is the most relatively democratic of them – the Royal Air Force. He is genuinely interested in his job and in continuing with it for as long as he can. He sees it as a career, though it is very likely it will come to an end as soon as his father succeeds and he himself becomes Prince of Wales, if not before.

His upbringing has been entirely different from his father's. While Charles was the son of an affectionate but preoccupied reigning sovereign, William's parents were both affectionate and available. He had from the beginning – and without any debate in the media – the opportunity to go to normal, if private, schools, attending a nearby day school then a boarding prep school followed by a major public school. He does not appear to have suffered in the way that Charles did from bullying or from others' fear of being seen to toady. He has a circle of friends who seem entirely average and more varied than one might think, although he could be expected to be most comfortable within the social class in which his background and interests lie.

In the case of William and Harry there was no formal committee to decide the course their education would take, regardless of their natural inclinations or abilities. Rather the priority was to give them an experience that was conventional and as sheltered as possible from both the media and the responsibilities of public life. There was, for instance, some talk of William attending with his father the handover of Hong Kong in June 1997. This was one of the major public events of the decade, but he said he did not yet feel ready for such duties, and it was left at that.

The choice of Eton for both boys' secondary education was surprising – and disappointing – to some who might have hoped for a less predictable, or conventional path. Though Gordonstoun has naturally featured in recent royal history, Charles's memories of his own time there are likely to have been decisive when it came to choosing his sons' school even though William, a more robust and less thoughtful young man than his father was, might ironically have fitted in better there. Eton, however, is not only a royal foundation but the school which some of his relatives – James Ogilvy, and Lord Frederick Windsor – had recently attended. It was particularly favoured by the Queen Mother, and Diana's father and brother had also been there. There was never, as far as is known, any serious suggestion that they should go to a local comprehensive school. The populist gestures made by the monarchy tend to be rather smaller and more subtle than that.

William managed the Common Entrance exam successfully; Harry found it more of a struggle. The school, whatever its historical associations with aristocracy, is academically very hard to get into and perhaps even harder to stay in. It requires its pupils, who have to learn to organize their time for themselves, to work according to personal motivation and not the demands of staff. There is such a heavy workload to get through that there is no time for idleness, and to keep up requires constant, sustained effort. It had been thought that Harry might be happier at Radley College, which is nearby, but he enrolled in the same house at the same school as William.

It cannot have helped either boy that during this formative time of their lives their parents divorced, the newspapers were filled with highly personal – and deeply embarrassing – revelations, and that many members of the public took sides with either their father or mother. After that, in the late summer of 1997, their mother suddenly died just as they were about to return to school, and they were required to attend their first official funeral. Though they naturally garnered immense public sympathy their father was vilified and they must have been aware of it too. At least their mother's death had ended a protracted and upsetting feud between their parents that would surely otherwise have carried on for many years to come.

Both of them spent happy years at Eton. Set in water meadows in the shadow of Windsor Castle, a cluster of venerable ancient buildings that represent probably the most historic few acres of English ground apart from Westminster, it would be a difficult place to dislike. William kept up with his academic work and excelled at sports, becoming 'Keeper', or Captain, of the water polo team. He ended his career as Captain of his house and a member of 'Pop', the gorgeously dressed prefectorial society. He did well enough in his A-levels (C in biology, B in history of art and A in geography) to go on to university.

Harry too found his forte, in the school's Combined Cadet Force. Destined by inclination to be a soldier, he followed this path and won the Sword of Honour for best cadet. Both princes played polo. Both grew up to be ordinary, pleasant young men.

William's education may have been 'elitist', but the process of applying to university and spending a gap year put him through the same experiences as thousands of other young men and women, and his life was at least comparable with theirs. His spent time doing military training in Belize, went to East Africa, and spent weeks in Chile with Raleigh International, sleeping in a communal room and carrying out chores that included cleaning the lavatory. He never complained about discomfort or hard work. People are now so accustomed to the notion that royalty are just like the rest of us that no one expected him to do other than 'muck in'.

It was similarly taken for granted, given the furore that had erupted when Prince Edward sought to go to Cambridge, that the notion of waving royalty through the gate without the need for proper qualifications was now over. Any member of the family who arrived at university under such circumstances would never have achieved credibility or respect. William had, in any case, another opportunity here to step outside the gilded world in which he had lived and try something new.

St Andrews, a small university on the east coast of Scotland, is a comfortable distance from Fleet Street, and indeed from any major city. Until recently it seemed half-forgotten, frozen in time. Founded six hundred years ago, it is the oldest in Britain after Oxford and Cambridge, and like them it is not a 'campus' university but a series of colleges scattered through the town. It is a place of high winds, high gables, narrow alleys, cobbled streets, ivy-covered walls and lamp-lit quadrangles. St Salvator's Hall, in which both William and Kate Middleton were to live, is all panelling and mullioned windows and founders' portraits set in stained glass As an environment, the town is magnificent. It has sea, cliffs, and a harbour as quaint as anything in Cornwall. There are long miles of golden beach, immortalized in the opening scene of the film *Chariots of Fire*. There are romantic ancient ruins, the rolling greensward of the world's most famous golf links, and vistas of distant, snow-capped mountains.

Socially, St Andrews is an unusual community. Lacking the diversions of a large city, cut off from the rest of the world, its student body becomes unusually close-knit. Surprising numbers of them form a very strong bond with both the place and their fellow students, sharing a sense of privilege at attending this university – a feeling of being in on a secret no one else knows. More of them marry each other than in any other British university, and after graduation they often continue the sense of fraternity that to outsiders seems like smug clique-ishness. St Andrews is unlike the other Scottish universities in that it has for a long time recruited its student body from far afield. It is so full of wealthy and public school-educated English that many Scots do not think of it as belonging to their country at all – a feeling that can be borne out by listening to the accents in the streets on any given day. It also attracts significant numbers of wealthy American 'preppies', and in many ways seems like an annexe of the Ivy League.

It was not as unfamiliar a place to William as many people might suppose. One of his cousins – the eldest son of the Duke of Kent – holds the title Earl of St Andrews. Another cousin, James Ogilvy, attended the university in the 1980s. William's housemaster at school, Andrew Gailey, had been at St Andrews, as had the headmaster, Eric Anderson. The first Old Etonian to attend the university did so in the 1790s, and in recent generations – at least since the sixties – there has been a well-beaten path between the school and the university. When William arrived, he had half a dozen old acquaintances at his elbow, all the time. He soon made new ones too. Though his circle remained largely that of the rich and privately educated, he had a certain 'blokishness' – a no-nonsense expectation that he would be treated like anyone else – that disarmed both snobs and critics. His fellow students gave him the codename 'Steve' so that eavesdropping journalists might not be aware of who was being discussed in pubs or coffee shops. The townspeople proved extremely protective, leaving him to wander the streets unpestered, and brushing aside the questions of any journalists in search of anecdotes. When he met Kate Middleton, they were able to pursue their friendship in private for a considerable time.

They graduated on the same day. William, with his upper second in geography, was dubbed 'the brainiest royal ever' by the press, and both his grandparents attended the ceremony. The next phase of his life would be devoted to the military. Harry, who was never university material, had already gone to Sandhurst. William was to join him there and, being junior, would have to salute him. Both of them thrived in this disciplined environment. They passed out successfully and their grandmother attended the graduation parades.

In what has become a militaristic age, dominated by foreign wars, both princes have kept entirely in step with the public mood as well as with family tradition by serving in the armed forces. The unprompted choice of both has been to join the Army or the Royal Air Force, as a long-term career and not merely as a time-filling activity for a few years. (William did initially sign up for a three-year commission, but extended it.) This has fitted in particularly well with a climate of opinion that expects royals to pay their way.

The determination of both of them to run the same risks as their comrades is well documented. Prince Harry succeeded in serving most of a tour in Afghanistan with his regiment, and is known to have trained as a helicopter pilot because this represents his best prospect of getting back into action. In the autumn of 2012 he succeeded in returning to 'theatre'. William, whose senior position in the line of succession makes it impossible for him to undertake a tour of duty, has found another highly useful, and acceptable, form of risk-taking. After undergoing training with the Royal Navy, he was seconded to the Army Air Corps and, presumably bitten by the flying bug, he transferred in 2009 to the RAF. Not only has this demonstrated commitment and enterprise, it has won him international plaudits (when he saved a Russian trawlerman he was thanked by the country's president) and enabled him to live a more-or-less ordinary life in North Wales. In the Service he uses the name William Wales, which has given rise to his punning nickname: 'Billy the Fish'.

The Cambridges live modestly, their only domestic staff consisting of a part-time cleaning woman. They could be the son and daughter-in-law of any middle-aged, middle-class British couple, causing their parents anxiety with their frenetic lifestyle. That they live like middle-class people requires no apology, and the attempt by the Left to turn this appellation into an insult has largely failed. The middle class, strategically situated in the centre of the social order, is the best place from which to view society. The longer they remain there, the better will be their insight into the lives of their future subjects.

Because of the experiences of Fergie and Diana and even Mark Phillips, it has become received wisdom that marriage by commoners into the royal family will prove difficult, and perhaps irretrievably so – that without a lifetime of conditioning, the adjustment simply cannot be made. But failure is not in the least inevitable, as was proved by the fact that the most popular and successful personality in the family for generations was the Queen Mother, who had had no royal background. Today there are other spouses who have quietly got on with both personal and official lives without making mistakes or being savaged by the press. The Duchess of Gloucester was a shy Dane who met her husband while they were both studying at Cambridge. Sophie, Countess of Wessex, has been happily married for more than a decade to Prince Edward and, although caught out once by a press-inspired scam, has lived a blameless life ever since. Her personality is nothing at all like those of the women who married her two brothers-in-law. Such is the tranquillity of the Wessexes' private life that many people do not know the names of their children – or indeed that they have any.

Kate Middleton is obviously suited by temperament to life in the royal family. She seems to have needed little more than minimal instruction in how to carry out the mundane but necessary tasks of 'the Firm' – greeting people, looking interested, talking superficially with strangers. No doubt important lessons were learned both by courtiers and by the family from the case of Diana. Whatever training the Duchess of Cambridge has received is likely to have been given informally by her husband. It helps, of course, that she is not yet the wife of the heir to the throne and that her official duties are balanced by spells of normality.

Nevertheless she has done very well, even in the eyes of critics in the press. She had several years, at university and afterward, in which to think about what life in the family would be like. Through numerous visits to their various homes, she was able to get to know her husband's relatives long before she became related to them. Prince William, mindful of his mother's experience, has gone out of his way to ensure that her transition from private individual to public figure has been as painless as possible. She herself is not sulky and brooding like Diana, and does not have the boisterousness that cost Sarah Ferguson her dignity. The first mishap to befall her, in September 2012, when a French magazine revealed topless photographs of her, saw her react with pained dignity – and legal action. Whereas pictures of Fergie in a similar state of semi-undress caused outrage because of her wild behaviour, the Duchess of Cambridge garnered considerable sympathy as an innocent victim of press harassment.

She has shown an equable temperament and has not been known to get angry – though such a side of her might become visible if she is not left alone by the media. She and William will have an important bargaining counter once they have children. Public interest will be immense, and they will be able to restrict access if there is a state of war between the Palace and the press. At any rate, the duchess seems to be pleasant, dutiful and suited by nature to her role. She and her husband are of the same generation. They share an interest in sport, and have a similar sense of humour. They have their education in common, which has given them the same circle of friends, and they even had the same gap-year experience in Chile. Whatever guardian angel watches over the House of Windsor has a talent for choosing ordinary, rather average people to marry into the family. She and William should make a very poplar king and queen because of that.

All of this augurs well for the monarchy in general. As for the prince himself, the signs are that he is from the same mould as his grandmother. Like Princess Elizabeth during her time as heir to the throne, he is dutiful, anxious to learn, somewhat earnest but not lacking in humour, only determined to take his role seriously and to perform his tasks well.

The differences in personality between William and Charles are significant. William has not yet acquired the wide-ranging interests of his father, and may never do so. Less sensitive perhaps (one could somehow not imagine him playing the cello), less interested in the arts and architecture, less passionate about the environment, he is also less likely to take sides, to voice strong or controversial opinions and thus become unpopular. While Charles was brought up largely by a single, exacting parent, William has had the guidance of two who were sympathetic and indulgent. He has had an education that was comfortably typical, at least for his class, and has been left alone to achieve whatever prizes his abilities could win him without the bending of rules or the altering of circumstances to make anything easier. He was able to marry for love and without being pestered or pressured to do so, as his father was, and he was very fortunate that the person he found was suited by temperament to the life she would lead.

He and she are well balanced, sensible and informal. Given more years in which to continue their present lifestyle, they may become even more like an average couple despite their official duties and constant media exposure.

Prince Harry, of whom nothing much has been expected, has attracted brickbats for his party-going, but also recently revealed an ability to communicate with the public that many had not expected. Early in 2012 he deputized for the queen on a tour of the Caribbean – his first-ever such duty. He proved to have a natural empathy with the crowds and a sense of humour that won him many admirers. 'Bookish he will never be,' as was said about his great-uncle, Edward VIII, but why should that matter? If he is good at the job the monarchy does – taking an interest in the lives of others, encouraging them, cheering them up – he can be forgiven the occasional embarrassing lapse. Here too the auspices are good.

What the subjects of the Windsors traditionally want is the sort of monarch they have had – with the single exception of Edward VIII – throughout the whole history of that house: quietly dutiful, personally modest, likeable – someone who can stand in the foreground to represent the nation, yet can equally well occupy the background so as not to hold back a country that is emphatically forward-looking. That is the best type of sovereign to preside over a people who are vigorous, democratic, iconoclastic yet conservative. Though the family will be perceived as dull for much of the time, they must provide their people with inspiration, entertainment, even occasional scandal. Above all, and in spite of any personal foibles or failings, they must uphold standards of behaviour that others feel no obligation to meet. The Windsors, through a combination of collective experience, common sense and personal inclination, have proved themselves to be very good at this. It has enabled them to adapt and thus to survive. They will continue to do both.

8

A MIDDLE-CLASS MONARCHY

*'It's vital that the monarchy keeps in touch with the people.
It's what I try and do.'*

Princess Diana

*'I want to see things evolve. The direction the monarchy
seems to be moving in – toward a more mainland European
model – is one I would feel sympathetic about.'*

Andrew Motion, former poet laureate

Monarchical government is as old as the notion of living in communities. In some societies the king was elected, or served a term of office in rotation with others (in one country – Poland – there was an elected monarchy until the eighteenth century), and in many he lived much like any other member of the community. By the Middle Ages the concept of kingly splendour had universally taken root, however. It was considered necessary in an unstable era to impress subjects, rival claimants and other countries with the wealth and might of a sovereign. Castles were as huge and imposing as the ruler's budget would permit. The number of retainers, and the gorgeousness of their livery, the brawn and ferocity of royal guards, all helped intimidate subjects, noblemen and foreign ambassadors alike. The notion of visual splendour was to reach its apogee with the Palace of Versailles in the reign of Louis XIV (1638–1715). More a small, aristocratic city than a single palace, it became an expression of the Sun King's majesty and was widely copied by other rulers – Drottningholm in Sweden was called 'the Versailles of the North'; the palace of Het Loo was 'the Versailles of the Netherlands'. Catherine the Great, Empress of Russia, was the only monarch to copy it on the same scale, and her palace at Tsarskoe Selo was specifically designed to outshine Louis XIV's creation.

Subjects wanted their monarch to live in splendour. They expected magnificence. In eras dominated by wars – and it has only been since 1945 that this spectre has vanished from western Europe – it was the prestige of the monarch, the impressiveness of his dwellings, the might of his armies, the flowering of culture at his court, that gave their country standing in the eyes of others, wooing allies and warning potential aggressors. A king who was kind to his people was a pleasant thing to have, but it was not as important as having a monarch who was feared by his neighbours, for that could ensure peace for his country.

Yet there have been sovereigns who won popularity with their subjects by the modest simplicity of their lives. One instance of this was Frederick the Great, king of Prussia from 1740–86. His kingdom was not rich, for its terrain was a sandy plain without natural resources, and the notion of royal ostentation did not sit easily with the austere national mindset. Frederick was only ever seen in one type of garment – a blue officer's coat, which he wore until it was in tatters before replacing it with an identical one. This enabled those subjects who owned only one coat to identify with him. Frederick was highly revered, though this had more to do with his considerable success in winning battles than with what he wore. Nevertheless his parsimony and canniness won general approval, and made him the subject of indulgent nostalgia after his death. An unlikeable man in reality, he is remembered with affection to this day.

His British contemporary, George III (1760–1820) had something of the same simplicity. In this he was following precedent. While other European sovereigns built vast monuments to their own glory, the kings of Great Britain lived in comparative, and perhaps even risible, modesty. Kensington Palace, in an unimportant village west of London, became the official home of the royal family (after the destruction by fire of Whitehall Palace in 1698) until Queen Victoria moved into Buckingham Palace in 1837. It looked like a slightly larger than average country manor house. George III chose to settle his family in an even smaller residence, Kew Palace. The monarchs also, of course, had Windsor Castle, which was and is the world's largest inhabited fortress, yet this was not usually their main or their permanent residence. The smallness of scale of the king's favourite dwelling seemed appropriate to a nation in which the real power rested with an elected Parliament and not with an absolute monarch.

As with the house, so with its occupants. Visitors to Kew Palace today are often surprised not only by the pokiness of the rooms but by the simplicity of George's family life as it has been reconstructed. The king, who was nicknamed 'Farmer George' because he had many of the characteristics of a small-scale country squire, led a domestic life that was not very different from that of his more prosperous subjects. This was much commented upon by both press and public, and it endeared him to his people. He even adopted a blue-and-scarlet coat – still sometimes worn as 'Windsor Dress' by the royal family and their servants – that was modelled on Frederick the Great's famous garment. Then, as now, an extravagant sovereign caused resentment among taxpayers and the notion of a massive, imposing royal palace or an over-sumptuous wardrobe smacked too much of Continental despotism. Had a king's plain living been characteristic of a weak sovereign or country it would have been viewed as a national embarrassment, but George presided over the world's wealthiest nation. His army and navy were mighty enough to be feared throughout the world. His was a simplicity of greatness and of choice rather than meekness or necessity.

Not all sovereigns, of course, were as home-loving as this. George's son, who reigned as Prince Regent from 1811 and as King George IV from 1820–30, was hated by the public. His vanity, extravagance and complicated love life gave a field-day to satirists and cartoonists, though the architectural monuments to his spendthrift nature – Brighton Pavilion, or the embellishments to Windsor Castle – have been much appreciated by posterity. It was not until the reign of George's granddaughter Victoria (1837–1901) that the British monarchy returned to a semblance of domestic ordinariness. The queen herself possessed a quiet and stable personality that would have influenced her court and British society, even had she not been married to a man who shared these characteristics in fuller measure. In 1840 she married Albert of Saxe-Coburg-Gotha, a minor German princeling. Earnest and largely humourless, he was – undeservedly – not popular with the British people, but he set the tone for Society in a manner that would dominate the Victorian age. He strongly disapproved of the hedonistic and immoral aristocratic circle that made up the Court, and set out to distance his wife from it. Imbued with the ideal of service and devoted to hard work, he acted as *de facto* co-ruler, not only advising the queen – a role he was not entitled to claim constitutionally – but working entirely in tandem with her, a situation encapsulated by their joint desk, which can still be seen at Osborne House.

Though Albert may not have endeared himself greatly to his wife's subjects, the personal lives led by the royal family struck a distinct chord with the public. This was a time of increased piety. An evangelical revival had swept away the raffish legacy of the Regency. Immorality was out of fashion.

The country was ready to be led by upright example, and royalty provided it. As well as a change in morals there was a shift in social and political power. Victoria's reign was the great age of the bourgeoisie. They, like Prince Albert, despised the self-indulgent hedonism of the aristocracy, and admired the virtues of work and self-improvement. Albert's interest in science and industry, manifest in his prominent role in the Great Exhibition, endeared him to the people who made and sold British goods. Accustomed to being despised by members of his class, they appreciated his patronage of new technology (railways and photography, to name but two areas), and his interest in them and their values. The queen, though not naturally as intelligent as her husband, shared this interest.

The British monarchy thus had a 'makeover' in the middle decades of the nineteenth century. Victoria and Albert had developed the tastes of the middle class, though they of course lived the life of the high aristocracy and no one expected them to do otherwise. Nevertheless it was appearances that counted. Their blameless natures made the monarchy more generally revered than it had been within living memory. Their mutual devotion and close family life established for the first time the notion – which has remained the case to the present day – that royalty should set a moral example and represent the best of its people's character.

Albert died in 1861. His widow, who grew steadily more entrenched in her social and moral conservatism, outlived him by forty years. She mourned him to the extent of disappearing into self-imposed purdah, absenting herself so effectively from national life that republicanism began to stir, and the monarchy sank into an unpopularity greater than it has ever known since. The situation was saved by her gradual reappearance and increasing age, which conferred on her almost mythical status.

The monarch who followed her to the throne, Edward VII, did not share her retiring nature, but he had an abiding love of splendour and spectacle. After his mother's reclusive reign he wanted royalty to be once again colourful, popular and visible. For his coronation in 1902, he asked the aristocracy to bring their liveried coaches to London so that these would add to the visual impact of the occasion, and they did. It was to be the last time these vehicles were seen *en masse*, and the last time a coronation was staged with such magnificence.

Edward went on as he had begun. The notion of royal spectacle had been given initial impetus by Queen Victoria's Diamond Jubilee in June 1897. Her funeral, his coronation and his own funeral were in similar vein (the latter occasion was attended by no less than nine other monarchs). He also gave out decorations generously, even carrying some minor ones in his pockets to hand out, and instituting a new award – the Order of Merit. Most importantly, he enhanced the physical surroundings in which state ceremonial took place; he had a new façade put on Buckingham Palace – a simple and dignified, if rather plain and dull affair that was designed to offset the Victoria Memorial, which he also had built. Edward had the Mall remade as a straight and wide triumphal avenue, with Admiralty Arch created at its eastern end, thus forming one of the comparatively few contrived areas in a city that is notoriously unplanned.

For all his reputation as a playboy, he was a conscientious king. While Victoria had only occasionally conducted the State Opening of Parliament and had not appeared at Trooping the Colour, Edward began to do these things with punctilious regularity, guaranteeing that the events became more popular and that his subjects could expect to see him on at least two occasions every year. In this, of course, he started a tradition that has been followed by his family ever since. His son, who succeeded him as King George V in 1910, combined Victoria's rectitude and sense of duty with Edward's feeling of obligation to provide the public with dignified and inspiring royal appearances.

The British Crown was, as has been suggested, a modest institution by comparison with its neighbours. The French

Court, from which other monarchs in Continental Europe tended to take their cue, had been a place of overwhelming magnificence under both the Bourbons and Napoleon. The Court of Spain was known to be the most rigidly protocol-bound and ceremonious of them all. The tsars of Russia lived and governed on a scale that was simply not possible for other monarchs – the size and number of their palaces, the wealth they commanded, the retinue of noblemen, ladies-in-waiting and gorgeously attired bodyguards that accompanied them, was sufficient to humble even the most self-assured foreign observer. The Court of Austria–Hungary, ruled until 1916 by the patriarchal Franz Joseph I who was just as venerable as Queen Victoria, spent far more on ceremony and banquets than its counterpart in Britain. The United Kingdom, whose royal family is now wealthier and more ceremonious that that of any other European monarchy, was a century ago – in an age when kings were thicker on the ground – outshone by several others. With its Yeomen of the Guard, Gentlemen at Arms, Household regiments and its quaint but splendid officials (Silver Stick-in-Waiting) it has always, of course, had the power to impress, but with that understatement that is characteristic of the British it has striven for a certain modesty too. Noisy extravagance did not sit well with the temper of its people or the mood of Parliament, which ran the country and decided, by democratic vote, what the monarch's income should be.

In other corners of Europe, the nature of monarchy was changing even before the Age of kings had ended. A turning point of sorts came in 1905 when Norway became independent of Sweden and chose to become a monarchy. In keeping with the new age, however, this king would have no political power, and would be a purely ceremonial figurehead uninvolved in the actual governance of the nation. The country invited a member of Europe's oldest ruling house, Denmark, to fill the position. Prince Carl, the thirty-three year old who accepted the throne and the title Haakon VII (to suggest continuity with medieval kings), did so on condition that he would live as much as possible like any Norwegian citizen. He was thus the harbinger of the 'bicycling monarchs' – the informal royalties that have since come to characterize Scandinavia and the Netherlands. Normality was sometimes relative, of course. (Both Haakon's son and grandson would be sent to Balliol College, Oxford.) Nevertheless, his son, who reigned as Olaf V (1957–91), devoutly practised this ordinariness too. He was famously photographed taking his skis on a train up to the slopes, apparently alone and unnoticed by other passengers. Olaf's son, now King Harald V, married a commoner – Sonja Haraldsen, whom he met informally – in 1968, a fact that caused considerable debate even in such a relaxed country. (They actually met in 1959. It took nine years to overcome the objectors.) By this time Britain had seen a royal marry a commoner – Princess Margaret had wed Antony Armstrong-Jones in 1960 – but he moved in Society, was related to the aristocracy and had the educational background of the upper class, while Miss Haraldsen was the daughter of a merchant. This was the first instance of a random romance between royalty and an ordinary member of the public, something that is now so universal as to excite no surprise.

Understandably, there are often rules that govern the choice of marriage partner for members of royal houses. In Japan, it is taken entirely for granted that any member of the imperial family must marry a Japanese. Public opinion would not stand for anything else. The matter is even more imperative if the spouse is to be the wife of the heir to the throne. There would be no question of Japan having, say, an American consort, as Jordan did with Queen Noor, the wife of King Hussein, or an Australian, as is the case with the crown prince of Denmark.

In Denmark, in fact, the rules are the exact opposite to Japan's. The royal family has an understanding that its members will never marry any Danish citizen. Though, as is the

case elsewhere, it is entirely possible for them to choose someone of any other social class, feeling against a home-grown
consort is intense, and within the royal family itself opposition is entrenched. In 1994 Crown Prince Frederik wished to
marry a beautiful, intelligent and companionable girl called
Katja Storkholm. The fact that she had once modelled under-
wear – which might have been viewed as a fatal handicap –
was seen merely as a minor embarrassment. In every way she
would have been a highly suitable princess. Most importantly, she and Frederik were genuinely in love. He proposed, she
accepted, but the engagement had to remain entirely secret.
The implacable disapproval of his parents, and of senior courtiers, killed off the relationship. His mother, Queen Marga-
rethe, who herself had married a French diplomat, simply
refused to grant permission, and there was nothing Frederik could do about it. The queen was quoted as saying with
regard to a foreign bride: 'There are many difficulties because
of the language. But you come with what the British call "no
strings attached". Of course you have a past, but that past is
not walking around the streets among us.' As if to further
emphasize this point, Frederik was eventually to find a wife
on the opposite side of the world. He would marry a young
woman called Mary Donaldson from Tasmania. They met in
a Sydney pub while he was attending the Olympics in 2000.
'Hi,' he said, 'I'm Fred, from Denmark.' It would be difficult
to imagine a monarchy more informal than that.

In small and easy-going countries, low-profile monarchy
has long since become normal. There was no need – in an era
before global terrorism – for large numbers of bodyguards,
and sovereigns could walk about the streets like anyone else.
King Frederik IX of Denmark – Prince Frederik's grandfather – once visited a public event in a Copenhagen park without a single person in attendance. 'Who looks after the king?'
an American journalist asked one bystander. 'We all do,' was
the reply. The lesson from this, doubtless noted in Courts
all over Europe, was that monarchy can be informal without

necessarily losing dignity. A royal family that is relaxed and accessible can reap immense rewards in popularity.

A Dutchman once explained that in his country any royal occasion, any state pageantry, would have people asking, 'But what's it all for?' The implication being that there is no point in making too great a fuss over these events. The majority of British people do not ask this question, and do not want this sort of monarchy. Proud of their history and their past status as a world power, they enjoy the monarchy's regular appearances at public events. They love splendour and they adore the notion – an immensely important national article of faith – that no other country can possibly compete with them in staging state ceremonial. (Ironically many members of the royal family, whose unlooked-for obligation it has been to participate in these events, absolutely hate them. Just like the crowds that line the Mall, they spend long periods of time standing and waiting.) They are proud of having the West's most elaborate, influential, vibrant and respected royal house. Like the people of Ancient China or Egypt they regard their own ruler as the only one of importance. When 'the queen' is spoken of in other parts of the world, the implication is clear that it is Elizabeth II who is being referred to, even though Denmark has had a reigning queen since 1972 and the Netherlands has been ruled by women since 1890.

Paradoxically, Queen Elizabeth's subjects like a certain distance in her even as they like the rest of their royal family to be to be less aloof. They expect dignity and, as was seen during the series of scandals that erupted during the 1990s, if they do not get it they feel betrayed and angry. With the resources the family has at its disposal – the advisers and officials who smooth their way and cover up their mistakes, the allowances made for them, the goodwill upon which they can call – their people expect better of them.

With an extensive family there will be members who can meet different public needs, reflect different qualities. When one or other is out of favour as a result of some misdeed, the others will remain popular and will thus keep up the overall standard. The older ones fit easily into the role of grandparents of the nation. George V, Queen Mary, Queen Elizabeth the Queen Mother, the Duke of Edinburgh and the present queen, have all provided a steadying, reassuring presence. It has naturally been for younger members of the family to supply glamour and excitement. The first to do this – the first royal 'media star', to use an unfortunate expression – was David, Prince of Wales, who later became Edward VIII. The notion of a member of the royal house being photographed and written about like a film star was entirely new at the beginning of the twenties, though it has become all too familiar in our own time. Coverage of family members is frequently intrusive and often inaccurate, but the mass media have been a benefit as well as a curse to the monarchy in recent decades. Though they have brought considerable anguish to members of the family they have also, for instance, made more widely known the fun-loving side of the queen's nature.

William and Harry – and now Kate – are naturally the royals who are identified with youth. They were shown endlessly on television watching the Olympics (the queen and Prince Philip featured only at the Opening Ceremony) in order to demonstrate that royalty is fully engaged with the preoccupations of the nation's young. William is a supporter of a football team – Aston Villa – that is unambiguously plebeian, and both young men wear chain-store clothing. William's wife, of course, fascinates many because she is an outsider who has made the transition to the inside. Some observers think her the most interesting of them all. 'If it weren't for Kate,' opines a largely hostile US website, 'they'd be a sorry lot.' Americans, as they did with Diana, have a special affection for those who marry into the family, provided they are attractive young women, of course. Neither Mark Phillips nor Timothy Laurence aroused noticeable interest across the Atlantic when they in turn became husband to Princess Anne. Perhaps it is embedded in the American psyche – it is after all a founding concept of their nation – to bestow their greatest admiration on those who have come from relative obscurity and moved upward, rather than those who have always been at the top.

If insight to the lives of the royal family is easier for the public than it used to be, the present generation is visibly freer and less hidebound than was the case, and they are much more at ease with us. Seeing them today, it seems incredible that within living memory they were forbidden by self-imposed rules from smiling or laughing in public, or injecting humour into speeches.

It is worth remembering, however, that the rules of society have changed in any case, making the lives of the young in general less hidebound. To cite one example: when William was elected to 'Pop' at Eton, the prefectorial society whose most conspicuous symbol is a colourful and self-designed waistcoat, the prince wore one bearing the slogan 'Groovy Baby', a reference to the then-fashionable Austin Powers spy films. Nobody raised an eyebrow at this. In the 1970s, when his father had put on a sweatshirt to play polo and it happened to bear the title of the film *A Bridge Too Far* (a serious war movie, as opposed to a vulgar spoof), he was reprimanded by courtiers on the grounds that 'royalty don't advertise'.

Monarchies need to know – and usually do, by virtue of long practice – when to be formal and when to unbend. In the modern era they must, after all, not only symbolize national virtue but seem like archetypal citizens. The trick is always to tread a fine line between the two. That so many dynasties survive in democratic countries is a testament to their success.

EPILOGUE

'If people don't want it, they won't have it.'
Prince Charles, on the monarchy

It is beyond doubt that if you dislike the royal family you have a hard time in Britain, especially if you live in the capital. Their image is everywhere. Not only can you not use a stamp or a coin without being reminded of them, but their faces are on thousands of other items – postcards, crockery, biscuit tins. (This is not their fault. They do not hold copyright regarding their own images, and anyone can thus make these souvenirs.) Their insignia, in the shape of the Royal Warrant, appears on everything from cereal packets to vacuum cleaners. Let there be any hint of a royal celebration and shop windows, magazine covers and public spaces will be saturated with them. On these high days and holidays the general, widespread hysteria must be positively sickening for those who do not share the enthusiasm, just as the World Cup is for those with no interest in football. There is no corner of the United Kingdom in which you can avoid it. As one critic railed during the jubilee celebrations of 2012, no view was permitted to appear in the media other than that the monarchy was worshipped, enjoyed, appreciated overwhelmingly by the British public.

And yet this reflects the genuine, uncontrived (fostered, but not contrived) desire of most of the British people, as shown in opinion polls.

The last major poll, by Mori in May 2012, found that a solid 80 per cent want to keep the monarchy, and while Conservative voters were predictably overwhelming in their support (96 per cent), so were Labour (74 per cent) and Liberal Democrats (84 per cent). The poll was taken just before the Diamond Jubilee, at a high point in the Crown's fortunes, yet even in its darkest days – in January 1997 a televised debate, *The Nation Decides*, included a telephone survey – support remained at 66 per cent. With two-thirds of the country in favour, there was little to comfort republicans.

June 2012: The Diamond Jubilee

A day of unseasonal chill and fitful sunshine that, before it is over, will have degenerated into wintry cold and almost solid sheets of rain. The usual crowds sit from dawn on the pavements or emerge, bleary-eyed, from pup-tents in St James's Park. As the hours pass there are more and more of them, still swapping yarns about where they have come from and what other occasions they have seen. As the numbers increase, the media awaken. As usual, the networks have decided that the crowd will be depicted as happily indomitable, determined to enjoy themselves in spite of the weather. This is what the audience both at home and overseas expect from the British – eccentric cheerfulness and a sense of carry-on-regardless. Presenters and cameramen from the television news channels go up and down the kerbsides, telling people what they are going to ask and what the answers must be ('When we say: "What keeps you going?" you're to answer: "Adrenalin!"') inciting them to wave and grin and cheer like morons as soon as the cameras are turned on. The hordes obey, and are rewarded with a thumbs-up: 'That was great!' Eventually, in mid-morning, the crowd will see a short motorcade that flashes past in minutes. 'Have I waited four hours for *that?*' asks one woman. Only in the afternoon, when the participants come back, will there be the bands and horses and gun-carriages that the spectators wanted. But it is frankly not very interesting, not a patch on 2002. This time most of the effort went into a river pageant, and for those on land there is only a short drive up Whitehall and along the Mall to look at. The crowd are bored. Magic sometimes fails to match expectations. And now the rain has come, threatening the fly-past by Second World War aircraft that is the traditional climax to these events.

Nevertheless when the family are back inside the Palace and the slow, almost stately surge of the crowd westward up the Mall begins, kept in check by a solid line of policemen, excitement mounts all over again. As always the climax, the moment more to be savoured than any other, is the appearance on the balcony of those who have been glimpsed in passing a short time earlier. The cheering will be deafening, the sense of goodwill and camaraderie and national unity will be fleeting but forthcoming, the notion of being a participant in something magnificent will bring some members of the crowd to tears. This is the single moment that will live in memory long after the early start, the discomfort and cold and boredom have been forgotten.

Despite such euphoria, there is an often-expressed view in the media that we have all had enough of this, that it will wither away through the increasing indifference of modern and forward-looking people, especially the young. In the days and weeks before the jubilee, and the wedding, there was much talk about the general lack of enthusiasm for these events. The perspective was always the same – that the queen's subjects are becoming more and more disenchanted with their constitutional arrangements, and that, by implication, there will not be such events in future because the monarchy will have gone. The foreign news coverage was especially dominated by this. Passers-by, stopped at random, opined that either the occasions meant nothing to them personally or they felt such celebrations were inappropriate at a time of recession and national austerity. On the days themselves, broadcasters even went in search of alternative celebrations – anti-weddings or jubilees – and found small groups of listless men and women doing nothing very much. Those they interviewed, almost invariably young and slovenly, are the sort of people who are against any established order anyway. A female Cambridge undergraduate – a self-confessed anarchist who would thus, by very definition, disapprove equally of every other form of government – was interviewed by American television. In the cut-glass tones of one educated in the Home Counties, she fulminated against the occasion with genuine passion if without any coherent arguments. Anyone watching this type of thing would have been aware of a palpable desperation as the networks looked for someone – anyone – who could present the alternative view. They did not manage to find a single spokesperson to put the case articulately or impressively.

On the afternoon of the river pageant there was a republican protest outside City Hall, close to the route that the vessels, and the royal family, would travel. Attendance was modest, despite the fact that participants had travelled from all over the United Kingdom and beyond (Swedish anti-monarchists, for some reason, were there). Peter Tatchell, an activist and unsuccessful parliamentary candidate, gave a speech in which he acknowledged that those present were a small minority (he was heckled throughout by chants of 'Long live the queen!' from loyalists) but compared the ending of the monarchy to the abolition of slavery, the gaining by women of the right to vote and the granting of equality to homosexuals. He pointed out that all of these had been unpopular, unfashionable causes but, because a small number of devoted activists had persevered with them, they had gradually won over the majority and succeeded in their objectives. To pretend that an extremely benign, and widely popular, institution of proven worth – such as the monarchy – is comparable with some denial of human rights is, at the least, very poor reasoning. After emphasizing that his objection was to the institution of monarchy and not the throne's current occupant, Tatchell went on to say that the queen has 'never made any sacrifices' and 'never suffered any hardship' – emphasizing that he appears to know little about her. If his speech sums up the current thinking of republicanism, it has overwhelmingly lost the argument.

Republicans are almost visibly disappointed that members of racial minorities are not more outraged by the royal family's ethnicity. In fact, among these groups the queen has long since won respect. As Head of the Commonwealth she is known to move easily among the leaders and peoples of the countries from which Britain's new communities are drawn. She is head of state in a number of them. Her views on racial discrimination – seen most clearly in her reaction to South African apartheid – are well known. However disenchanted minority citizens may become with British governments or other institutions, the monarchy is not a target of their anger. One historian, Philip Howard, has neatly summed up the sovereign's position thus: 'Constitutional monarchy is, paradoxically, a democratic institution: by giving the official head of state no power, it makes her a representative of all her subjects, particularly the weaker and the powerless.' Perhaps minority citizens sense this, or know it, while those who are indignant on their behalf do not. She is all things to all men. That is the beauty of it.

The notion that 'this is the twenty-first century' is perhaps the most ludicrous 'argument' of the lot, though it is much used by the lazy and the unthinking. What has the date on the calendar to do with whether an institution is useful and effective? The idea that change is compulsory whether or not it is for the better, simply because time has moved on, is a very quick recipe for disaster. We would be left with nothing very useful at all if we got rid of tried and proven things just because they have been around for a long time. Does anyone suggest we abolish the International Red Cross because it was founded as long ago as 1859? Or the Olympics because they hark back to Ancient Greece? Parliament was first summoned in England in 1295, yet one does not hear people saying: 'But this is the twenty-first century! Why do we still have a constituent assembly that dates from over seven hundred years ago?' Institutions such as schools and businesses are proud to advertise the date at which they began, because it suggests that by having been in existence a long time they have not only proved trustworthy but have given satisfaction, gained valuable experience and adapted to suit changing needs. Why should the monarchy, which has done all of these things, not be judged by the same criteria and take the same pride?

There is also an argument produced by republicans that monarchy prevents any person, anywhere, from becoming Britain's head of state – that there can be no 'log cabin to White House' dream, as there is in the United States. Yet the position of British prime minister is not exactly negligible. It is one of the world's great offices, bringing with it tremendous power and prestige. It was sufficient to satisfy the ambitions of Churchill, Disraeli and Pitt the Elder. Harold Wilson, a working-class boy from Yorkshire, actually lived that dream when he was photographed as a child outside Number 10 Downing Street. He was to return forty years later as the occupant, and twice to serve as prime minister. To anyone of reasonable ambitions the premiership would surely be enough to satisfy them. (Today, in addition, children could grow up wanting to be president of the European Council.) The post of prime minister has the added attraction that it gives its occupant the opportunity to exercise power without its usual accompaniment – the need to preside over hours of mind-numbing official entertaining and protocol. It could be argued that the monarchy has taken on all the dull bits of being in office, saving others the trouble. It is also worth remembering, since politics attracts people with considerable self-regard, that the presence of a monarch keeps in check the egos of ambitious statesmen. When MPs attend the queen's garden parties, as they do each summer, it is noticeable how little interest their presence arouses.

Republicans often cannot understand why others do not share their zeal or their perpetual resentment. They seize avidly on any small reverse for the House of Windsor as evidence that victory is imminent. Every time Prince Philip makes one of his trademark *faux pas* they react with spluttering indignation. What the shrill and humourless apostles of political correctness do not realize is that a great many members of the public do not think such incidents worthy of anger. Knowing that these throwaway remarks are unintentional and not meant to offend, they might even find them funny, and may well enjoy the notion that public figures can successfully get away with defying the straitjacket of current orthodoxy. Every instance of Prince Philip or Prince Harry speaking out of turn (often when the media had no business to be eavesdropping in the first place) is trumpeted by newspapers, and may pursue them for years afterward. The public, however, tend to forgive, or simply not to hold it against them in the first place.

There was considerable smirking among progressives when, following the death of the Queen Mother in 2002, there was no immediate rush to sign books of condolence for her. At least one newspaper featured a photograph of a deserted crush-barrier next to St James's Palace where thousands had been expected, and asked if she did not deserve better after a lifetime of public service. The prophecy that this showed a terminal decline in the popularity of monarchy was to prove seriously premature. Though crowds had been slow to gather, after that they came in very significant numbers. They queued for anything up to nine hours to pass her coffin while she lay in state in Westminster Hall, and over a million lined the streets on the day of her funeral. It was not only a matter of her personal popularity, it was a quiet but effective riposte from the people of Britain to those who predicted that apathy would be their only reaction.

One thing that critics also seriously underestimate is the sheer entertainment that the royal family provide. Everyone knows who they are. The public have followed the doings of the principal characters all their lives. They like to know how the younger generation are getting on at school and university, what they will go on to do for a living, how they meet their spouses and when and where they are going to settle down. Births and other new arrivals are greeted with interest. Any comparison of the Windsors with a soap opera – a comment first made in the fifties – need not be seen as derogatory. They are indeed like a long-running television series, but such programmes are immensely popular with millions (far more people watch them than would vote for any single political party or support any movement), and are a very important part of national life. The characters in the royal family, like those in *Coronation Street*, are expected to earn the attention of viewers through their entertainment value – by being interesting, loveable, villainous, eccentric, controversial, by both leading and following social trends.

More importantly, the entire mindset of the British people is unsympathetic to the notion of removing the monarchy. Not that there are not intelligent and articulate people who disagree with the system, but these are not in anything like a majority, and they are not likely to be. The great mass of the populace is against them. The feelings of the public, whether conscious or subconscious but reflected in the results of opinion polls over decades, are in favour of an institution they respect and a non-political head of state to whom the Civil Service, the armed forces, politicians and the judiciary owe allegiance.

Many people – probably the majority – in any country are more interested in their own affairs than in the doings of the government except when these impinge upon their lives. Americans may well think about the presidency only every four years when they are subjected to electioneering. So it is with the monarchy. It is quietly there for the whole of British people's lives, taken for granted. Only when some great occasion makes it conspicuous do the general public start to think about it. When a royal occasion is coming up, the preparations always start slowly. They gather momentum gradually, until at last, on the day or the weekend itself, there is an explosion of enthusiasm. That is, again, not contrived – nobody tells these millions to celebrate – it is simply true that the party mood is not and cannot be sustained over weeks. That is why a number of people interviewed beforehand sound apathetic. They have not yet made their plans, or thought about the matter properly. They may go along to see the festivities, they may not. It would probably be the same in any free nation. What anti-monarchists see as apathy among the great majority is more accurately a quiet and undemonstrative approval of the way things are, and an inability to see any good reason to change them. In the opposite corner, what is actually passive indifference is sometimes angled to suggest positive, even passionate, views.

Foreign news coverage often has its own peculiar perspective. In 1969 when Prince Charles was invested as Prince of Wales at Caernarfon Castle, media in the Soviet Union – wishing to present the monarchy as unpopular and despotic – conveyed the impression that bombs were going off all over the Principality (there were two, planted by attention-seeking nationalists, and neither was anywhere near the event). Less dramatically, the angle is often to show the quaintness of British tradition, but sometimes it is to suggest – because such things make a good news story – that the institution is about to collapse. Watch this television coverage or read this newspaper, the media is saying, because the event it records may never happen again. The whole thing may soon vanish.

This is not going to happen, suddenly or soon. The monarchy is an older institution than almost any other. It has already withstood a successful revolution that got rid of it for a dozen years, yet it came back invigorated as if nothing had happened. It has survived a host of unpopular sovereigns, major scandals, national emergencies. Two long and costly wars simply – and greatly – increased its popularity. It out-lasted the upheavals that swept away most of the European thrones, and the age of Bolshevik revolution that followed. It also came through the Great Depression. It has, in other words, already faced every type of attack, in more serious forms than are experienced today. If these things could not shift, or even seriously threaten it, why would the grumbling of present-day malcontents succeed in its abolition?

It is very unlikely that a monarchy would ever be aban-doned in peacetime and in normal circumstances. The Euro-pean Crowns that have fallen have all been toppled, directly or indirectly, by violence. The French emperor through a dis-astrous war with Prussia; the German kings and emperor, and the Habsburg dynasty of Austria–Hungary, through the loss of the First World War; the Romanovs through Russia's col-lapse after three years of the same war. Two other countries, Italy and Greece, lost their monarchies through plebiscite, but only after either war or military coup had rendered the Crown ineffectual. Other countries – Romania, Bulgaria and Yugoslavia – became Communist. No similar circumstance has arisen in Britain. The loss of some monarchies has no les-sons to teach a country whose conditions are so different.

The abdication of Edward VIII in 1936, which was the grav-est test it has faced in a century, simply enhanced the popu-larity of his successor, George VI, for whom the nation felt a surge of sympathy. As an institution, the Crown has come largely unscathed through the era of debunking and has even weathered the latest scandals in the 1990s. It just is not true that this form of government is on the verge of collapse or that anything will seriously alter the way Britain is governed. If mature democracies throughout the world – Canada, Aus-tralia, New Zealand – still opt for monarchical government despite the distance between themselves and Buckingham Palace, is the country in which the House of Windsor actu-ally resides likely to abolish them? They will not fade from history, but what we can be sure of is that they will adapt, and go on adapting. They always have, and they have survived. It's what they do.

It is usually the elderly, and especially women, who favour the monarchy. Their connection is, naturally and principally, a sentimental one. They have grown up with this family, they recall the milestones in the queen's life and may have been married or had children at approximately the same times. They are the group least likely to want to see change and the one most likely to appreciate the old-fashioned virtues that royalty represents. They are also the most prepared to recognize the element of selfless duty that has characterized the lives of the queen and her husband. They are, on the other hand, more likely than the rest of society to wonder what will become of the monarchy once the present generation that has championed these values has gone from the scene.

It is the young – as seen in the results of surveys – whose negative views on the monarchy are taken to indicate that its days are numbered. After all, if a sample of the next generation is so lacklustre in its support, so uninterested, so impatient, does this not mean that thirty years hence, when that generation will be running the country, the monarchy will be cast off like an old shoe? The thing about young people is that they get older. As they gain experience, they begin to see the point of things that made little sense to them before. As they enter the workforce and become participants in society instead of spectators, they realize the value of structure and stability and continuity and – in the shape of the honours system – reward. A great many of those who voiced negative views at the time of the latest celebrations may well find themselves cheering on equivalent occasions in the future.

As for the idea that in a time of austerity money should not be spent on celebrations, that has been shown to be both unfair and unpopular. A host of royal events – the queen's wedding in 1947, the Coronation in 1953, the Silver Jubilee in 1977 – have been planned with the notion that austerity was necessary in view of the financial situation. In every one of these cases it has been the pressure of public opinion that has forced the organizers to think on a larger scale. It is a proven fact that in times of economic and societal gloom (and 1977 was about as bad as things could get) the British want a party to forget their troubles. It is the people, more than the monarchy, who crave this splendour. For all our cynicism and our preoccupation with everyday concerns, we enjoy these occasions. They provide, as they always did, milestones in the life of the nation and of individuals. Even the most sceptical can be susceptible to the tug of national pride.

The thing about monarchy is that it can play the long game. It is there for decades, generations, centuries. Its faults are buried by time and forgotten. It has constant chances to redeem its errors, to reinvent itself, to win back approval through new deeds or initiatives, or through the arrival of new people. Because it has faced many of its problems before, it has a wealth of precedent upon which to call in solving them. With the sentiments expressed today about Charles's fitness to rule – at least insofar as they refer to his personal morality – there is a feeling that we have been here before, since they are uncannily similar to views heard in the reign of Queen Victoria with regard to her eldest son, Albert Edward. There was exactly the same sense then, expressed word for word, that while the monarch had never put a foot wrong and that the monarchy would survive until her death, there was likely to be a review of the situation once she was gone.

Compared to Edward VII, Charles's indiscretions are mild. He was unfaithful to his marriage vows only once, and then because he had made a mistake in his choice of wife and was sharing his life with someone he found uncongenial and abrasive, and who took a similar view of him. Having now married a woman whose sympathetic personality complements his own, he has attracted no further scandal or rumour. His predecessor was by contrast a serial adulterer and gambler in an age that was far more censorious of moral lapses than our own. Edward was widely hated by middle Britain for his louche companions, his patronage of the Turf, his hedonistic lifestyle and his flaunting of mistresses under the nose of his popular and long-suffering wife, Alexandra. Yet he became an extremely successful and much-loved king. Why could Charles not do the same?

The oft-heard argument that the royal family is 'out of touch' with ordinary life has been losing ground for an entire generation, and now simply does not bear repetition (just as their increasingly wide choice of spouses will make irrelevant any jibes that they are 'inbred'). While the queen, as a child and a young woman, did not attend school or look for a job, her grandchildren and their spouses have done these things. All but one of her children married middle-class people, who had some experience of working prior to joining the family, and who had lived anonymous lives. Her grandson William, after joining the – admittedly socially exclusive – Royal Horse Guards as an officer, found a useful role in the more democratic Royal Air Force as a search and rescue helicopter pilot. This is a skilled job and is not without risks. While doing it he lives in relative obscurity in a remote corner of his grandmother's realm. No one will be able to accuse him in the future of not having lived in close proximity to his subjects or seen at first hand their problems. And this is obviously what he wants to do. There is every reason to expect that the next generation of royals will earn their way as a matter of course. The notion that they get what they want because of who they are has often been something that others have foisted upon them rather than a stance they have taken for themselves.

Some of the great positions they hold are equally accessible to more or less anyone. There have been members of the family who have been Chancellors of universities – Prince Philip of Cambridge, the Queen Mother and now Princess Anne of London. These are popular appointments and have been conscientiously filled by their incumbents, but the majority of such positions go to commoners and it is of course equally possible to have Chancellors who are 'the people's choice'. At the University of Durham the post is currently held by Bill Bryson, an American travel writer, who appears to have won the job on the basis of a single kind reference to the city in one of his books. There can, in other words, co-exist both royalty and democracy. There is room for both.

The queen and her husband – indeed her whole family – have been gently mocked with comments on how middle-class they are. *Private Eye*, the satirical magazine, christened the monarch and her husband 'Brenda and Keith' for their resemblance to archetypal next-door neighbours. Princess Margaret was similarly dubbed 'Yvonne', the sort of name, according to satirists, a suburban hairdresser would have and one that was seen as fitting her lifestyle, her friends and her outlook. Prince Charles was 'Brian' and Princess Diana was 'Cheryl', a name typical of a supermarket check-out girl. These nicknames came into widespread use, well beyond the university-graduate readership of *Private Eye*, and can still be heard today. If they were inspired by the family's resemblance to a middle-class family, why are the royals simultaneously accused of being 'out of touch'?

The family has recruited, through marriage, members of the middle class – the centre of the social order – who have been accustomed to leading ordinary lives. The royals themselves, while they may never have queued in a Jobcentre, have had other valid experiences. Several of them have fought in wars: George VI at Jutland, Prince Philip in the Mediterranean, Prince Andrew in the Falklands, Prince Harry in Afghanistan. They have also, through an unending series of visits to cities, factories, housing estates, seen more of everyday Britain, its homes and streets and places of work, than most politicians and most members of the public do. Though these encounters are contrived – they could not be anything else, given security concerns – they allow a more comprehensive picture of the nation to be formed than many appreciate.

Through a combination of advice, necessity and, above all,

personal inclination, the present generation of young royalty is to a large extent avoiding the mistakes of the previous one. Their detractors might be on firmer ground if the monarchy stayed the same, but it provides a constantly moving target. What is said about it one year is seen to be inaccurate and irrelevant by the following one. The House of Windsor is far more well informed about the state of public opinion than most of us think. It can disarm criticism not only by deliberate action but by natural desire. For example, the two sons of Prince Charles have shown every indication of wanting to live like other people. When sharing a flat while undertaking flying training with the armed forces, they bantered in a television interview about who was worst at remembering to wash the dishes.

Both of them, like other members of their family, have undergone a military training that has often been extremely tough, and their background has been of no help. That they have come through this suggests that they have already paid their debts to 'normality'. Even their vices – the much-photographed visits to nightclubs that will become rarer as they get older and settle down – merely serve to remind the public that they do the same things as other young men.

Not everyone is impressed by the informality that characterizes the contemporary royal family and there is a sense in which they can seem too ordinary, for the line between approachability and absurdity can be a thin one. The American website *Yahoo! Sports* reported during the Olympics that: 'The queen acted in an Opening Ceremony video. The rest of them mugged it up for every camera available in a shameless bit of look-at-us-we're-normal-fans. What is it they do again?' Critics may see it as shameless but it is their duty, after all, to be seen on important public occasions. If they were at fault for looking excited and enthusiastic during the proceedings, imagine the carping if they had seemed bored instead!

When news of the Duchess of Cambridge's pregnancy was announced, Andrew Morton wrote that: 'The prince or princess born next summer will be the most proletarian, and English, since . . . Alfred the Great. [He or she] will boast miners, fish-and-chip shop owners, carpenters and bakers among the bloodline.' This may be true, and it will doubtless increase public approval, but it will make no difference to the young person's upbringing, which will be in accordance with the traditions of the monarchy.

Now, it is clear, the way is fully open for any young woman to join the royal family, regardless of background. In a genera-tion's time a royal bride could easily be not middle class but working class, not from a well-heeled commuter village but from a council estate. If she were, and if she met her husband through some chance encounter, both the media and the public would be delighted, for they now expect such romances. Who-ever she was, she would need exceptional qualities of patience and stamina, for she could well be subject to an exhaustive makeover that would leave little of her tastes or personality intact. Nevertheless a nation that is now accustomed to decid-ing, through its votes on television talent shows, who will win recording contracts or leading roles in West End musicals would be comfortable with the notion of having royals chosen from among its own.

The popularization of the monarchy has now gone as far as it can. The royals are as informal and as just-like-the-rest-of-us as they are able, or likely, to get. However casually they dress in off-duty moments, whatever slang they use or teams they support, however many celebrities they are seen with, there will continue to be distance between them and their subjects. This will be the result of their wealth, the duties they perform, the uniforms in which they dress and the def-erence of the entourage that surrounds them. It is a very good thing that this distance is there. There must always be more magic than daylight.

Anti-monarchical arguments come down to two things: the cost of the monarchy and the fact that under this system no ordinary person can aspire to be head of state. Part of the trouble republicans experience is the fact that they have no clear ideas about what they would replace the monarchy with. They offer little but a reprise of the drab Puritanism that followed the beheading of Charles I, and certainly not any clear and straightforward plan as to how the country could be governed. As a republican website points out: 'The method by which the head of state should be chosen has not been agreed upon, with some favouring an elected president, some an appointed head of state with little power, and others supporting the idea of leaving the political system as it is but without a monarch.'

When there are complaints about the cost of the royal family, the amount that they bring into the economy is often wantonly ignored. The annual cost to the public of maintaining them has been estimated at something over £41 million, about 51p per taxpayer, though anti-monarchists have estimated a figure five times as much. Yet this is seldom balanced by an estimate of their earnings for Britain. Sometimes they are derided as a 'tourist attraction', though this aspect is not to be sneezed at. The sale of wedding memorabilia in 2011 injected £163 million into the British economy. The royals bring more visitors to Britain than any other attraction, and for this reason alone casting them off would be quickly regretted. It is not simply the amount earned by the television rights for the great public occasions, but the vast expenditure on train and plane tickets, hotel beds, restaurant meals, souvenirs, books and magazine sales, that would be lost. The invisible earnings too from those who, hearing or reading about them, and seeing their weddings and funerals and anniversaries on television around the globe, decide to visit Britain in the months or years ahead, make any talk of their cost to the taxpayer seem rather one-sided.

Without them would Britain opt for an executive president as there is in France or the United States, wielding political power and giving jobs to cronies? Every republican seems adamant that this is not what the country wants. The notion would go entirely against the grain of British thinking. The British prime minister is too established a figure of authority, and it would be difficult for any other official to achieve acceptance if inserted above that. The alternative is a ceremonial president, such as exists in several neighbouring countries. The job tends to become an elephant's graveyard for senior politicians, a reward for long service. They have little to do other than greeting official visitors, launching occasional ships and presiding over, without participating in, sessions of Parliament. Their elections arouse little excitement and a significant number of citizens know nothing about them. It is also important that any such person has a political past. If they are a former Conservative politician, they will be disliked by Labour supporters, and so on. It would mean that the head of state was not politically neutral, as is the case with the queen. They would owe favours, or would support government initiatives, or would have been responsible for unpopular legislation in the past, and none of these things would help.

The third option is one which has been seriously considered, despite the fact that it would be highly impractical. This is that the head of state be chosen, or appointed, to represent the nation for an annual term and recruited from any walk of life – perhaps applications would be considered by a committee and based on nominations from members of the public. There would without question be a strong element of farce in any such process. Many of them would, by definition, be people 'in the news' – the sort of nine-days' wonder thrown up by media exposure. While there are many entertainers, sports personalities and courageous sufferers from illness who have won the nation's heart or become part of popular folklore, they would not cut a credible figure in the world of international affairs. Candidates would include those whose names or faces were most familiar to the masses, and therefore footballers, television personalities, celebrity chefs, pop singers and greedy executives would feature heavily. The process of nomination, and voting, would almost certainly become corrupt to the extent that it would swiftly lose all credibility. People chosen who were not celebrities, including no doubt the occasional housewife (astonished at being proposed by her neighbours) to show how democratic the whole thing was, would excite little public interest. Even the well known would cause a few raised eyebrows.

One has only to imagine David and Victoria Beckham waving from the balcony of Buckingham Palace, Elton John hosting a state banquet for the president of Uganda (in whose country same sex relations are illegal), Cheryl Cole (whose regional dialect would surely challenge the translators!) addressing a session of the United Nations or Jamie Oliver receiving the credentials of a foreign ambassador ('Cheers, mate!'), to realize that this might not work. Any number of people who have talent and who have won recognition within their profession simply do not have the gifts of presence, patience, dignity, intelligence or self-control that are necessary to be an effective national leader. Indeed the last of these is something that celebrity prima donnas notoriously lack. A person who had earned fame within Britain but was entirely unknown outside (*Coronation Street*, for instance, is not watched by Americans) might well not cut a very awe-inspiring figure on the international stage.

In addition there is the issue of continuity. Every year or, if the system were less rigid, perhaps every few years, a new incumbent would have to be educated from scratch in the tasks of office and start all over again, making contacts and friendships and gaining experience. A great many thoughtful people want the country to be represented by the best that it can produce – good manners, good intentions, no questionable past or connections, a sense of history, an ability to speak well on important national occasions – an entire range of old-fashioned virtues. Past monarchs either had these qualities naturally or were able to acquire them.

Nevertheless a sort of 'Buggins' turn' authority figure exists in some societies. In Scotland, the queen is represented by a High Commissioner at the General Assembly of the Church of Scotland – an annual gathering in Edinburgh to discuss Church business. The post is filled by some suitably worthy, or important, Scot, who for the two weeks of the Assembly acts as sovereign – living at Holyrood, travelling by carriage, receiving salutes from soldiers, visiting schools or hospitals and opening bazaars. It has a serious purpose but it is a fantasy existence, not 'king for a day' but king for a fortnight. Though the position was once held by the novelist John Buchan, the appointees are more usually unfamiliar to the public, and their term of office arouses little interest.

One country is permanently run like this. Switzerland is ruled by a committee of seven people, who act in rotation as president. Many citizens, let alone foreigners, have no idea who the incumbent is, and the officials themselves are virtually invisible. A Swiss recalled seeing his country's head of state on a crowded commuter train one morning. Unable to get a seat, the man was perched on the steps of the double-decker carriage, typing on his laptop, unnoticed by those around him. This may be precisely the type of national leader that some British levellers want, but it simply does not fit with the people's wishes or their sense of nationality. They crave pomp, tradition, majesty, and they will not give up these things. When they did have a republic, in the 1650s, it is interesting to notice that the head of state – Oliver Cromwell, the 'Lord Protector' – came to behave more and more like a king. The royal palaces, which had been sold off (Windsor Castle was turned into apartments), were bought back by the government and once again became the residences of the leadership. Servants were again attired in livery with coats-of-arms (though the colour chosen was grey rather than the scarlet of the Stuarts) and state banquets resumed. When Cromwell died, he was even succeeded by his son. What republicans today do not apparently realize is something that was obvious enough during the years of the Commonwealth – that the new regime would be constantly and unfavourably compared to the old (especially if it increasingly took on the same trappings), and that there would be an unending chorus of complaint that things were not as grand, as convincing, as worthy of respect, as much fun, as they had been in the past. Any modern republican government would have a mountain to climb in winning loyalty, and maintaining it could prove even more challenging.

With a short-term, honorary presidency there might be the risk of competing demands from different groups within society. The lobbying, the pressurizing, the shambles that would result, could be extremely socially divisive, necessitating each time the sort of unpleasant class war that is seen every half-decade in General Elections. And people would get thoroughly sick of it, as they do with politics when they are exposed to too much of it. Whatever the talents of the famous and whoever they were, it would take very little time before the thinking public became outraged by the loss of national dignity. The novelty would wear off almost at once, and another restoration of the monarchy could well be the result.

The last time, it took twelve years before the people of Britain invited back their royal family. This time it could be two or even one. It simply is the case that no one else – no individual, no family – has anything like the same experience, the expertise, the training, the social and political neutrality, or, even remotely, the international prestige of the British monarchy. The vast momentum of history and precedent and experience and connections to other peoples that the Windsors can deploy makes any alternative seem confusing, amateurish and pointless. It would be a good deal more difficult to rebuild the reputation and integrity of the country if it were lost.

The monarchy makes perfect sense as a constitutional lynch-pin. Politically neutral, immune to bribes because it has no need to accept them, it keeps the balance between different parties, different factions, different special interests. Because all are excluded, none are excluded. Its favour cannot be bought and it cannot be politically influenced.

It is important to remember that at no time in modern history has any parliamentary party dared to suggest the abolition of the monarchy. Those who actually take part in government, as opposed to those who protest in the streets, very often come to appreciate how useful an institution it is. For all the flirting with the question of the Crown's future by home-grown pundits and foreign analysts of British society, none have suggested that the demise of monarchy is imminent, or even foreseeable. For all the hot air talked on television and in the newspapers, for all the periodic opinion polls that show dips in support, there has never been an attempt by any elected party to dethrone the sovereign. No politician or party would take the risk, it would be such a vote loser.

Those who expect to seize the opportunity of the present monarch's eventual death to end the practice of hereditary rule have miscalculated. Her demise, whenever it happens, may well occur quite suddenly, and there will certainly not be time to dream up and put into practice an entire new constitutional system. The notion of ignoring Charles and crowning his eldest son the next king would cause endless legal dispute and William himself, who wishes to continue his career in the RAF for as long as possible, is unlikely to accept any such suggestion. The general attitude may then be one of waiting to see what sort of monarch Charles will be rather than wishing to throw him out untested. Critics have, however, not reckoned with the power of custom, the appeal of the familiar, the love of tradition and celebration, the vast wave of sentiment and gratitude that will follow the departure of Elizabeth II – and appreciation of the many things that the Prince of Wales has already done. King Charles III will come to the throne on a tide of inherited goodwill. And he will not be the last King of England.

While it would take a revolution to overthrow the monarchy, there has already been a quiet one within the institution itself. It has been going on for most of a century, gradual and often unnoticed. It has been carried out not by a mob at the Palace gates, but by those within. It has been so successful that it has calmed annoyance, disarmed criticism and survived detraction. It will continue, for the royal family will carry on learning the lessons of history and adapting to reflect the better instincts of the people over whom it rules.

INDEX